Global Cities at Work

Global Cities at Work

New Migrant Divisions of Labour

JANE WILLS, KAVITA DATTA,
YARA EVANS, JOANNA HERBERT,
JON MAY and CATHY McILWAINE

PlutoPress
www.plutobooks.com

First published 2010 by Pluto Press
345 Archway Road, London N6 5AA and
175 Fifth Avenue, New York, NY 10010

www.plutobooks.com

Distributed in the United States of America exclusively by
Palgrave Macmillan, a division of St. Martin's Press LLC,
175 Fifth Avenue, New York, NY 10010

British Library Cataloguing in Publication Data
A catalogue record for this book is available from the British Library

ISBN   978 0 7453 2799 0   Hardback
ISBN   978 0 7453 2798 3   Paperback

Library of Congress Cataloging in Publication Data applied for

This book is printed on paper suitable for recycling and made from fully managed and
sustained forest sources. Logging, pulping and manufacturing processes are expected to
conform to the environmental standards of the country of origin.

10 9 8 7 6 5 4 3 2 1

Designed and produced for Pluto Press by
Chase Publishing Services Ltd, 33 Livonia Road, Sidmouth, EX10 9JB England
Typeset from disk by Stanford DTP Services, Northampton, England
Printed and bound in the European Union by
CPI Antony Rowe, Chippenham and Eastbourne

CONTENTS

LIST OF TABLES

LIST OF FIGURES

LIST OF PHOTOS

LIST OF ABBREVIATIONS AND ACRONYMS

APS – Annual Population Survey
ASHE – Annual Survey of Hours and Earnings
BUILD – Baltimoreans United in Leadership Development
CANUK – Central Association of Nigerians in the United Kingdom
CIS – Construction Industry Scheme
COIC – Commission on Integration and Cohesion
DCLG – Department of Communities and Local Government
DFID – Department for International Development
EPZ – Export Processing Zone
EU – European Union
FDI – Foreign Direct Investment
FIRE – Finance, Insurance and Real Estate
GLA – Greater London Authority
IAF – Industrial Areas Foundation
ILR – Indefinite Leave to Remain
IMF – International Monetary Fund
IOM – International Organisation for Migration
IPPR – Institute for Public Policy Research
IWA – Indian Workers Association
LFS – Labour Force Survey
LLW – London Living Wage
MDGs – Millennium Development Goals
MOT – Ministry of Transport
MTBs – Money-Transfer Businesses
NES – New Earnings Survey
NHS – National Health Service
NMW – National Minimum Wage
NVQ – National Vocational Qualification
OC – Occupational Categories
ODA – Overseas Development Assistance
RPI – Retail Price Index
SAP – Structural Adjustment Programme
SOC – Standard Occupational Classification
TUPE – Transfer of Undertakings (Protection of Employment) regulations

TUC – Trades Union Congress
UK – United Kingdom
US – United States of America
WRS – Worker Registration Scheme

ACKNOWLEDGEMENTS

The research on which this book is based was funded by the Economic and Social Research Council (ESRC Awards RES00230694 Global Cities at Work and RES148250046 Work, Identity and New Forms of Political Mobilisation: An Assessment of Broad-Based Organising and London's Living Wage campaign). We are very grateful for this support and would like to thank all those involved in administering, refereeing and evaluating the projects. Our research also benefited from early financial input from the Greater London Authority, Oxfam, UNISON and Queen Mary, University of London, for which we are grateful.

Our Global Cities at Work project benefited enormously from the input of an advisory team that comprised Nathalie Branosky (from Inclusion), Don Flynn (from the Migrant Rights Network), Declan Gaffney (from the Greater London Authority), Deborah Littman (from London Citizens and UNISON) and Laurie Heselden (from the Southern and Eastern Region of the Trades Union Congress). The Living Wage research project was similarly supported by the participants in the ESRC Identities Programme, and particularly its director, Professor Margie Wetherell, from the Open University.

In 2006 we were lucky enough to find a number of senior managers at one cleaning contractor in London who felt able to grant us access to the cleaning staff employed in one building at Canary Wharf. This provided us with invaluable insight into London's migrant division of labour – and we are very grateful to everybody involved. Just prior to this, we also met a senior manager at one of the banks on the Wharf, and they too opened their doors to a photography project. We are particularly grateful to the photographer Chris Clunn for his wonderful work, and for his permission to reproduce some of his images on the cover, as well as later on in the book. We are also very grateful to photographer Chris Jepson for the other pictures we have used in the book.

We are also indebted to a great group of enthusiastic and committed young researchers and community organisers who worked on our project as part of their training with London Citizens in July 2005. Nana Adu-Kwapong, Alana Bates, Elaine Ho, Catherine Finney, Ciara Silke, Marisol Reyes, Tracey McAndrews, Kombo Lovemore, Amir Malik, Mohammed Ali and Anna Majcherek spent a month standing outside workplaces, riding underground trains and attending union meetings in order to collect some of the data we use in this book. Boguslaw Potoczny, Monika Percic and Eva Matamba also provided excellent service by later conducting research interviews with people in the Bosnian, Croatian, Congolese, Polish and Slovenian communities in London. We would also like to thank Yiannis Kaplanis from the London School of Economics who provided us with access to the large data sets that we used in this project – without his expertise we would have missed the big picture that has added so much to our work. We are also very grateful to Ed Oliver, the Cartographer based in the Department of Geography, Queen Mary, University of London, who has done such a brilliant job producing all the Figures we use in this book. Thanks are also due to Kerry Cable and her colleagues at Business Friend, who completed all the interview transcriptions that we used in this work.

Some of the data and arguments that we present in this book have been aired before – albeit partially – in a variety of conference presentations, workshops and seminars, academic journals and books. Though they are too numerous to list in full, we would like to thank all those who provided the opportunities for us to present our work, and who contributed to its development through their questions. We would especially like to acknowledge the valuable input of the editors and referees of the following journals: *British Journal of Industrial Relations*; *European Urban and Regional Studies*; *International Development Planning Review*; *Just Labor*; *Cambridge Journal of Regions, Economy and Society*; and *Transactions of the Institute of British Geography*. We also received excellent feedback from Adrian Smith, Alison Stenning and Katie Willis in relation to our chapter for their book *Social Justice and Neo-liberalism: Global perspectives* (Zed, 2009); from Neil Coe and Andrew Jones in relation to a chapter we wrote for *The Economic Geography of the UK* (Sage, 2010); and from Andy Pike, Andrés Rodríguez-Pose and John Tomaney for a chapter in their *Handbook of Local and Regional Development* (Routledge, 2010).

We feel particularly blessed to have had the opportunity to work together at Queen Mary, University of London, and are grateful for the intellectual and emotional support of our colleagues in the Department of Geography. Warm thanks go to Alison Blunt, Marg Buckley, Steve Cummins, Isabel Dyck, Eszter Gillay, Jason Go, Beth Greenhough, Al James, Roger Lee, Helen McLurg, Konstantinos Melachroinos, Jenny Murray, Catherine Nash, Miles Ogborn, Philip Ogden, Alastair Owens, Bronwyn Parry, David Pinder, Simon Reid-Henry, Marta Timoncini, Martin Sokol, Nigel Spence, Adrian Smith and Donald Wu who have all been an enormous support. We have been further sustained by our relationship with London Citizens, and would like to thank Matthew Bolton, Catherine Howarth, Deborah Littman, Neil Jameson and Paul Regan for their ongoing enthusiasm for the work that we do.

We each have some more personal acknowledgements. Jane would like to thank Jim, Agnes and Eric for putting up with this book, as well as Greta, Ann and John, who do so much by loving their grandchildren, including stocking the fridge.

Kavita owes a special debt of gratitude for Priya and Kinza's love and support, and for Aashna's insights into being a 'Londoner' and the daughter of a migrant. Yara owes an eternal debt of gratitude to Nair, Virginia and Arary who, by lovingly supporting her move to London, enabled her to experience many of the vicissitudes of life as an immigrant. Joanna is indebted to Anshuman for his constant love and support. Jon would like to thank, as always, Vicki, Max and Mo, without whom none of this kind of stuff would ever be possible, but also Chris and Lorna and the New Zealand Whanau for their help and support with this one. Cathy would like to thank Lee, Max and Alex for all their love and support.

Finally, a project like this has most obviously depended on the hundreds of people who agreed to be interviewed, welcoming us into their lives. Although we have anonymised everyone in the text that follows, we are very grateful to everyone who took part, and hope we have done some justice to the things that were said.

London, May 2009

1

DEREGULATION, MIGRATION AND THE NEW WORLD OF WORK

The metaphors for immigration are usually aquatic: we talk of floods and tides, of being swamped or drowned. We might do better to think of Britain as a lake refreshed by one stream that bubbles in and another that trickles out. The fish might squabble and at times attack one another; conditions sometimes favour the pike, sometimes the minnow. Every so often the incoming stream stirs the still pond, but over time, the lake adapts and develops a new, unexpected ecology. Without the oxygen generated by fresh water, it would stagnate.

Robert Winder (2004: 5)

As Winders implies, the history of the UK cannot be understood without full appreciation of the history of immigration. In this book, we explore the nature of contemporary immigration and its role in labour-market change in the UK through the lens of the capital city. We look at the nature of the low-paid labour market that keeps London working, unpacking the extraordinary story of the city's new migrant division of labour. Although it has gone largely unremarked, London now depends on an army of foreign-born workers to clean its offices, care for its sick, make beds, and serve at its restaurants and bars. Many have arrived outside the official channels of the immigration system, coming to make London their home. While migrants have long populated the lower echelons of the London labour market, supplying the workers who do the dirty, dangerous and difficult jobs, we posit that something new has been going on over the past two decades or so. Most clearly in relation to its rise to global-city status, London has become almost wholly reliant on foreign-born workers to do the city's 'bottom-end' jobs. We suggest that this labour market is a product of the model of economic development that has dominated the global political economy during the same period. In what has become known as neo-liberal economic management, the market – and particularly subcontracting – has been used to push down the wages and conditions of work in jobs like cleaning, care and construction. At the same time, the export of this model of economic development to the rest of the world has helped to create both the necessity and the desire for people to migrate across international borders in search of work. In this chapter, we show how these developments have culminated in a new labour market, and a new migrant division of labour, in London.

This book has been written to illuminate the lives of the foreign-born workers who find themselves part of London's migrant division of labour. We draw on extensive new research material that, for the first time, tells the story of London's changing low-paid labour market and the people who keep the city afloat. While this population necessarily contains settled immigrants as well as newer arrivals, we use the term 'migrant division of labour' to capture the importance of this foreign-born labour supply. However, we also seek to locate these developments in their broader context, and we use this opening chapter and the final sections of the book to explore the wider implications of the migrant division of labour – for the city, the nation, and the rest of the world.

In this chapter we set the scene for the arguments that follow by focusing on the related developments of deregulated employment and increased population mobility. In so doing, we explain why the migrant has become the embodiment of the good worker in so many parts of the world. We look at the ways in which the British state has responded to increased employer demand for low-paid workers and to increased global population mobility, recasting the post-war immigration regime with a new approach to 'manage' migration. We then move on to make some background arguments about the tensions that can exist between migrants and established working-class communities in poorer parts of the country. While this is not the focus of the research we have done, it forms an important part of the story behind developments in a city like London today. In the penultimate section we introduce our study of London, setting out how and why we chose to explore these contemporary developments and their implications for politics and policy through the lens of our capital city. The final section then introduces the rest of the book.

The Necessary Connection: Labour Deregulation and International Migration

During the past 30 years the UK has been responsible for developing and exporting a particular model of the economy to the rest of the world. Much of what is now known as neo-liberalism began – in tandem with developments in the rest of the world (Harvey 2005) – as a series of experiments conducted to do battle with our own working class. When, in 1979, Margaret Thatcher and ministers like Norman Tebbit were elected on the promise of solving 'the British disease', they had their sights on unionised workers in car factories, mines and the docks. Politicians were determined to liberate the labour market for managers who had lost their mettle and abandoned their right to manage. As Norman Tebbit declared in his role as secretary of state for trade and industry at the height of the miners' strike in 1984: 'Unless the ball and chain, the irons and the handcuffs of traditional trades union attitudes are struck off we will continue to be handicapped in the race for markets, customers, orders and jobs.'

The contemporary reification of neo-liberalism has tended to obscure its origins on the battlefield of the British class war. During the 1980s, police and pickets regularly made war across industrial landscapes that have since become part of the heritage industry. Groups of organised workers were picked off one by one, from the steel and car industries to the mines and dockyards. New laws made it harder to organise, and much more difficult to secure the support and resolve needed to mount industrial action. Yet while direct legislation played a key role in the mounting class war, the Conservatives launched a much more deadly weapon against workers in the form of privatisation. As early as 1983, managers in the National Health Service (NHS) were expected to practise 'market testing' to save money by subcontracting their 'non-essential' staff like cleaners, cooks and security guards. The same approach was later applied to local government in the form of compulsory competitive tendering, and many more workers were exposed to the winds of the market. The women cooking and serving meals to school children and the men emptying our bins joined the hospital cleaners on the sharp end of a new form of employment. Alongside the wholesale privatisation of the state-owned utilities (gas, telecommunications and water) and the means of transport (docks, buses and trains), many thousands of workers were transferred from the public to the private sector, with dramatic implications for the nature of work.

Once the genie was out of the bottle, privatisation very quickly took hold. Councils, hospitals, schools and universities could provide services with inbuilt cost deflation. Regular re-tendering and intense competition between contractors meant that wages, conditions and staffing were kept at minimal levels, and managers no longer had the burden of responsibility for employing their staff. New workers could be taken on without the troublesome costs of annual increments, sick pay or overtime rates. Moreover, there was little that trade unions could do to negotiate when their members were now employed by contractors, with no legal access to the managers who really determined the nature of work. While the British disease was being fought front-stage outside the collieries of the country, it was being won back-stage through the deadly assault of the market. Millions of workers were being disciplined through exposure to the pressures of competition. No longer protected by the political opportunity structure of the state, these workers experienced real cuts in their terms and conditions of work, with knock-on psychological effects on those watching from behind the parapet walls.

By the time Tony Blair came to power in May 1997, Britain's organised working class had all but vanished, and what was left was easily vanquished by New Labour itself. For example, the latest research shows that as many as 93 per cent of private sector workplaces in Britain are now outsourcing at least one of their activities (White et al. 2004: 25). Driven by the desire to cut costs and shed the risks of employment, all public sector employers are doing the same – including our art galleries, hospitals, schools, swimming pools and universities. Moreover, what started as a series of ad hoc experiments to unleash the market as a force for reform in the UK has become something called 'global neo-liberalism', with subcontracting as its favoured form of employment. Indeed, Mrs Thatcher's greatest and deadliest legacy is undoubtedly witnessed in the industrial powerhouses of the developing world. Multinational firms have used subcontracting to expand their activities, developing complex chains of production that involve suppliers in different parts of the world. In what academics have called 'global commodity chains' or 'global production networks', the brand-name companies at the top of these chains employ few, if any, of the workers producing their goods, and corporate elites have been able to liberate themselves from any responsibility for workers employed in the chain (Hale and Wills 2005, Henderson et al. 2002, Gereffi and Korzeniewicz 1994). Multinational corporations have sought to keep costs down by ensuring that suppliers that get too expensive or troublesome are ditched, with little thought for the impact this has on workers and their communities.

Over the past 30 years, subcontracting has thus become a key part of a booming global economy that has largely evaded the collective power of labour. Indeed, economic growth has occurred alongside a reduction in workers' share of overall wealth. Productivity – and profitability – bargaining are things of the past: quaint relics of the golden age of corporatism. In the global North, many of the low-paid jobs created by subcontracting have been devalued to the point that it is hard to find people to fill them; and in the global South, many millions earn less than they need to survive. Indeed, if London and the UK were one of the first test sites for the development of neo-liberal policies, many countries in the global South were much more deeply affected. Warmly embraced by international financial institutions like the World Bank and IMF, programmes of neo-liberal reform were introduced in many countries in the aftermath of the oil and debt crisis and the so-called 'lost decade of development' of the 1980s. Echoing the political experiments pioneered in the UK during the 1980s, and outlined above, governments in the global South were encouraged to reduce state expenditure, privatise state assets, liberalise markets, reduce import tariffs, and welcome inward investment. In what became known as 'structural adjustment', a model of social and economic 'reform' born in the corridors of the World Bank in Washington was visited upon struggling nation-states in the developing world (Bayart 1993, Beckman 1992, Simon 2008). Finance and debt reduction became dependent upon take-up of these policies, and recipient countries had little choice but to accept the medicine doled out from on high. During the period 1980–89, for example,

171 structural adjustment programmes were introduced in sub-Saharan Africa alone, with a further 57 initiated by the end of 1996 (Simon 2001). The impact of these policies was almost immediately and uniformly severe in countries that lacked welfare systems, with devastating consequences for the poor, vulnerable and marginalised.

The introduction of these reforms also paved the way for the establishment of export processing zones (EPZs) in those countries which had a comparative advantage over their competitors in the form of semi-skilled cheap labour supplies, reasonable infrastructure, and state-level support. These locations became key nodes in global subcontracting chains and were associated with the migration of low-order jobs from the global North to the South, where they attracted a new generation of young, mainly female, labour into factory work (Kelly 2000, Klein 2002). Driven by the needs of the export market and the 'real employers' at the top of the contracting chain, these jobs were often associated with enforced overtime, poor health and safety, and relatively low rates of pay (Chant and McIlwaine 1995, Hale and Wills 2005). Moreover, while EPZs initially fuelled internal migration, they also opened the door for international migration – not only within the global South, but also from the global South to the North.

While the precise details of implementation varied in each case, these policies and practices tended to increase unemployment (particularly in the public sector and in those activities exposed to international competition) and inequality (as those able to exploit the opportunities associated with global subcontracting chains and new sources of investment secured economic advantage). In tandem with the extension of market relations and the development of new communication infrastructure, such policies also tended to increase international migration. As Douglas Massey and colleagues (1998: 277) put it in their overview of migration: 'International migration does not stem from a lack of economic development, but from development itself.' Thus, rates of international migration have grown considerably since the 1980s, such that countries like Ghana have now lost up to one in five of their adults overseas (Mohan et al. 2000, Peil 1995). Since the 1990s, a similar exodus has affected the countries of central and eastern Europe – most notably, Poland, where millions of workers have moved abroad (Iglicka 2005). In many cases, these population movements have been sanctioned and even encouraged by national governments struggling with mass unemployment and shortages of foreign exchange (see also Chapter 6; and for more detailed arguments in relation to Ghana and Poland, see May et al. 2008).

The economic experiments pioneered in the UK in the 1980s, and which produced a new model of employment, have also provided the engine for economic globalisation and increased rates of national and international migration. Subcontracting has been pivotal in making it easier for multinational corporations to exploit the opportunities associated with new sources of cheap labour in the global

South, without the risks of direct employment. These activities have both fuelled economic growth in the global South – extending local markets and the desire for material goods, along with the money and physical infrastructure needed to move – and generated the widening inequalities and impoverishment that have further encouraged international migration. Indeed, although there is a long history of workers moving between the countries of the global South, it is the direction of flows that has shifted during the last 30 years: neo-liberal globalisation has helped to fuel transnational migration from the South to the North. There is a necessary connection between the impact of new forms of global political economy – and subcontracting in particular – and increased rates of global migration (International Organisation for Migration 2008).

Processes of economic globalisation associated with subcontracted employment have thus placed the migrant at the centre of the contemporary labour process. While subcontracting is now the paradigmatic form of employment across the world, the migrant is the world's paradigmatic worker. Moreover, while migrants are drawn into employment for economic reasons, they also have major political advantages as a labour supply. Even those who cross borders legally find themselves politically disenfranchised. Without citizenship, they will likely encounter restrictions on their access to employment, welfare and the political process. In relation to the UK, even those who have been able to secure a job in advance cannot leave this position without securing another; new arrivals from eastern Europe cannot stop working to take up state benefits without working for more than a year; and those who do not have the papers to work have no choice but to do anything in order to live. Migrant workers are attractive to employers precisely because they are migrants.

Migrants, Marx and Labour Reserves

Despite its critics, Marx's concept of the reserve army of labour remains remarkably salient in explaining such dynamics. Writing in the late nineteenth century, Marx highlighted the requirement for employers to have a ready supply of labour in the event of increased demand. Crucially, this surplus labour-power could be hired and fired to meet employer demand without the costs and time involved in social reproduction. In Volume 1 of *Capital*, Marx quoted Merrivale, a professor of political economy who later went on to work for the English Colonial Office, to illuminate the importance of employers having 'a mass of human material always ready for exploitation' (Marx 1954 [1887]: 592):

> However rapid reproduction may be, it takes at all events, the space of a generation to replace the loss of adult power [needed to fill shortages in the labour market]. Now, the profits of our manufacturers depend mainly on the power of making use of the prosperous

market when demand is brisk, and thus compensating themselves for the interval during which it is slack. This power is secured to them only by the command of machinery and of manual labour. *They must have hands ready by them, they must be able to increase the activity of their operations when required, and to slacken it again, according to the state of the market, or they cannot possibly maintain that pre-eminence in the race of competition on which the wealth of the country is funded.* (Merrivale, quoted in Marx, 1954 [1887]: 594, emphasis added)

At that time, Marx argued that surplus labour-power tended to be locally available, made up either from those already on the margins of the labour market ('the stagnant labour supply') or those attracted to that place from different parts of the country ('the floating and latent labour supply'). Marx's notion of the reserve army of labour was thus conceived on a regional and/or national scale; without the welfare state that was to be developed during the twentieth century, the potential labour supply at both local and national scales was always large and more than able to meet employer demand.

In contrast, the welfare entitlements afforded today to citizens of a country like the UK, coupled with developments in transport and communications associated with globalisation, have reconfigured the geography of the reserve army of labour. While the country's already-existing latent workforce may be better off claiming benefits than going to work, others from across the world may choose to travel very long distances, sometimes at great risk, in the hope of securing a job. Moreover, while foreign-born workers deploy a 'dual frame of reference', making favourable comparisons of the wages on offer in the global North relative to those available at home, their widespread exclusion from state welfare benefits leaves them with little choice but to accept the jobs that native workers decline (Piore 1979, Waldinger and Lichter 2003). The uneven geography of wages, prices and welfare makes their decision a positive one, just as it also explains the lack of work incentives for those already present within the UK. Such a geography means that foreigners will be hungry for the work that native workers reject.

Marx's concept of a reserve army of labour was first revisited in relation to migrant labour by scholars and activists during the years after the Second World War, when immigration provided a crucial fillip to economic activity across the nations of Europe (Braverman 1974, Castles and Kosack 1973, Piore 1979). At the time, full employment fuelled the demand for both female and foreign-born labour. As 'native' workers moved up the employment hierarchy, women and immigrants filled the gaps created below. New Commonwealth immigrants coming to the UK filled very particular niches in the labour market in low-paid manufacturing jobs (particularly in textiles in cities like Bradford, Leeds and Leicester) and low-paid services (particularly in health and transport in cities like Birmingham, London and Manchester).

In contrast, today's immigration takes place in the context of significant potential supplies of locally available labour. In the wake of de-industrialisation, economic inactivity rates among the working-age population have remained stubbornly high in many parts of the UK. Moreover, as we have seen, many low-paid jobs have been subject to downward pressure on wages and conditions as a result of subcontracting and associated market competition. Whereas the first wave of post-war immigration took place alongside widespread upward mobility for the general population between 1950 and the late 1970s, high levels of immigration more recently have coincided with relatively high rates of unemployment and downward pressure on the wages and conditions of work for those in non-professional jobs. Thus, whereas the international reserve army of labour had the potential to improve the relative position of local working-class communities in the 1960s, buttressing the belief that Britons were a labour aristocracy and largely protected from the insecurity found in the rest of the world, the UK's new immigrants are more likely to be viewed as a threat for jobs and resources. Even though immigration was still seen as a problem during the 1960s and 1970s, particularly in relation to housing and welfare, public sentiment later relaxed (see also Herbert 2008a, Ratcliffe 1981, Rex and Moore 1967, Rex and Tomlinson 1979, S. Smith 1989). In contemporary Britain, immigration has shot up the list of voter concerns, with an opinion poll conducted in February 2008 indicating that more than 40 per cent of the British electorate felt that race relations and immigration were their most pressing concern (Ipsos MORI 2008). Unprecedented levels of immigration have triggered increased public anxiety, putting pressure on the government to act. While employers are generally keen to proselytise the advantages of immigration, albeit with a strong preference for temporary schemes, the majority of the voting populace have a growing appetite for much stronger immigration controls. These pressures and the responses made by the British government are outlined in more detail below.

Partial Liberalisation: The United Kingdom's New Immigration Regime

As we have seen, structural shifts in global political economy have fuelled increased rates of population displacement and movement in recent years. The International Organisation for Migration (IOM) (2008: 2) estimates that, in 2005, some 191 million people were living outside their country of birth – a figure two-and-a-half times the number in 1965 – and the trend looks set to continue. Migration is now recognised as one of the most critical challenges facing the world. As the IOM declared in 2006:

> Migration is one of the defining issues of the twenty-first century. It is now an essential, inevitable and potentially beneficial component of the economic and social life of every

country and region. The question is no longer whether to have migration, but rather how to manage migration effectively so as to enhance its positive and reduce its negative impacts. Well-informed choices by migrants, governments, home and host communities, civil society, and the private sector can help realize the positive potential of migration in social, economic and political terms.

Yet, while international migration continues to increase as workers move to fill the jobs created by the subcontracted global economy, politicians remain accountable to a national electorate. Internal divisions over the issue of immigration will thus inevitably pull them two ways: both in favour of, and against, immigration controls (Hollifield 1992). Indeed, for Zolberg, the existence of the nation-state itself depends upon efforts to limit immigration, even if this becomes a growing challenge in the context of economic globalisation:

> Arising from the aggregate policies of the states of the international system, and undertaken in response to domestic considerations as well as interactively in response to each other's policies, the restrictive immigration regime prevails worldwide because it constitutes a *sine qua non* for maintaining the Westphalian international state system, as well as the privileged position of the core states amid highly unequal conditions. (Zolberg 1999: 83)

In this context, states like the UK have been pushed by different interest groups to 'manage' immigration to a lesser or greater extent (Freeman 1995). Indeed, however committed they are to economic liberalism, politicians rarely adopt the pure political liberalism that would abandon any immigration controls. Rather, most have opted for some form of increasing, and largely hierarchical and carefully stratified, forms of control.

In the post-war years, British governments sought to respond to the challenges of population movement by limiting immigration almost as soon as they could.[1] While recognised labour shortages provoked ministerial backing for the European Voluntary Workers Programme to attract displaced people from the Baltic States, Ukraine and Yugoslavia to work in the years immediately after the Second World War, the government began legislating to limit access to would-be immigrants as early as 1962 (Hatton and Wheatley-Price 2005, McDowell 2005). Thus,

---

1. It is important to note that, although the British government stepped up its activity in relation to immigration after the Second World War, there was already a legacy of immigration control. The first legislation was as early as 1905, when the Aliens Act refused entry to those who were not self-supporting and targeted 'undesirable aliens' – paupers, lunatics, vagrants. It was specifically aimed at destitute Jews. This Act was extended in 1914 and 1918, and in 1919 a new Aliens Act was introduced giving immigration officers and the Home Office the authority to refuse entry or deport any alien in the interests of the public good. Tony Kushner (2004) has argued that this is important because it is often wrongly assumed that the history of British racism dates back no further than 1945, or that Britain's race relations problems are attributable solely to migration from the New Commonwealth.

the Commonwealth Immigrants Act (1962) differentiated between those with prior offers of employment, who were granted A-grade vouchers, those who had recognised skills, who could apply for B-grade vouchers, and those who were classed as unskilled, and who could only secure one of a few thousand C-grade vouchers that were available for a couple of years.

Policy also moved swiftly to racialise migrant streams to the UK. Most obviously, the Commonwealth Immigrant Act (1968) prioritised those would-be immigrants whose grandparents were born in the UK – largely now living in the Old Commonwealth – over those without ancestors born within the UK. As Robert Miles put it in relation to the history of Commonwealth immigration to the UK: 'the British state has signified and thereby ranked migrants to Britain by reference to certain phenotypical features (notably skin colour) and has attributed negative characteristics to those defined as "coloured" and negative consequences to their presence in Britain' (1988: 434). Indeed, in the wake of 'race riots' in Liverpool in 1948, Deptford and Birmingham in 1949, and Nottingham and Notting Hill in 1958, immigration fast became associated with the issue – and perceived as a problem – of race.[2] As a result, the post-war years saw the development of a bifurcated policy regime in the UK that sought to limit immigration while also looking to manage race relations with those who had already arrived. In fact, given that the principle of free movement of some Europeans had to be accepted in the wake of British membership of the European Economic Community (EEC) in 1973, the focus of British immigration policy quickly became one of hindering entrants from beyond the EEC. In the context of a very restricted immigration regime, the nation then slowly and very unevenly came to terms with its immigrant 'other'. A reluctant multiculturalism at home was matched with a policy of zero immigration from beyond the EEC (see also Chapter 7).

During the 1980s, the UK's immigration regime was largely developed reactively in response to the growing pressures associated with increased demand for entry to the UK. The geopolitical realignments associated with the end of the Cold War stimulated much greater global population movements, not least due to new political freedoms, civil wars and the penetration of market relations. In addition, as we have seen, economic globalisation and the development of complex global supply chains to source goods from the developing world also increased the incentive to move. Such population mobility subverted the state from within, and many migrants found their way into countries like the UK despite the restrictive official regime. Reflecting the insecurity of the post–Cold War world, which in

2. In this volume, all references to race and racialised identities are to be understood as provisional. We recognise the social construction of racial categories and their apparent naturalisation (see Murji and Solomos 2005). Part of our concern, illustrated most clearly in Chapter 4, has been to look at the context in which the processes through which racial categorisation takes place become significant.

itself was partly fuelled by aggressive neo-liberal reform, increasing numbers of people migrated from war-torn and unstable countries and claimed asylum. Indeed, the number of asylum-seekers coming to Britain increased dramatically during the 1980s and 1990s, regularly exceeding 30,000 a year (Home Office 2008, Watson and Danzelman 1998). While refusal levels were high, the state was ill-equipped to detain and deport those denied refugee status, some of whom would later regularise themselves through alternative means. In addition, family reunification and increased flows of international students added to the numbers moving to the UK, and, as we explore in relation to London in Chapters 2 and 3, relatively lax visa and border controls also allowed significant numbers of migrants to arrive 'under the radar' of the state altogether.

It was in this context that New Labour began to develop a new approach to the management of immigration. In a departure from the post-war consensus, ministers began to extol the economic virtues of immigration and the importance of attracting talent to the UK. In her speech to the Institute for Public Policy Research (IPPR) in September 2000, for example, the immigration minister Barbara Roche signalled this dramatic shift in policy by declaring: 'We are in competition for the brightest and best talents. The market for skilled labour is a global market and not necessarily a buyers' market.' Drawing parallels with the effective use of immigration as a strategy for economic development in countries like the US, Canada and Australia, Roche anticipated a torrent of future legislation enacted by New Labour in the following years. In a scaled-up version of Richard Florida's (2002) arguments about the role of the creative class in the dynamism of conurbations, the UK government sought to open its borders to those who were seen as sufficiently highly skilled and entrepreneurial that they would contribute to the wealth of the nation. Rather than limiting immigration per se, the government sought to manage it for economic advantage. In contrast to the state-based immigration control of the post-war period, the British government adopted a market-led approach to immigration reform (Favell and Hansen 2002; see also Flynn 2005). As a result, and in contrast to the previous century, the UK has been a country of net immigration since the early 1990s (see Figure 1.1).

This new approach to 'managed' migration has culminated in the implementation of a points-based immigration regime that is similar to the one already operating in Australia. As outlined in Table 1.1, the highly skilled migrants at the top of this hierarchy (in Tier 1) have full rights to the labour market and the benefit system. They are welcome to stay and work for as long as they like, backed up with a pathway to citizenship should they want to remain. Those who are granted access to work for a particular employer in an identified shortage sector (which depends on research and analysis conducted by the Migration Advisory Committee) have to have a requisite level of English language skills to fulfil the terms of Tier 2. These workers have no rights to use the benefit system, although they do have the

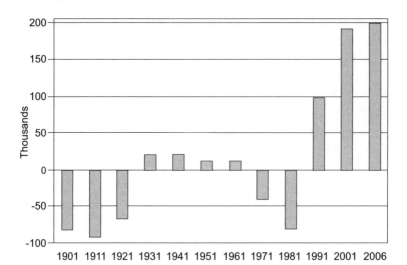

Notes: Includes civilian migration and other adjustments. Ten year averages
are used before 1931 and between 1951 and 1970. A twenty year
average is used between 1931 and 1950. Data prior to 1971 are for
calendar years, data for 1971 onwards are mid-year estimates.

Sources: 1901–97, Hicks and Allen (1999: 7); 1998–2006, ONS (2008).

Figure 1.1   Net migration to the UK, 1901–2006

right to apply for citizenship if they sustain their employment for more than five years. In Tier 3, there is no space for relatively unskilled workers from outside the EU to gain access to employment and citizenship within the UK. Instead, the government now expects all unskilled vacancies to be filled by migrants from the wider EU. Those from outside the EU can only gain access to the UK's labour market through family reunification, as international students, or as refugees. Indeed, those running educational courses for international students (under Tier 4) are now expected to sponsor and monitor the activities of their students for violations of immigration control. Students are expected to attend their classes and to limit their work to 20 hours a week during term-time, and unless they satisfy particular criteria, to leave the country once their course is complete.

In many ways, this new system represents little change for the would-be unskilled migrant from beyond the EU. There have been very limited opportunities for unskilled non-Europeans without family contacts or grounds for asylum to enter the British labour market since the abandonment of the grade C vouchers that were instituted by the 1962 Commonwealth Immigrant Act and the enforcement of patriality after 1968. The limited sector-based schemes that briefly existed for those working in agriculture, hospitality and food processing under the terms of the Nationality, Immigration and Asylum Act (2002) were abolished in 2005, and

Table 1.1   The UK's points-based immigration regime

	Description	*Terms of entry*
Tier 1	Highly skilled individuals to contribute to growth and productivity.	Based on qualifications, previous earnings, age and other criteria. Granted unrestricted access to the labour market and benefits for two years with dependants. Extension, settlement and citizenship can follow reassessment.
Tier 2	Skilled workers with a job offer to fill gaps in the UK labour force.	Job offer in shortage area or where not displacing a UK/EU worker. Job must be at NVQ3 or above and have been advertised. Employers act as sponsor. The recruit has to meet English-language requirements and can only change employer if they reapply for a new permit. If they meet the points demanded by Tier 1, they can subsequently bring dependants and secure unrestricted access to the labour market and benefit system. It is possible to apply for settlement after five years in the UK.
Tier 3	Limited numbers of low skilled workers needed to fill specific temporary labour shortages.	Quota-based, operator-led, time-limited schemes will run subject to review involving countries with which the UK has a robust returns arrangement. Expected to include only migrants from the A2 states (Bulgaria and Romania).
Tier 4	Students	Dependent upon sponsorship and granted only for the period of the course. Tighter controls over the institutions able to sponsor students. Can work 20 hours a week and full-time in holidays.
Tier 5	Youth mobility and temporary workers: people allowed to work in the UK for a limited period of time to satisfy primarily non-economic objectives.	Includes Commonwealth Working Holiday Makers' scheme and au pairs. For 18–30-year-olds for up to 24 months. Can work for 12 of the 24 months. No rights for dependants, no right to switch to a different Tier. Sponsorship required from national governments with agreed returns policy and reciprocal relationships with the UK. Limited additional options for temporary workers in the creative and sporting sectors, for voluntary work, religious activities, international exchange and agreements.

Source: Home Office (2006)

in any case rarely recruited from beyond the wider Europe, including Ukraine. For the past 40 years, so-called unskilled migrants from outside the EU have only been able to enter Britain through family reunification, the asylum system, as international students, as tourists, or clandestinely in the back of a lorry or under a train.

Thus, although the UK is now somewhat more open to foreigners, selling itself as a cosmopolitan country at the heart of economic globalisation, the nation's borders are no more open to the unskilled from outside the EU than in the past. Indeed, while the British government has opened the labour market to millions of potential migrants from the wider EU, it remains firmly – and increasingly – hostile to those from further afield. Following the accession of Cyprus, Malta, Estonia, Croatia, the Czech Republic, Hungary, Lithuania, Poland, Slovakia and Slovenia (the latter eight eastern European countries being known as the Accession 8 or A8) in May 2004, unprecedented numbers of Europeans have arrived to work in the UK. Many of these workers are located in low-skilled jobs (see Fig. 1.2); and for their first year, at least, they have no access to the welfare regime. These workers – who are often more skilled than their position in the British labour market suggests – have transformed labour markets across the UK, often settling in locations with little history and experience of immigration (Anderson et al. 2006, Drinkwater et al. 2009, Stenning and Dawley 2009; see also Chapter 8). There has been no parallel development for non-white unskilled would-be migrants from beyond the EU.

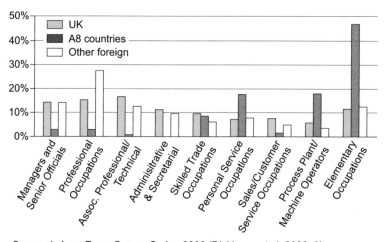

Source: Labour Force Survey Spring 2006 (Dickinson et al. 2008: 8).

Figure 1.2   The occupational distribution of migrant workers in the UK economy, 2006

In fact, the openness to migrants from within the EU has been accompanied by a parallel tightening of immigration controls in relation to other groups. British immigration policy has been developed in the interests of the economy with 'borders that are open to those who bring skills, talent, business and creativity that boost our economy, yet closed to those who might cause us harm or seek to enter illegally' (Home Office and Commonwealth Office 2007: 2). As the government has very limited power to control arrivals from within the EU, and only time-limited options with regard to the new accession states of Bulgaria and Romania and any others that follow, there have been increased controls over those perceived as unskilled from outside the borders of Europe. In what Somerville (2007) calls the 'paradox of contemporary immigration reform', New Labour have freed up immigration control for a global and European elite, while simultaneously introducing greater restrictions on those seeking asylum or economic opportunity from further afield. A new form of 'carceral cosmopolitanism' (Sparke 2006) has developed that involves more security checks (particularly through the visa regime, newly introduced biometric identity cards, and border controls), workplace raids, dispersal, detention and deportation (Bloch and Schuster 2005). While the UK's elite prides itself on its sophisticated cosmopolitan culture and anti-racist beliefs, it has presided over (or at least tolerated) a new carceral economy that involves thousands of people being imprisoned – or worse – because of the type of passport they have.

The UK now has as many as nine Immigration Removal Centres and four Short-Term Holding Centres housing failed asylum seekers and irregular migrants, many of whom do not have the papers needed for identification or deportation abroad. Moreover, these detainees are the tip of a much bigger iceberg, with analysts estimating that there are currently something in the region of half a million people living and working illegally in the UK, and that most of these are in London (LSE 2009, Woodbridge 2001). Many of these individuals were able to slip quietly across borders – often on tourist or student visas – during the past 20 years. Others failed in their claim for asylum but were never removed; and yet others arrived in a container, lorry or train (Black et al. 2006). These people have mostly found employment – and we will introduce some of those doing the low-paid jobs in London later in this book – and have sought to make the UK their home. Some have been able to regularise themselves through marriage, childbirth or the fall-out of the asylum system, but others now find themselves the targets of an increasingly aggressive immigration regime. Prior to 1996, there was no sanction on employers hiring irregular migrants, and even after 1996 there was little capacity or appetite for enforcing the law. Between 2002 and 2006, just 27 employers were found guilty of hiring irregular migrants, and workers could expect to escape undetected at work (House of Lords 2008: 28). In contrast, 6,000 workplace visits were undertaken in 2007, with as many as 91 employers fined for employing workers in violation of immigration controls during the first nine months of 2008 (Migrant Rights Network 2008). While such policies have not yet stopped people trying to enter the UK illegally, with current estimates suggesting that at least 1,000 people a year die trying to reach the EU (Legrain 2007), the new regime is making it much harder for irregular migrants and their would-be employers.

In countries like France, Italy and Spain, similar changes in policy have provoked political organisation and demands for the regularisation of migrants (Iskander 2007, Jordan and Düvell 2002, Lautenthal 2007, Levinson 2005, Ryan 2005). Despite differences in the national politico-institutional contexts involved, changes in the law and increased surveillance have forced irregular migrants out of the shadows in a desperate plea to be heard. In most cases, governments have responded with limited opportunities for regularisation, and in Spain – long a country of emigration – amnesties have covered as many as 1.3 million workers (Levinson 2005). Given that the British government is now exposing the scale and significance of irregular working through its own policies, illuminating the extent to which our economy depends on such labour, not to mention the costs of detention and deportation – estimated at £11,000 per head (IPPR 2006) – it is likely that the demand for regularisation in the UK will only increase. Indeed, as has been suggested by grassroots organisations like London Citizens and the Joint Council for the Welfare of Immigrants (JCWI), and as we explore in more detail in Chapter 7, 'For managed migration to succeed, it is logical that it starts with managing the people who are already here through a regularisation programme' (JCWI 2006: 11).

Since 1988, long-term residents who can prove their presence in the UK for at least 14 years, and those with children born in the country more than seven years previously, have been able to apply for Indefinite Leave to Remain (ILR). Likewise, in 1998 concessions were made to clear a large backlog of asylum cases and to enhance the ability of migrant domestic workers to leave abusive employers. Another exercise followed in 2003, allowing those with dependent children and four years of residence to remain in the UK. But there is, as yet, little appetite for further reform. Rather, the government is responding to public anxiety about high rates of immigration, as well as growing support for the British National Party, not with a regularisation programme but by visibly stepping up its border controls. It is thus tempting to suggest that, now that employers have a strong supply of low-waged labour from central and eastern Europe, they no longer need workers from further afield. Now that employers can recruit 'white' Europeans, the state has been able to crack down on those from beyond the EU who were doing the work – albeit without the correct papers – before this new labour supply materialised.

While recent years have seen a reconfiguration of the immigration regime, the New Labour government has also moved to reconfigure the national debate about multiculturalism (Lewis and Neal 2005). In the wake of increased public concern about immigration and the possibility of home-grown terrorism, debate has shifted towards the importance of shared values and community cohesion (Muir 2008). There is now greater emphasis on integration through the acquisition of English-language skills, citizenship tests and ceremonies, and on the duty of state-funded bodies to promote trans-cultural links. Just as the post-war immigration regime had a bifurcated approach that linked immigration control to race relations at home, the new managed migration regime links increased immigration flows to the need for integration at home. But integration has so far largely been interpreted as a duty to be imposed only on migrants. Despite occasional nods in the direction of two-way traffic, the emphasis has been on learning English, basic knowledge about the UK, and swearing allegiance to the Queen. For some, this smacks of a return to the demand for assimilation that has long provided a strand of debate within the UK (Back et al. 2002). However, it is also likely that many, particularly those from central and eastern Europe, will neither choose to stay nor take up citizenship. The government's policy of integration is unlikely to work among those who are uncommitted to long-term residence, and research suggests that only 60 per cent of those eligible to do so will actually take up citizenship; indeed, it is ironic that migrants from the global South are much more likely to take up citizenship, were it on offer. Given the presence of large numbers of Europeans and irregular migrants, however, cohesion on the basis of citizenship is likely to fail. As Rutter and her colleagues (2008: 23) suggest, the challenge will instead be to 'devise ways of facilitating the integration of new migrants, promoting active citizenship and developing local and national attachments through policies that go beyond naturalisation'.

In relation to such changes, there are also obvious material reasons why the people who live in closest proximity to the UK's new arrivals may in any case be unlikely to extend the hand of friendship. Whether for reasons of cost, because of established diasporic communities, or the government's efforts to disperse asylum seekers across the UK, new migrants tend to settle in the areas of poorest housing (Phillimore and Goodson 2006). Indeed, the seven areas identified for asylum dispersal are all within the poorest 20 areas of the UK, presenting increased competition for local services and low-paid, often informal employment. As we outline below, the conjuncture of a deregulated labour market with the arrival of new migrants has created tensions between different groups of migrants, as well as between migrants and the settled population. In a period of economic recession, and without efforts to improve job quality, these pressures are only likely to grow.

A New Class of Division Within the UK

Tensions over immigration have tended to be greatest in the poorest parts of Britain. Those communities already facing the challenge of surviving in a subcontracted, deflationary economy with poor employment prospects and diminishing service provision have understandably been the most likely to view immigration as a real threat. In their research to explore the reception and integration of new migrant communities in different localities across the UK, the Institute for Public Policy Research and the Commission for Racial Equality (IPPR-CRE 2007) found a clear link between attitudes towards immigration and economic status. Those living in relatively affluent areas, with tight labour markets and above-average levels of skills (in this case, Edinburgh, Perth and Kinross, in Scotland) did not see migrants as a threat to their lives. In contrast, those living in relatively poor areas, with high rates of unemployment, high levels of homelessness and/or overcrowding, and below-average levels of skills (in this case Birmingham, and Barking and Dagenham) were much more concerned about increased rates of immigration. Indeed, at the time of research, the people living in the London Borough of Barking and Dagenham – itself already an increasingly multicultural area – had a job density rate of just 0.53 jobs per resident aged 16–64, and a 30 per cent economic inactivity rate. In an area where just 15 per cent of the population had skill levels above NVQ level 4, low-waged workers and would-be workers were naturally worried about the impact of new arrivals who represented direct competition for low-waged employment. Other research has also highlighted the extent to which people have been fearful of articulating their concerns about immigration in what they perceive to be a 'politically correct' public culture that defends the rights of the migrant – and particularly non-white populations – over their own (Clarke et al. 2008, G. Dench et al. 2006, Valentine 2008).

More than this, however, there is also a very real danger that immigrants can be used as a stick to beat any sense of entitlement and respect out of the local working class. Employers are increasingly open about their preference for foreign-born workers – with those from eastern Europe proving particularly popular – over local people in the hiring queue (S. Dench et al. 2006). When a representative from the Confederation of British Industry contributed to the enquiry into the economic impact of immigration hosted by the House of Lords' Select Committee on Economic Affairs, for example, she declared:

> If you have a choice between two individuals, one of whom seems really enthusiastic about work, who wants to get on … who wants to learn and wants to move on and wants to perform well, then you are going to choose that individual with that positive attitude. If those positive attitudes are coming more from migrant workers than the UK-born, then I am afraid you are going to go for the migrant workers. We know what the solution to that disadvantage would be: a bit more enthusiasm from the indigenous worker. (Susan Anderson, quoted in House of Lords 2008: 33)

Such comments were further endorsed by other contributions made by Sainsbury's and a representative from the Recruitment and Employment Confederation, who suggested that the UK has 'an attitude gap rather than a skills gap' (ibid.: 33). Employers prefer migrants because they are apparently eager and more willing to work than their British counterparts.

In this regard, the House of Lords report is also clear that, without the supply of migrant labour, British employers would have to increase wages and improve conditions in order to draw in the locally based, latent labour supply. While acknowledging the real impact this would have on the cost of goods and services and the likely implications for levels of taxation, the Lords also noted that rising costs might also stimulate more determined efforts to improve productivity by investing in training, new technology and improved management.[3] In their report, the Lords and their advisors therefore raised anxieties over the impact of immigration on training and workforce development, with the risk that those without skills would be further disadvantaged in the future:

> Immigration, encouraged as a 'quick fix' in response to perceived labour and skills shortages, reduces employers' incentives to consider and invest in alternatives. It will also reduce domestic workers' incentives to acquire the training and skills necessary to do certain jobs. Consequently, immigration designed to address short-term shortages may have the unintended consequence of creating the conditions that encourage shortages of local workers in the longer term. (House of Lords 2008: 39)

Thus the UK faces a conundrum: stubborn and rising levels of unemployment alongside a strong migrant labour supply. While the UK's native workers have proved reluctant to take up the low-paid jobs that have been so devalued over the past 30 years, partly as a result of increased subcontracting (Lindsay and McQuaid 2004), employers have increasingly taken on migrant workers instead. 'Natives' and migrants are thus differentially positioned in the labour market, not least because of their differential entitlement to use the benefit system. Moreover, New Labour's efforts to 'make work pay' have been wholly inadequate to substitute for the benefit system. While the national minimum wage has been set at the level the market will bear, and is backed up by a complicated system of household-based tax credits, these measures have been insufficient to entice a sizeable proportion of the local latent labour reserve back into work. Indeed, migrants have been paying the taxes that help to pay for 'locals' to sit on the dole.

Moreover, while an alternative labour supply has allowed employers to articulate their perceived views about the UK's lazy, workshy proletariat, it has also allowed political commentators to bemoan their 'own' working class. At its most extreme, there has been an outbreak of naked class hatred in newspapers like the *Daily Mail*, one of whose most established commentators felt able, in 1994, to write the following about the so-called underclass within the UK:

3. These arguments parallel the long-established debate about the implementation of minimum employment standards in the UK. For more than 100 years, social reformers have argued that increased wages and improved conditions will stimulate increases in productivity and efficiency (see Metcalf 2007, Oldroyd 1894, Seebohm Rowntree 1918, Webb and Webb 1911).

This self-loathing, self-destructive tranche of the population is far less assimilable into morally conservative social life than any immigrant group ... Those ethnic minorities which bring with them religion, cultural dignity, and a sense of family will find a way. The only bar to their steady progress will be the mindless hatred of [the] indigenous working-classes, who loathe them precisely for their cultural integrity ... I fear that long after Britain has become a successful multi-racial society it will be plagued by this diminishing (but increasingly alienated) detritus of the Industrial Revolution. (Quoted in Skeggs 2003: 9)

Such vitriol is found in milder form on reality TV and in popular jokes about 'chavs'. The cultural distance between the middle and working class has widened, and the balance of power means that the poor have little opportunity to answer back (Mount 2004).

Thus, in popular narratives, the good – and enterprising – migrant is invariably counterposed to the lazy – and benefit-dependent – native. Echoing the way that subcontracted capitalism has allowed the powerful to wash their hands of responsibility for those they really employ, immigration has allowed some employers, commentators and politicians to wash their hands of their 'own' working class (including the British Asian and black communities that are presumably now seen as ex-enterprising). Indeed, it is no coincidence that the working class has been racialised as white just when it is less white than it has ever been in its history.[4] The fact that black and minority ethnic Britons are often just as worried about immigration as their white brothers and sisters is an inconvenience that is generally pushed to one side (although see Hudson et al. 2007). By identifying the 'white' working class as the problem, the commentariat have helped to pathologise particular communities as problematic, distracting attention from the core issues of jobs, housing, welfare and opportunity.

Thus, we would argue that immigration has exposed some rather unpleasant truths about our low-paid labour market and the inadequacy of the national minimum wage and tax credits that are supposed to entice people back into work. There have also been shocking spill-over effects into systems of cultural production, exposing the persistent – and widening – class antagonism at the

4. Interestingly, similar processes in the US have highlighted the exclusion of the black (African-American) working class, and of men in particular. As Waldinger and Lichter (2003: 20) put it in the context of their research in Los Angeles, 'The large-scale immigrant arrival is not doing anything good for less-skilled African-American workers. Moreover, the availability of the immigrants facilitates the activation of employers' preferences, which lead them to seek out workers from the group they perceive least likely to give trouble.' At the end of the book they highlight the extent to which '[e]mployers in the low-skilled sector previously held *negative* attitudes towards blacks as people but *positive* preferences for blacks as workers for the least desirable jobs. Today, however, both attributes *and* preferences are negative' (ibid.: 170, emphasis in original). There are striking parallels with what has happened to the white working class in the UK today (Mount 2004, Skeggs 2003).

heart of British society. In this context, there is a real danger that migrants and locals can be played off against each other when, in reality, both have the same material interests in good, well-paid jobs and improved service provision. Indeed, if it were possible to improve the quality of local employment, and thus increase the labour-market participation of local people, it is likely that the demand for migrants would start to decline. Given that the government is unable to stem in-migration rates from the wider EU – even if it wished to do so – improving job quality would likely reduce the demand for migrants much more than increased immigration control. Moreover, without such efforts, and in times of recession, tensions with migrants are likely to mount (see Chapter 8).

Low-Waged Labour in London

These dramatic changes in the UK's political economy, culture and class politics are most clearly evident in London. During the past 30 years London's labour market has been transformed; as we explore in Chapter 2, the city now relies more than ever on its business and financial services sector. Firms in this sector have led the way in promoting the model of neo-liberal economic 'reform' that has so radically changed the economies of the global South and encouraged mass migration. They have also applied the same principles to the management of their own activities in London, contracting out many of the jobs (in cleaning, catering and security work, for example, but also in information technology, payroll and human resources) created by the expansion of this sector.

In light of the arguments presented in the previous section, it is therefore no coincidence that, alongside these changes in London's economy and labour market, the past couple of decades have also seen a dramatic growth in the city's foreign-born population. In 1986, 18 per cent of Londoners (approximately 1.17 million people) were born overseas. By 2006, just under a third (31 per cent) of the city's population and just over a third (35 per cent) of its working-age population were foreign-born, putting London in a very similar position to New York, where 40 per cent of the city's population recorded a different country of birth at the last census (Lambert 2000; see also Price and Benton-Short 2007). Moreover, while a significant minority (16 per cent) of London's recent migrants originated in high-income countries, and many work for the city's finance houses and legal offices, the vast majority have come to London from low-income countries (62 per cent) or through the asylum system (22 per cent). Many of these migrants are now to be found in the least desirable jobs (Gordon and Whitehead 2007). As outlined in the following chapter, even official statistics (which are known to underplay the presence of foreign-born workers and to give a poor account of changes in low-paid employment) suggest that as many as half of those filling London's elementary occupations (working as cleaners, porters and security guards) were born overseas (Spence 2005).

Such developments raise important questions about the impact of these changes on the city's population. The restructuring of London's economy and labour market has profound implications for Londoners – not least because unemployment levels have remained stubbornly high, and rates of child poverty are among the highest of any region in the UK (HM Treasury 2006, 2007). Many locals, including foreign-born but naturalised citizens, have voted with their feet and abandoned the low-waged economy in favour of benefits and/or informal employment (Katungi et al. 2006). Despite its economic boom, the city experienced a 7 per cent *decline* in employment rates for those without qualifications between 1997 and 2006 (HM Treasury 2007: 19). Recent research suggests that – prior to the current recession at least – the government's efforts to 'make work pay' were having less impact in London than in the rest of the country. Whereas economic activity rates had risen outside London, they remained as low as 60 per cent in boroughs like Hackney, Newham and Tower Hamlets (HM Treasury 2007: 21; see Fig. 1.3). Young people – and those with low skills and parenting responsibilities, in particular – were much less likely to work than their counterparts outside the capital.

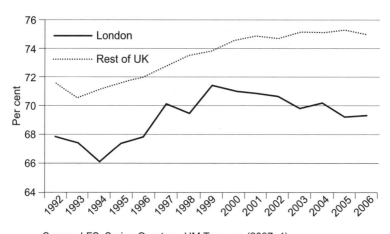

Source: LFS, Spring Quarters, HM Treasury (2007: 4).

Figure 1.3   Employment rates in London and the rest of the UK, 1992–2006

Of course, both the cost of living and the cost of going to work (including transport and childcare) are much higher in London, and this partly explains these trends in employment (see Fig. 1.4). But data also suggest that the wage premium afforded to Londoners compared with those working outside the capital has fallen sharply for those doing the lowest-paid work. Data presented in the next chapter show that, whereas in the past Londoners were able to secure a premium that reflected the higher cost of living and working in the capital, this differential has fallen very sharply in recent years (see also Bivand et al. 2003, Gordon and Whitehead 2007). Indeed, as the government's own analysts point out, low-paid Londoners have been hardest hit by the twin processes of global economic restructuring and increased migration:

> Labour market competition brings important productivity benefits to the economy. However, the contention [here] is that the nature of competition in the market for low-skilled jobs in Inner London is reducing the employment chances of local residents, particularly as they have little access to alternative labour markets. (HM Treasury 2007: 47)

Doreen Massey (2007) has documented some of the implications of London's role as what she calls a 'world city'. While the city has been an engine-house of many of the ideas and practices that later became known as global neo-liberalism, and though its elites have benefited from the resultant political–economic restructuring at home and in the rest of the world, the city also exemplifies the negative impacts of the model of capitalism it has done so much to export. Thus London contains staggering contrasts of wealth, poverty and power. It also relies on increasing numbers of foreign-born workers to do the jobs that locals cannot be persuaded to do. Indeed, as we have seen, many of London's local workers

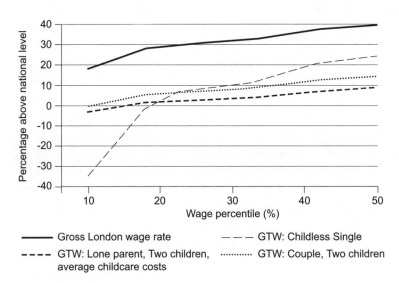

Source: Annual Survey of Hours and Earnings, 2005, HM Treasury (2006: 35).

Figure 1.4   London's real gain to work and hourly earnings relative to the rest of the UK, 2005

have been bypassed by the shift to global neo-liberalism and its impact on the local labour market. As Massey argues,

> London's poor ... and those without higher-level skills are caught in the cross-fire of the city's representation. On the one hand the employment generated by the new growth is not for them; it is a different class project entirely. This is London 'global city' as a capital of neoliberalisation. On the other hand, as their old jobs disappear, other workers arrive from around the planet to compete for the few economic opportunities that do remain for them. This is London 'global city' as cultural mixity. The old London working class (already ethnically mixed), caught between two world citydoms, feels itself under threat from both directions. (Massey 2007: 64–5)

The inequalities evident in contemporary London have a particular geography. The areas of greatest poverty are precisely those where in-migrants are most likely to settle when they arrive (Eade 2000). These are places of cheaper housing, and of established diasporic communities with the social networks needed to find accommodation and work. Thus the boroughs of Brent, Haringey, Hackney, Lambeth, Newham and Tower Hamlets are on the frontline of London's new migrant division of labour and its local effects. As we explore again in relation to our own data in Chapter 3, these are the boroughs with the largest migrant communities, the largest numbers of unemployed residents, and the greatest demand for services. They are the places where London's multiculturalism and the challenges of labour market deregulation are most obvious and acute.

This geography has been remarkably persistent, with London's eastern boroughs especially having a long history of accommodating both poor and foreign-born populations. In the 1860s, for example, the Victorians were increasingly fearful of east London's 'residuum', or what Gareth Stedman-Jones (1971) described as 'outcast London'. At that time, London was a port, a centre for conspicuous consumption, and a consumer-driven society. With parallels to today, the city was in industrial decline and production was vulnerable to competition from the expanding factories of the industrial north. Those goods that were made in London were subject to 'sweating' through subcontracting – often to small workshops and outworkers – with its attendant impact on wages and conditions of work. Much work was seasonal, and this increased the likelihood of the higher skilled 'bumping down' the labour market and displacing those less fortunate than themselves. The city had a chronic over-supply of low-skilled workers, and in a sector like dock-work there were at least three times as many workers as jobs (Stedman-Jones 1971: 53). As many as 10 per cent of the working population were 'surplus' to requirements, amounting to a 'stagnant' reserve army of labour of something like 400,000 people (ibid.: 56). Supply of and demand for labour were completely out of line with each other, and poverty increased people's need to stay put. Londoners needed to be known locally in order to gain access to the few jobs that were available, and, when there was no work, to secure enough credit and/or public relief to survive.

As might be expected, wages in many sectors fell over time, and just as Mike Davis (2006) asks in relation to contemporary cities in the global South, it was hard to see how people could live. Moreover, tensions between national groups were a constant issue in London. To our chagrin, we discovered that the British Brothers' League had its first large meeting in the People's Palace, now part of our own University, in January 1902. In words that could as easily have been articulated by a representative of today's British National Party, A. T. Williams declared:

> I don't care for statistics. God has given me a pair of eyes in my head – and as I walk through Mile End or Cable Street, as I walk about your streets, I see homes have changed; I see good old names of tradesmen have gone, and in their place are foreign names – the names of those who have ousted Englishmen into the cold. (*East London Advertiser*, quoted in Holmes 1997: 17)

During Victorian times, the dominant discourse about poverty offered a fore-echo of that of today's *Daily Mail*, outlined above. Commentators suggested that London's poor were a moral problem – that they were morally degenerate, lazy and stupid – and that any charity should be increasingly linked to control. The 'deserving' were separated from the 'undeserving', and the latter were targeted for moral reform. Indeed, following the Trafalgar Square riot of 1886 and an increased thirst for socialist and collective politics, there was widespread fear that the poor would 'infect' the wider city, polluting the minds of respectable folk. In the last decade of the nineteenth century, many commentators thus began to welcome the growth of trade unionism as a route to social control. In his definitive history of this period, Stedman-Jones argued that the 1889 dock strike was particularly emblematic of this shift in consciousness. Some public authorities read the strike as a positive sign that the poor were becoming more self-disciplined, controlled and controllable. Moreover, the influence of religious figures like Cardinal Manning suggested that unions offered a route to bring the poor into the fold of the respectable working class, and could be part of the solution to the problem of 'outcast London'.

Similarly, today, efforts to organise London's poor communities find favour with public officials. As we outline towards the end of this book, a new coalition of faith, labour and community organisations called London Citizens has played a significant role in organising poor workers around the quality of local employment (demanding a living wage), housing and immigration reform (making a demand to turn 'strangers into citizens' through a one-off regularisation). Our analysis suggests that it is no accident that these issues are at the top of the political agenda in the poorest places in London.

In the early years of the twenty-first century, London again has an over-supply of low-skilled labour. Large parts of the low-waged economy are still 'sweated' through subcontracting, a practice that is now more widely adopted than at any time in the past, putting downward pressure on the terms and conditions of work. Moreover, employers have been able to tap new sources of cheap labour that help to keep wages down; and whereas in the nineteenth century these reserve armies were of local origin, they are now largely foreign-born. The changing role of the state means that welfare payments allow the entitled poor to survive (just) outside the formal labour market, whereas the foreign-born have no choice but to work. In what follows, we explore the implications of this situation for the migrant workers involved. We highlight the nature of the low-paid labour market and the views and experiences of employers. We also explore the wider impact of this labour market on the home countries of migrants. Indeed, while our focus is on the migrant workers doing low-paid jobs in London, we seek to locate these developments in their wider context, exploring the implications for policy and politics. Between 2005 and 2007, we designed and implemented a large research project in London to explore these issues. A brief summary of our methods and activities is presented below.

The Research Presented in this Book

The material presented in this book was generated by the Global Cities at Work project that was based at Queen Mary, University of London, and funded by the Economic and Social Research Council, between 2005 and 2007. It has been further supplemented by a related project exploring the London Living Wage campaign and the broad-based community coalition, London Citizens, which has led the campaign since 2001 (see also Wills 2008, 2009). The Global Cities at Work project sought to capture developments taking place on a number of scales, including London's labour market as a whole, particular sectors of London's low-paid economy, in single workplaces, and for individual workers. Early on in the project we decided to focus on five sectors of the low-paid economy that were known to employ large numbers of migrants. These were cleaning (offices and London Underground), hospitality (hotels and catering), domiciliary care, food processing, and construction. This research involved analysis of the Labour Force Survey and the Annual Survey of Hours and Earnings; the design and implementation of a large-scale questionnaire survey; interviews conducted with employers, policy-makers and community organisations; and in-depth interviews with migrant workers themselves. The project produced a number of analyses of large data sets, a new database comprising responses from 429 migrant workers, and 134 interview transcripts (for full details, see Appendix 1).

Following on from the material introduced here, Chapter 2 documents in more detail the changes in London's economy and its emergence as a global city. We outline the evolution of the city's migrant division of labour and illustrate the growing dependence of the city on foreign-born labour. Chapter 3 puts flesh on the bones of this argument by telling the stories of migrant workers who have come to live in the city. We outline the characteristics of the people behind the headlines, exploring why they have come to London and how they engage in the labour market, and their experiences of low-paid employment in London today. In Chapter 4 we locate these stories in their historical context. Given that the city has long been a magnet for international migration, and has well-established ethnic and gender divisions of labour, we highlight what is new about contemporary forms of labour-market segmentation in London. We pay particular attention to the role of immigration status, the evolving issue of race, and the re-gendering of some low-paid jobs – particularly in the cleaning and care sectors – in the context of this new labour supply.

In Chapter 5 we explore how people survive on low pay, and we use concepts developed in the global South and in central and eastern Europe to understand the ways in which transnational communities get by in an expensive city like London. In Chapter 6, we further advance these arguments by looking at the wider implications of migration for development in the rest of the world. We explore the impact of remittance-sending on families 'at home', and the extent to which remittances can be understood as the bottom-up development that has long eluded national governments in the global South. Chapter 7 returns to London to look at the political organisation and influence of migrant communities living in the city. We argue that recent developments in London have opened up new opportunities for political organising on the basis of coalitions involving faith and labour organisations, as demonstrated by the campaign for a living wage and the demand for regularisation. Finally, Chapter 8 takes up these issues as part of a wider argument about the role of migrant labour in contemporary capitalism, and about the possibilities for creating just geographies of (im)migration today.

2

GLOBAL CITY LABOUR MARKETS AND LONDON'S NEW MIGRANT DIVISION OF LABOUR

London is now the world's financial centre. [But] the world's financial centre would not exist if it weren't for migrant workers. Both to do the banking and the trading but also [the] cleaning ...

Representative of the Institute for Public Policy Research

Exactly what constitutes a 'global city' is a matter of some debate. For some, only those cities playing a quite particular role in the world economy – the 'command and control' points of the new global economy, to use the words of the best known exponent of the 'global cities hypothesis' – are to be awarded this status (Sassen 1991). By such criteria, there is no doubt that London qualifies as a global city. At least 30 per cent of global foreign exchange turnover, as well as 40 per cent of activity in the world's foreign equities market and more than 70 per cent of the world's Eurobond trading takes place in London (Massey 2007: 34). In 2004 the City of London alone (as opposed to Greater London) was home to more than 2,000 financial institutions, and had more than 7,000 companies providing business services support (*Economic Development* 2006). As the Corporation of London has put it, in a statement that may be read as usefully as a sales pitch as a simple statement of fact:

> The City of London is at the heart of the world's financial markets. It is a unique concentration of international expertise and capital, with a supportive legal and regulatory system, an advanced communications and information technology infrastructure and an unrivalled concentration of professional services.[1]

Exactly why a city's 'global' status should be determined according to these rather than other criteria (levels of manufacturing output, population size, political or

1. <www.cityoflondon.gov.uk/Corporation/business_city>, last accessed 11 March 2008.

military 'reach', or religious significance, for example) is not entirely clear. What is clear is that attempts to categorise the world's cities in such ways have important effects. Within the academy, for example, discussions of 'global cities' have become increasingly narrow in recent years, focused around a handful of Northern hemisphere cities (London, New York, Tokyo, Los Angeles, Paris and Frankfurt) that clearly fulfil these rather limited criteria, even if they would certainly fail to register according to other possible measures of global significance (Robinson 2002). This is despite the fact that six out of ten of the world's most populous urban regions lie in the global South, in whose cities more than half of the world's population now live (Davis 2006, UNFPA 2007). Moreover, and as Benton-Short and colleagues recognise, 'a city's ranking in the global urban hierarchy is [far] more than an academic exercise' (2005: 946). As cities increasingly compete one with another, notions of 'global citydom' based on finance and business exert a powerful pull, 'pressur[ing] urban governments and managers around the world into striving for this self-same ["global city" status]' (Massey 2007: 35), irrespective of whether such an objective is achievable, let alone desirable.

Partly because of the exclusions built into such definitions, others have sought instead to define the 'global city' according to quite different criteria. Here, rather than seeking to trace a city's position in a network of financial flows and economic decision-making, the focus is on a city's position in the new networks of international migration that have brought ever greater diversity to the cities of both the global North and South, and which connect one city to another (see for example Benton-Short et al. 2005, Henry et al. 2002). On these criteria, too, London clearly 'makes it'. Over the past 10 to 15 years the city's population has become far more diverse, to the extent that it may now best be described as exemplifying what Steven Vertovec (2007b) has called 'super-diversity'. As Price and Benton-Short note in their discussion of London as a 'hyper-diverse' city, 'nearly every country in the world has an immigrant in London' (2007: 113). In fact, London is home to people from no fewer than 179 different countries – out of a total of between 192 and 195, depending upon whose definition of statehood one accepts (GLA 2005a) – and more than 300 languages are spoken in its schools (Baker and Mohieldeen 2000).

These apparently rather different takes on London's 'global city' status are of course not so far removed from one another as they may at first appear. Holding them together is the figure of the migrant worker. The reliance of London's financial institutions and business services industries on the continuing flow of highly skilled labour from overseas is now well known (Beaverstock and Smith 1996). Less well known is the extent to which London's economy as a whole is now dependent upon the labour power of low-paid workers from across the world.

Cross-cutting the divisions of social class, gender and ethnicity that have long been a feature of London's labour market, there is now a distinctive migrant division of labour at the bottom end of London's labour market (see May et al. 2007). For example, using data that almost certainly underestimate the extent of such a phenomenon, the Greater London Authority (GLA) have estimated that almost half (46 per cent) of London's 'elementary occupations' (household domestics, contract cleaners, bottlers, canners, sandwich makers, postal workers, waiters, hotel housekeepers, traffic wardens, and hospital porters) are now filled by workers who were born abroad (Spence 2005: 61). It is these workers and their families that constitute London's new 'super-diversity' and who keep London working: cleaning the city's banks when the financiers have gone home, clearing litter from the city's trains and buses, caring for the city's elderly, and providing cheaper goods and services for millions of ordinary Londoners.

In this chapter we elaborate upon and attempt to explain the emergence of this new migrant division of labour. The argument is in five parts. Firstly, we review the existing literature on global city labour markets and summarise key changes to London's economy and labour market over the past 30 years. In accordance with the 'global city hypothesis', we show that London's labour market is characterised by processes of both income and occupational polarisation – processes that have resulted in a growing divide between an expanding cohort of professional and managerial workers, on the one hand, and a growing number of low-paid workers and the economically inactive on the other. Secondly, we document recent changes in London's population, charting the emergence of a situation of super-diversity, and demonstrate the growing role that migrant workers play in this polarising labour market. Drawing on new analyses of the Annual Survey of Hours and Earnings and the Labour Force Survey, we trace the emergence of a distinctive migrant division of labour at the bottom end of the London labour market over the last decade or so.

In the third, fourth and fifth parts we revisit earlier analyses of the role of migrant workers in the labour markets of the 'advanced' capitalist economies. Substantiating the arguments introduced in the previous chapter, we attempt to explain the emergence of London's new migrant division of labour – going back to our argument about the reserve army of labour and highlighting the triple effect of employer demand, local entitlement to welfare, and national immigration and economic 'reform' in shaping developments in London's labour market. We draw on interviews with employers, employer associations, policy analysts and community groups to explore why London's low-wage employers have increasingly turned to migrants rather than native workers, framing their narratives in accounts of a 'dual frame of reference' (Waldinger and Lichter 2003) and theories of the 'hiring queue' (Model 2002).

Rather than viewing the emergence of a migrant division of labour in London as the by-product of broader processes of 'global' economic restructuring over which politicians and policy makers have little control, we focus upon the active production of these divisions. We argue that the emergence of a new migrant division of labour in London is the result of a convergence – and the (sometimes unforeseen) consequences – of the semi-autonomous actions of policy-makers, politicians, employers and migrant workers themselves.

The Global Cities Hypothesis and the Transformation of London's Economy

For the past 20 years or so academic debate on global city labour markets has mainly been framed by variations of the 'global cities hypothesis'. First outlined by Friedman and Wolff (1982), and subsequently elaborated by Saskia Sassen (1991, 2001), the broad contours of this thesis are now relatively well known. Briefly, following a period of global economic restructuring in the 1970s and early 1980s, a small number of cities – the eponymous global cities – were understood to have emerged as key sites of 'command and control' in the new global economy. These were centres both of the world's financial system and of the headquarters of an increasing number of transnational and multinational companies. For Sassen, such cities formed a new network of organisational and financial control – making them increasingly closely connected to each other, and to spaces of production spread across the globe, rather than to other cities or regions in their relevant national economies.

Such cities were also argued to be characterised by the decline of manufacturing employment – as a result of its dispersal to the global South and to newly indus-trializing countries – and an increase in service-sector employment, with especially rapid growth in those sectors associated with the activities of 'command and control': the so-called FIRE (finance, insurance and real estate) industries. Whereas manufacturing employment tends to cluster around middle-income occupations, service-sector employment tends instead to be characterised by a clustering at both the top and the bottom end of the occupational and income hierarchies. Thus, as the employment base of global cities has shifted, the occupational and income structures of these cities is also thought to have been transformed, from something like an egg to something more akin to an hourglass. The result, and indeed the 'primary social fact about world city formation', is therefore argued to be 'the polarisation of [these cities'] social class divisions' (Friedman and Wolff 1982: 322). Although similar trends are apparent elsewhere, such polarisation is held to be especially marked in global cities, with cities otherwise as different as London, New York and Tokyo apparently displaying remarkably similar economic profiles and social structures (Sassen 1991, 2001).

For Sassen, the increasing inequalities evident in global cities are therefore a direct result of these new patterns of employment, with growth at the top end of the labour market fuelling growth at the bottom. While new offices and banks need security staff and cleaners, a new managerial and professional elite demands restaurant workers and bar staff, nannies and domestics (Sassen 1996).

Importantly, a significant proportion of these low-wage jobs are argued to be filled by migrants, with the worst of them falling to those who have little choice but to accept the worst pay and conditions. These are people whose immigration status renders them ineligible for welfare, or irregular migrants exploited by unscrupulous employers in the 'grey' economy.

Recent changes to London's economy broadly echo the changes outlined in the 'global cities hypothesis'. For example, once a city with a significant light manufacturing base (with 32 per cent of its employment in manufacturing in 1961), nine out of ten (91 per cent) of London's workers are now employed in the service industries (Hamnett 2003: 31, Prothero 2007: 43). Indeed, the decline in manufacturing employment may be even more dramatic than these figures suggest. As many as half of the city's 'manufacturing' jobs can now be accounted for by those working in the head offices of companies producing goods elsewhere (Banks and Scanlon 2000). While manufacturing employment has fallen sharply, London's banking, insurance and business services sectors have grown dramatically over recent decades – adding some 167,000 jobs to the London economy between 1981 and 1991, and thereby taking these sectors' share to almost one third (32 per cent) of the city's total employment in 2005 (Hamnett 2003: 34, Prothero 2007: 43; see Fig. 2.1).

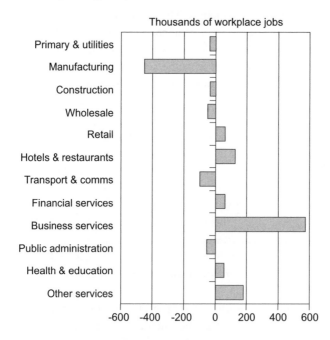

Source: Piggott (2008: 54).

Figure 2.1   Change in employment in London, by sector, 1981–2004

Notwithstanding these broader changes to its economy, however, the conventional view has been that London's social structure has not (yet) polarised in the manner suggested by Sassen and her colleagues. Rather, most argue that, although London certainly witnessed *income* polarisation through the 1980s and 1990s, there is no evidence that this was accompanied by the kind of *occupational* polarisation that might be expected to accompany it. Instead, studies have pointed to a rapid professionalisation of the London labour force over the last 20 or 30 years. This has involved an absolute increase in the number of managers and professionals at the top end of the occupational hierarchy and an absolute and relative decline in every other socio-economic group, including those employed in 'bottom-end' jobs (Buck 1994, Buck et al. 2002, GLA 2002, 2005a, Hamnett 1994a, 1996, 2003, Hamnett and Cross 1998).

For these authors, it is therefore processes of professionalisation that have led to the recent explosion of income inequality in London, not least because – reflecting global competition for top-level positions – wages have risen much faster for managerial and professional workers in recent decades than for anyone else. As HM Treasury (2006: 34) put it in their overview of the London labour market: 'In recent years, wages at the lower end of the income distribution have grown more slowly in London than elsewhere, while those at the top have grown faster.' As a result, and as the data in Fig. 2.2 demonstrate, income inequality in London has widened to a dramatic extent, and much more so than in the rest of

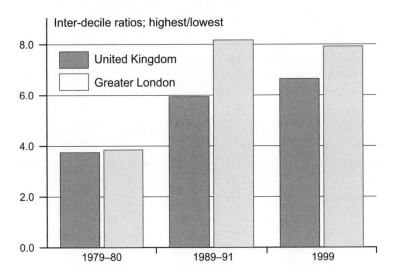

Source: Buck et al. (2002: 157).

Figure 2.2   Inequality in London, households by richest/poorest deciles, 1979–80, 1989–91 and 1999

the UK. In 1999, for example, the richest 10 per cent of the population in London had about eight times more income than the poorest 10 per cent – a rate that had doubled since 1979.

In the best-known attempt to elaborate on this apparent disjuncture between processes of income and occupational polarisation, Chris Hamnett has pointed to important variations in the welfare state regimes and levels of immigration found in different countries (Hamnett 1994b, 1996). Hamnett has argued that one reason that London appears not to have experienced the same levels of growth at the bottom end of the labour market as have some US cities is because it lacks the large-scale supply of cheap migrant labour found in cities like New York and Los Angeles. At the same time, a more generous welfare safety net protects people from the worst excesses of low-paid employment. Hence he concludes that

> in many European countries [recent processes of economic restructuring] are more likely to create a large and growing unemployed and economically inactive group excluded from the labour force rather than ... a large, low-skilled and low-paid labour force. While this may be true in the US, with its large and growing immigrant labour force, willing to work for low wages (possibly forced to because of the limited nature of welfare provision) it is not necessarily true of all Western capitalist countries. (Hamnett 1996: 1411)

And, he argues, it is certainly not true of London (see also Hamnett 2003).

We would accept that there are good reasons to be suspicious of the narrative of economic and social change posited by the 'global cities hypothesis' (for a review of contrasting empirical findings on social polarisation in different global cities see Norgaard 2003; for a conceptual critique see White 1998). In the first place, as Doreen Massey has argued, 'what emerges most emphatically from any detailed examination of London's economy is [in fact] its sheer diversity' (Massey 2007: 41). It is this diversity, rather than only the FIRE industries, that have been the engine of London's economic growth in recent years (Gordon 2004). It is also clear that London cannot be understood as somehow 'floating free' of the wider British economy, as Sassen and others suggest – not least because, while the continued growth of the city's economy is clearly dependent on the movement of workers from the wider UK (Fielding 1992), London also continues to export more goods and services to the 'rest of the UK' (28.5 per cent of its export market) than it does overseas (12.3 per cent of exports), with this differential holding even in the case of the export of financial and business services (Gordon 2004: 5, cited in Massey 2007: 38). Finally, it is also clear that, although the number of professional and managerial jobs in London has grown very significantly in recent years, the total number of people in work has actually fallen, as Hamnett and others point out (GLA 2002, Hamnett 2003: 65).

But there is also growing evidence to suggest that the gap between London's 'haves' and 'have-nots' is not only a result of the divide between those enjoying the fruits of professionalisation and those excluded from work in the new economy. Alongside the growing numbers of London's managers and professionals on the one hand, and economically inactive households on the other, there is also a growing number of 'working poor'. Working with data from the New Earnings Survey, for example, Yiannis Kaplanis has examined changes in the employment shares of jobs in different wage-bands between 1991 and 2001 (see Fig. 2.3). In line with previous studies, his analysis shows a very significant increase in the proportion of workers at the top end of the London labour market over that decade. But it also shows a smaller but still significant rise in the proportion of workers at the very bottom end – and a falling-out of the middle. As proponents of the 'global cities hypothesis' suggest, such trends are much more developed in London than in the rest of the UK – where similar polarisation is evident but less marked (Kaplanis 2007; see also Goos and Manning 2003).

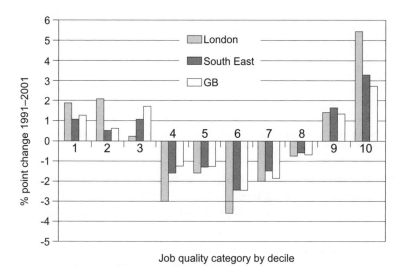

Source: Kaplanis (2007: 29).

Figure 2.3   Employment change by job quality, London and the UK, 1981–91

But it is important to note that, while there has been a growth in the relative size of the low-wage labour market in London during this period, this growth has not been accompanied by any increase in relative levels of pay. Whereas job growth might usually be expected to stimulate wage inflation, there are particular reasons why this has not happened in London. To explore these trends, we conducted original analysis of the Annual Survey of Hours and Earnings to map changes in the remuneration paid for key low-wage occupations in London, compared to the rest of the UK. This analysis shows that, while the wage differential was already lower than average for those in lower-paid occupations at the start of the period (1993), rates had fallen further behind by 2001 (see Table 2.1). Indeed, whereas, on average, London's employees earned £2.88 more per hour than their counterparts outside the city in 2001, the differential for catering assistants had fallen to just £0.54 by this date (from £0.85 in 1993), while for chefs, cooks, care assistants and cleaners it was as much as £1 per hour less than the London average.

Table 2.1   The London–UK differential in wage rates for low-paying jobs (1993 and 2001)

	London 1993	UK 1993	Differential 1993	London 2001	UK 2001	Differential 2001
Hospitality						
OC Job title						
620 chefs, cooks	6.3	5.1	1.2	6.71	5.48	1.23
953 catering assistants	5.25	4.4	0.85	5.17	4.63	0.54
Care						
OC Job title						
644 care assistants	7	5.05	1.95	6.78	5.45	1.33
Cleaning						
OC Job title						
958 cleaners, domestics	5.4	4.45	0.95	5.55	4.63	0.92
All All	10.14	7.52	2.62	11.09	8.21	2.88

Source: Author's analysis of the New Earnings Survey (1993) and Annual Survey of Hours and Earnings (2001) using Occupational Categories (OC) as indicated (see also Appendix 2)

Our data also show that, during this period, wages for the lowest-paid in London failed to keep up with changes in the pay of other workers in London, and others doing the same jobs outside London. Indeed, real wages actually *fell* for catering assistants, cleaners and domestics, care assistants and chefs working in London over this period (see Table 2.2). Between 1993 and 2000, for example, real wages for all those working in London increased by £0.50 per hour. But catering assistants lost £0.48 per hour, care assistants lost £0.43 per hour and cleaners lost £0.12 per hour over the same period. This contrasts sharply with the real wage increases for workers in the same occupations outside London. Beyond the capital, catering assistants gained £0.13 and care assistants £0.17 per hour. And such trends have worsened in recent years. While working Londoners gained an average of £0.71 per hour in their real earnings between 2001 and 2005, chefs and cooks lost £0.17 per hour (reversing real growth in the previous period), catering assistants lost a staggering £1.66 per hour, and cleaners lost £0.44 per hour. Only care assistants did better during this period, increasing their real earnings by more than their counterparts in the rest of the UK.

Contrary to accepted wisdom, it would therefore appear that London's labour market is indeed now coming to resemble an hour-glass rather than an egg.

More accurately, perhaps, we might suggest that London's labour market is now exhibiting clear signs both of occupational polarisation – with a growing proportion of both very highly paid and very poorly paid jobs – and of bifurcation at the bottom end, with high levels of economic inactivity sitting alongside a growth in the proportion of those in low-paid work, many of whom have seen their real wages *fall* in recent years.

Table 2.2   Changes in real hourly earnings in low-paid occupations, 1993–2000, 2001–05, London and the UK

		1993–2000		2001–05	
		London	UK	London	UK
Hospitality					
OC	Job title				
620	chefs, cooks	0.49	0.31	−0.17	0.35
953	catering assistants	−0.48	0.13	−1.66	0.21
Care					
OC	Job title				
644	care assistants	−0.43	0.17	1.65	0.74
Cleaning					
OC	Job title				
958	cleaners, domestics	−0.12	0.1	−0.44	0.42
All	All	0.5	0.42	0.71	0.21

Source: Authors' analysis of the New Earnings Survey (1993–2000) and Annual Survey of Hours and Earnings (2001–05) using Occupational Categories (OC) as indicated; wages adjusted in relation to the RPI for the first year of each pair (see also Appendix 2).

These shocking trends can be explained by the twin processes of labour-market deregulation and increased global population mobility. As outlined in the previous chapter, subcontracting and labour-market deregulation have held down wages and conditions in occupations like cleaning, construction, hospitality and food processing. Indeed, our research in these sectors – outlined in more detail in the following chapter – reveals that all were engaged in some form of subcontracted employment. In care, workers were employed by private companies or not-for-profit organisations that tendered to local authorities for service provision (Wills 2003). In cleaning too, workers were employed by subcontractors delivering services to a range of public and private employers. In construction, workers were enmeshed in a complex system of labour supply, either being employed by small-scale contractors or working on a self-employed basis. In the hospitality sector we discovered a process we have called 'subcontracting by stealth' (Evans et al. 2007a), whereby in-house jobs were slowly being replaced by the use of agency workers. Even in food-processing, factory workers were found to be supplying large chains like Starbucks and Tesco, even though they were contracted with a much smaller firm that had to compete for the work. Thus, in every case, workers' employers were having to bid for work on a regular basis, and this kept wages, conditions and staffing levels at a minimum. Moreover, even if they were protected by TUPE (the Transfer of Undertakings Protection of Employment regulations), newer colleagues would invariably be employed on inferior levels of pay.

But, as we have already suggested, divisions in London's labour market are also now increasingly structured by a new divide: between London's 'native' population (some of whom are themselves settled immigrants) and a new population of migrant workers who have made their way to London as part of a general increase in global population mobility. It is the presence of the latter that helps to explain the apparent conundrum of London having high levels of economic inactivity alongside a growing low-paid workforce. Put simply, there is a new migrant division of labour in London, with workers from abroad taking on the growing number of low-paid jobs at the bottom end of London's labour market.

Super-Diversity and London's New Migrant Division of Labour

> We haven't actually got a London labour market. We've got a series of labour markets.
> (Representative of the Greater London Authority)

As we showed in Chapter 1, it is no longer possible to argue that the UK lacks the large-scale supply of (cheap) migrant labour found in countries like the United States. Having slowed in the 1980s, levels of immigration into the UK rose very significantly through the 1990s. Of those who had arrived in the UK by 2001, 42 per cent had settled in London (Spence 2005: 17). The resulting changes in London's population have been dramatic. In the last 20 years the proportion of London's population born abroad has doubled. By 2006, just under a third (31 per cent) of the city's population and just over a third (35 per cent) of its working-age population were born overseas (ibid.: 31), putting London in a very similar position to New York, where 40 per cent of the city's population recorded a different country of birth at the last census (Lambert 2000; see also Price and Benton-Short 2007). While a significant minority (16 per cent) of London's recent migrants originated in high-income countries, the vast majority have come to London from low-income countries (62 per cent) or via the asylum system (22 per cent) (Gordon and Whitehead 2007).

As Steven Vertovec has argued, 'One of the most noteworthy features of "the new migration" is the multiplicity of immigrant's countries of origin' (Vertovec 2007b: 1029). By 2002, people from the New Commonwealth countries accounted for just 20 per cent of British immigrants, with many of the new groups arriving in London coming from countries with no specific historical – or colonial – ties to Britain (see Fig. 2.4). In addition to the very diverse countries of origin (and religion and language) included in these new flows, people were also taking increasingly diverse routes into the country. Coinciding with increasing immigration, the 1990s saw a significant expansion in the number of ways in which people could legally enter Britain (as highly skilled workers, those with work permits, students, sector-based migrants, family members, and asylum seekers), with each pathway carrying quite different conditions of entry and entitlements to work and residence. As we saw in the previous chapter in relation to the points-based immigration regime, these range from full access to work and benefits for the highly skilled to the right to work only in designated industries, with no recourse to public funds, for the low-skilled (House of Lords 2008: 18). The same period also saw a significant increase in the number of people either entering the UK without permission, or remaining in contravention of their original immigration status, with the Home Office estimating there to be half a million 'irregular' migrants in Britain by 2001 (Woodbridge 2001; see also LSE 2009, IPPR 2006).

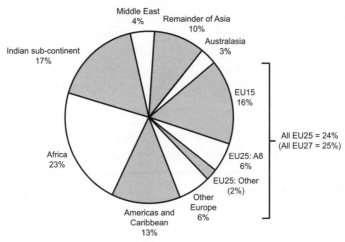

Foreign-born by country of birth, geographic groupings[1], London residents, 2006[2, 3, 4]

[1]   A8 are Eastern European countries that joined the EU in 2004, namely Czech Republic, Estonia, Hungary, Latvia, Lithuania, Poland, Slovakia, Slovenia. EU15 are 15 member states who formed the European Union prior to enlargement in 2004, namely Austria, Belgium, Denmark, Finland, France, Germany, Greece, Ireland, Italy, Luxembourg, Netherlands, Portugal, Spain, Sweden, United Kingdom. The two other countries that make up the EU27 are Bulgaria and Romania who joined the EU in January 2007. Indian subcontinent is defined here as India, Pakistan and Bangladesh.
[2]   Data based on relatively small samples (ie <200) are shown in brackets to emphasise the higher levels of sampling variability attached to these estimates.
[3]   Base: 2.3m (All born outside UK)
[4]   Migrants include all people born outside the UK and have lived in the UK for at least one year.

Source: Piggott (2008: 30).

Figure 2.4   Foreign-born London residents, by country of birth and geographic grouping, 2006

The concept of 'super-diversity' thus refers to both the diversity in the countries of origin, language, religion and culture to be found among London's new migrant groups, and to the different legal statuses held by different individuals. A person's immigration status (defining their rights to both residency and work) can be crucial in determining their labour-market position – a point developed in later chapters. As the House of Lords (2008: 18) indicated in its recent report, 'Immigration status is important ... because it determines an immigrant's rights in the UK, including rights in the labour market, access to welfare benefits and rights to family-reunion, and rights to stay permanently in the UK and acquire British citizenship.' As Vertovec explains, a key feature of 'super-diversity' is therefore that

> there may be widely differing statuses *within* groups of the same ethnic or national origin. For example, among Somalis in the UK – and in any single locality – we will find British citizens, refugees, asylum-seekers, persons granted exceptional leave to remain, undocumented migrants, and people granted refugee status in another European country but who subsequently moved to Britain. (Vertovec 2007b: 1039)

The experience of earlier immigrants from New Commonwealth countries thus contrasts sharply with the trajectory faced by new arrivals in Britain today. As Lydia Morris has argued, the last decade has seen the emergence in Britain of 'an expanding army of actively recruited migrant labour [alongside] an underground population of both rejected asylum-seekers and undocumented migrants existing with minimal rights in the interstices of the informal economy' (Morris 2002: 25).

Yet it is also precisely this differentiation, caused partly by differential immigration status, that renders it impossible to limit our understanding of London's new migrant division of labour to tales of 'irregulars' working in the 'grey economy'. Indeed, one of the most problematic aspects of previous accounts of global city labour markets is the rather limited role ascribed to migrant workers (see Samers 2002). For Sassen (1991, 2001), for example, migrant workers are to be found in three main parts of the economy: first, servicing the advanced producer services industries, and the lifestyles of these industries' new managerial and professional elite; second, filling the positions vacated by native workers in a downgraded manufacturing sector (where employers have sought to take advantage of a new 'international' division of labour without moving abroad); and, finally, producing the cheaper goods and services required by migrant workers themselves in the so-called 'ethnic economy' (Sassen 1996). Many of these jobs in personal services, manufacturing and in the ethnic economy are understood as lying on the fringes of legality, with workers employed 'off the books', and with employers taking advantage of those with 'irregular' immigration status to force down pay and conditions of work (see also Cox and Watt 2002).

Some of London's new migrant workers undoubtedly work in such conditions (see Jordan and Düvell 2002, Lagnado 2004), and a very significant number are living and working in London illegally (see, for example, Evans et al. 2007b). But migrants now play a much fuller role in London's economy than these accounts would suggest, with the foreign-born now found in every sector and every kind of workplace: in manufacturing and services, working off the books for small employers, and employed under contract by large multinational companies and by the public sector. Indeed, the GLA estimate that 28 per cent of London's manufacturing workforce, 23 per cent of the city's construction workers, 32 per cent of its wholesale and retail workers, 35 per cent of those working in health and social care, and almost 60 per cent of those in the hotel and restaurant trade were born abroad (Spence 2005: 68).

It is also important to emphasise that not all of those coming to London from overseas end up in London's low-wage economy. Tracking the labour market experiences of London's new migrants, Gordon and Whitehead (2007) have charted the very different labour-market outcomes of those coming to London from high-income countries and those coming from low-income countries or through the asylum system. Broadly speaking, patterns of employment among these different groups reflect the status afforded to the nation involved, with clear differences in labour-market outcomes between those from the EU15, the Old Commonwealth, the US, Japan and Korea, on the one hand, and those from low-wage and asylum countries (sub-Saharan Africa, Asia, Latin America and the east-central European accession states) on the other. Hence, while the former are in fact over-represented at the top end of the London labour market, the latter are very heavily over-represented at the bottom (see Table 2.3).

Table 2.3   The distribution of migrants across higher- and low-paid jobs in London, by time in the UK and by origin, 2005/06

Region of Origin	Years in UK	Bottom quintile (<£9/hr)	2nd quintile (£9– £11.50/hr)	3rd quintile (£11.50– £15.80/hr)	4th quintile (£15.80– £20.80/hr)	5th quintile (>£20.80/hr)
Non-migrants		21%	20%	21%	19%	20%
High-wage	0–3	18%	14%	12%	21%	35%
	>3	25%	19%	16%	17%	22%
Asylum	0–3	31%	24%	14%	21%	22%
	>3	23%	20%	14%	21%	22%

Source: Gordon and Whitehead (2007: 51).

Note: Gordon and Whitehead divide migrant workers into those from 'high-wage' countries, by which they mean the EU15, the Old Commonwealth, the US, Japan and Korea; 'asylum' countries, by which they mean Albania, Bosnia, Croatia, Ethiopia, Iran, Iraq, Lebanon, Macedonia, Romania, Sierra Leone, Somalia, Sri Lanka, Zimbabwe and two 'other Yugoslavia' and 'other Middle East' groups; and 'other low-wage' countries, which includes the rest of the world.

Importantly, these data also show some movement up the labour hierarchy after the first few years in Britain for some who arrive in the UK from low-wage countries. Even so, nearly half (48 per cent) of those coming to London from low-wage and asylum countries remain in the bottom fifth of London's labour market after their first three years in the country.

More generally, the extent to which London's low-wage economy is now reliant on foreign-born workers and the speed of change is startling. While official data indicate that some 46 per cent of the jobs at the very bottom of London's occupational hierarchy were filled by migrants in 2001 (Spence 2005: 61), our more recent and fine-grained analysis of the Labour Force Survey suggests that this reliance on migrant workers is considerably higher in some sectors of the economy, and that there has been an upward trend for more than a decade. For example, in 1993/94, just over 40 per cent of London's cleaners were born abroad. By 2004/05 the figure had climbed to almost 70 per cent. Similar rates are evident among chefs and cooks, catering assistants and care assistants – to the extent that it is increasingly evident that some parts of London's low-wage economy could in fact no longer function without the labour of migrants (see Table 2.4, Fig. 2.5).

Table 2.4 Total employment and the proportion of foreign-born labour, by occupation, London, 1993/94, 1999/2000, 2001/02, 2004/05

Occupation	1993/94 (000s)	%FB	1999/2000 (000s)	%FB	2001/02 (000s)	%FB	2004/05 (000s)	%FB
Chefs, cooks	29	51	34	61	31	67	38	76
Catering assistants	27	42	25	52	38	55	39	62
Care assistants	22	n/a	41	48	36	38	35	56
Cleaners	64	41	55	46	52	61	51	69
All London	2,894	25	3,262	27	3,349	30	3,375	34
UK	24,449	7	26,687	8	27,114	9	27,599	10

Note: FB = foreign-born. The reclassification of occupational categories in 2000 means that the data for the two periods are not directly comparable (see also Appendix 2).

Source: Original analysis of the Labour Force Survey/Annual Population Survey.

Such trends are in sharp contrast to the situation in the rest of the UK. Whereas there has been an increase in rates of immigration across the UK during the past 20 years, and immigrants are similarly located in low-wage jobs outside London, these trends are most pronounced within the capital. Indeed, when the data analysis presented in Table 2.4 and Fig. 2.5 is replicated for the country as a whole, London at first appears completely at odds with the rest of the UK (see Table 2.5). Outside London, for example, the proportion of the workforce who were foreign-born increased by just 3 percentage points between 1993/94 and 2004/05. Moreover, although rates were rising, fewer than 30 per cent of all cooks and chefs, and fewer than 20 per cent of catering assistants, care assistants and cleaners were foreign-born as late as 2004/05. But, while the migrant division of labour is clearly much more developed in London than in the UK as a whole,

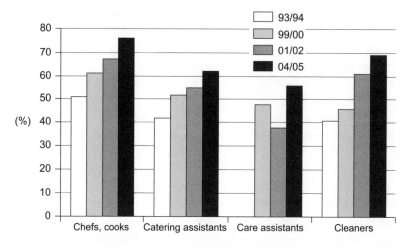

Source: Authors' analysis of the Labour Force Survey, London (1993/94 – 2004/05)
NB: The reclassification of occupational categories in 2000 means that the data
    for the two periods are not directly comparable.

Figure 2.5 The proportion of employees who are foreign-born, by selected occupations,
London, 1993/94 to 2004/05

the rest of the economy is certainly beginning to experience similar changes (and
for an example in the manufacturing sector – see Mackenzie and Forde 2009).
We would therefore argue that our data actually suggest that trends in London
may best be understood as offering a foretaste of developments that are likely to
become much further entrenched in the UK as a whole in coming years.

Table 2.5 Total employment and the proportion of foreign-born labour, by occupation, UK,
1993/94, 1999/2000, 2001/02, 2004/05

Occupation	1993/94 (000s)	%FB	1999/2000 (000s)	%FB	2001/02 (000s)	%FB	2004/05 (000s)	%FB
Chefs, cooks	224	16	244	19	248	20	242	26
Catering assistants	204	10	225	10	388	11	371	15
Care assistants	371	7	537	9	543	8	590	11
Cleaners	740	7	638	8	594	10	541	14
UK	24,449	7	26,687	8	27,114	9	27,599	10

Note: FB = foreign-born. The reclassification of occupational categories in 2000 means that the data for the
two periods are not directly comparable (see also Appendix 2).

Source: Original analysis of the Labour Force Survey/Annual Population Survey.

In an important contrast to cities like Los Angeles – where the low-wage
economy is characterised by the presence of a large number of workers from a
small number of countries (notably Mexico, Guatemala and El Salvador – see

Lopez et al. 1996) – London's low-wage labour market is characterised by much greater diversity. Even so, there is some indication of growing specialisation and segmentation at the bottom end of the labour market, with particular national groups being concentrated in specific parts of the economy and in particular jobs. For example, official statistics indicate that as many as 39 per cent of the Ecuadorians of working age living in London, 33 per cent of the Colombians, and 33 per cent of the Portuguese work in elementary occupations. As many as 41 per cent of working-age people born in Slovakia now living in London are recorded as working in personal services – as nursery nurses, housekeepers and care assistants. Filipinos are heavily concentrated in the health and social care sectors (where data indicate that 31 per cent of London's Filipino population are employed), and 25 per cent of Afghans work as sales assistants or check-out operators (Spence 2005: 64). As we show in the following chapter, we have found strong concentrations of Ghanaians and Nigerians in cleaning and care, and concentrations of eastern European workers in hospitality jobs. Our own research with a particular part of London's Brazilian community, outlined more fully in the following chapter, also found upwards of 32 per cent of adults (from a sample of 423 people) working as cleaners (see also Evans et al. 2007b: 12, McIlwaine 2007a).

Thus it is clear that London has growing divisions between rich and poor, employed and unemployed, settled and foreign-born, as well as between and within migrant communities themselves. These divisions are reflected in London's migrant division of labour. In what follows we unpack the mechanisms behind these divisions and the reasons why they have come to be manifested in London's labour market today.

London's New Labour Reserve

The growing role of migrant workers in Britain's low-paid economy has sparked a raft of new research, including everything from econometric analyses of the impact of increased immigration on the British labour market (Bell 1997, Dustmann and Fabbri 2005, Schmitt and Wadsworth 2007, Wheatley-Price 2001) to the role of migrant workers in different sectors of the economy (for agriculture see McKay and Winkleman-Gleed 2005, Rogaly 2006; for hospitality see Batnitzky et al. 2008, Mathews and Ruhs 2007, Wright and Pollert 2006; for domestic workers see Anderson 2007) and the experiences of different national groups and those in different immigration categories (Beaverstock 2004, Black et al. 2005, McGregor 2007, Raghuram 2004, Raghuram and Kofman 2004, Vasta and Kandilige 2007). Although such work has provided invaluable insights into the dynamics operating in particular sectors, or the experiences of different groups, it has yet to cohere into a broader conceptual framework through which we might explain exactly how and why it is that migrants have come to play such a key role in the low-wage labour market. In an attempt to provide exactly such a framework, we have therefore gone back to re-examine earlier attempts to conceptualise the relationships between immigration and labour-market change to see what, if anything, such accounts might add to our understanding of London's new divides.

As we outlined in the previous chapter, we have found it particularly useful to go back to Marx's theory of the reserve army of labour, and the influential readings of this work that were developed in the context of post-war immigration to Europe. Labour shortages after the Second World War led employers in countries like Britain to lobby government to try and attract workers to fill these shortages. In tandem with the development of guest-worker schemes in a number of other European nations, the British government endorsed limited recruitment from beyond the UK (Winder 2004). While labour shortages enabled 'natives' to secure better forms of employment, immigrants arrived to fill the most dangerous, dirty or disadvantaged occupations – with concentrations of African-Caribbean workers in the National Health Service and London Transport, for example, and of Indian, Pakistani and Bangladeshi workers in Britain's factories and mills (Castles and Kosack 1973, Hollifield 2004, Jackson 1992, Miles 1982, Ryan 2005).

This situation prompted scholars to focus on employer demand as a key determinant of immigration. At a time when Marxist ideas were widely adopted in the social sciences, scholars argued that immigration was functional to capitalism – that it was driven by employer demand for cheap and pliable labour, and dependent upon surplus populations (or 'reserve armies') from the former colonies. The extent to which destination states opened their borders to this 'reserve' was itself argued to be dependent upon the nature of the class compromise between capital and labour within any particular state. While a well organised 'native' working class might be able to defend its terms and conditions of employment and keep immigrants out, a weak working class could do little to influence state immigration policies (Castles and Kosack 1973, Hjarnø 2003, Miles 1988, Miles and Brown 1989).

In one of the most sophisticated and well-known arguments from this period, Piore (1979) posited that there was an inherent role for immigrant labour in advanced capitalist economies. He argued that labour-dependent employers in tight labour markets with limited margins could not simply increase wage levels to attract natives into work. Raising wages at the bottom would mean demand for wage rises elsewhere, potentially leading to structural inflation – and although this is somewhat questionable after the experience of implementing minimum-wage legislation in the UK (see Wills 2004), there is never a strong appetite for increasing wages for these kinds of jobs.

In addition, however, Piore argued that employers needed to find workers with the motivation to work. Immigrants fitted the bill, as they often arrived with poor language skills and low levels of education, and had few alternative sources of work. Immigrants were thus recruited in the wake of the 'natives' who were moving out of such jobs. Moreover, immigrants were then argued to be further confined by racism and wider socio-economic disadvantage to remain in 'bottom-end' jobs. Such analyses were later extended by the notion of the segmented labour market, in which a combination of personal characteristics and employer discrimi-nation corralled individuals into particular kinds of employment – (re)producing locally contingent gender and ethnic divisions of labour – an issue we explore further in Chapter 4 (Edwards et al. 1975, Leontaridi 1998, Peck 1996).

Whilst research into the relationships between immigration and employment was in vogue in British social science during the 1970s, it has since rather slipped off the agenda. By the 1980s, notions of a 'reserve army of labour', and the primacy of employer demand and the 'class contract' in shaping the deployment of that reserve, were widely viewed as products of an increasingly discredited Marxist approach. With Marxism under fire within the academy, beyond the academy immigration was slowing. As it did so scholars began to focus their attention on the experiences of those who had now settled in Britain, turning away from questions of immigration to focus instead on questions of race. While the labour-market experiences of different minority ethnic groups formed a key part of this work (Iganski and Payne 1996, Jones 1993, Modood et al. 1997, Virdee 2006), scholars also began to look at other aspects of immigrant identities, including gender, and the development of new political formations. Led by scholars at the Centre for Contemporary Cultural Studies at Birmingham University in the 1980s, this work aimed to create more positive representations of the black British diaspora than had previously been the case (Gilroy 1987).

Yet Piore's reading of the migrant division of labour that emerged in Britain in the 1960s and 1970s has clear resonances with the situation unfolding in London today. Now, as then, levels of immigration have been rising and a growing number of migrant workers are to be found in the most difficult and demanding occupations – in jobs with low levels of pay and minimum status. At the same time, and as we intimated in the previous chapter, there are also important differences in the role and impact of contemporary immigration. Not the least of these is that today's labour market is characterised by sometimes extensive pockets of low levels of economic activity among the low-skilled, because – in the context of the deregulation and devaluation of many low-paid jobs – the benefits system can be more attractive than work for those who are able to claim. Given the costs of going to work in London, those with relatively low levels of skills who can claim benefits – particularly if they couple this with caring responsibilities – are the least likely to work. Indeed, data from HM Treasury (2006: 35; 2007: 62) indicate that the 'gain to work' is much lower for lone parents, mothers in couples, and single people in the lowest-paid occupations in London than it is in the rest of the country. Wages have to be much higher in London than elsewhere to make going to work worthwhile (see Chapter 1). For example, using 2004/05 data, HM Treasury (2007: 68) identifies entry pay levels for mothers in London as at least £2 higher per hour than in the rest of the country. The costs of transport and childcare mean that a mother working full-time would have needed to earn £8.50 per hour (compared to £6.50 outside London) and £8 per hour part-time (compared to £5 outside London) in 2004/05, to make employment worthwhile.

Moreover, given the increased liberalisation of immigration controls, particularly in relation to the wider EU, together with the relatively weak border control that was practised during the 1980s and 1990s, there is a clear oversupply of low-wage workers in the capital. Prior to the current recession, the British Treasury (2007: 52–3) suggested that there were as many as three low-skilled workers for every low-skilled job in London, making wages and conditions much less likely to rise over time. The slack labour market also created a tendency for 'bumping down', whereby skilled workers ended up taking less-skilled jobs for lack of alternatives. The rate of bumping down in London is again much higher than in the rest of the country, and HM Treasury (2007: 52) suggest that as many as 37 per cent of higher-skilled workers in London are found in lower-skilled jobs, compared to a rate of 24 per cent in the rest of the country.

In contrast to Piore's analysis, in the current period London's reserve army of labour has therefore developed to meet employer demand despite, rather than because of, a locally-based latent labour supply. This situation can be understood as reflecting a desire among employers to get the job done without having to increase wages or improve conditions of work. It is also facilitated by the dynamism of migrants themselves. Indeed, immigrants are rightly celebrated for their motivation to cross borders, sometimes in conditions of great danger, in pursuit of a new and better life. While some commentators tend to focus on such ingenuity as evidence of a new social movement capable of eroding the state from within (see for example Chambers 1994, Hardt and Negri 2005), others highlight the extent to which capital benefits from the exploitation of unprotected labour power from the poorest parts of the world (Legrain 2007).

The remainder of this chapter demonstrates that the situation in London reflects both aspects of immigrant labour supply. While employers have been able to fill their vacancies for low-wage jobs, this has been facilitated by the very dynamism of the workers themselves. Just as Chalcraft (2007) found in his research into the situation facing Syrian migrants in Lebanon, for example, processes of class-based exploitation are facilitated by the persistence, resilience and ingenuity of those who migrate looking for work. As we outline below, migrants' strong motivation to work and better themselves is a key explanation for their position in low-wage labour markets in London. Moreover, the presence of so many would-be workers – and the differentiations between them in terms of immigration status, language, nationality, ethnicity, race and gender – only serves to increase employers' ability to discriminate over those whom they want to employ. Before exploring these dynamics, and the complex hierarchies in London's hiring queue that they give rise to, however, we will first elaborate on the role that the British state has played in the production of London's new migrant division of labour.

Immigration, Labour Market Change and the Limits of Public Policy

One of the criticisms levelled at Piore and other scholars working on the relationships between migration and labour reserves in the 1970s and 1980s was the apparent functionalism of such accounts. Most notably, while Piore himself offered a sophisticated reading of the struggles between labour and capital that influence state policy, the role of employer demand in such accounts too often implied a direct relationship between the requirements of employers and state immigration policy. This assumed that clear and coherent immigration policies were formulated in response to the demands of employers – such that labour shortages encouraged the (partial) opening of borders, and labour surpluses their closure. At worst, such accounts can lend analyses of immigration policy a conspiratorial air. At best, they imply a coherence and control over immigration policy, and of the relationships between immigration and labour-market policies, that are hardly demonstrated in practice (Castles 2004, Cornelius 2005, Düvell and Jordan 2003).

Thus, while it is tempting to see the rapid growth in the number of migrant workers in London in the last decade or so as the result of a deliberate attempt by government to use immigration policy to create a replacement workforce in a period of labour shortage, it is in fact remarkably difficult to sustain such a narrative. It is true, for example, that by the mid-1990s employers were reporting significant labour shortages at both the top and bottom ends of London's labour market, even while levels of economic inactivity remained high (GLA 2002, Learning and Skills Council 2005). It is also clear that, in the face of continuing difficulties in filling vacancies, employers began to lobby government to ease the restrictions on the use of overseas workers. As a result, the number of work permits issued to foreign-born workers increased very dramatically in this period: from around 40,000 a year in the mid-1990s, to over 200,000 a year in 2004 (Flynn 2005). Moreover, between 1993 and 2003 the number of foreign workers in the UK as a whole increased by no less than 62 per cent – rising to 1.5 million migrants (Sriskandarajah et al. 2004).

Yet, as we showed in Chapter 1, these workers were divided between a number of immigration categories (including highly-skilled migrants, work-permit holders, working holiday–makers, and special visa holders), only a small number of which might be expected to have fed directly into London's low-wage economy – most notably, perhaps, those on very short-term, sector-based schemes covering hotels, catering, and the food-processing sectors. Indeed, when set against the numbers of people coming into the UK by other means in this period, the significance of work-related immigration channels disappears in the shadows. In 2002, for example, some 369,000 foreign students entered the UK, and the same year saw 103,100 applications for asylum (accounting for some 26.5 per cent of all non-British immigration that year). Likewise, in 2004 there were 95,000 grants of settlement for spouses and dependants – far more than the limited number of places offered to overseas workers through sector-based schemes (Vertovec 2007b: 1036–7). Thus, our research suggests that the rapid rise in the number of foreign-born workers employed in London's low-wage economy documented here stems from this wider increase in immigration to the UK, rather than from any particular policy related to immigration for low-wage employment itself.

Moreover, while most analysts agree that business exerted increasing influence over British immigration policy following the election of the New Labour government in May 1997, it was not the only voice shaping policy. As we saw in the previous chapter, the New Labour government's relaxation of the immigration system fitted with their wider pro-business agenda, but it also had other roots – as a senior analyst at the influential Institute for Public Policy Research made clear during an interview with us for our research:

> I think government listens to people such as big business or business representatives, obviously the press, predominantly the tabloid press, the reactionary right-wing press, but not always. I think the unions have had an important role in shaping government policy in this area, or certainly [in] reassuring government about what it's doing. The European Union can't be ignored in the shaping of the UK's migration policy ... So ... in Whitehall, in Westminster, a whole bunch of people who make policy, or who write policy, on migration ... are connected, or sitting in this web ... And it's changed. Because I think if you look at what happened ten years ago and this government coming in and liberalising many avenues of economic migration to this country, one could argue that it was done because they felt the Conservative Party had been unfair in its immigration policy, marriage rules, and all sorts of things, so they went about ... making a more progressive set of policies. They also said: 'We're planning economic growth, we want to expand public services, we want to access these people, so let's liberalise our migration policy regime.' Business they wanted to keep happy ... So, you know, the move by this government was [to] climb up the liberal agenda on migration, [though] since then ... it's been a slippery slope downwards.

As this quotation suggests, it appears that, far from immigration policy being used to actively recruit a new labour reserve, as Piore would suggest, the emergence of very significant numbers of overseas workers in London's low-wage economy at this time occurred largely 'under the radar' of government. A senior official at the Department for Work and Pensions recognised this, telling us in an interview that, despite appearances,

> We've never had a policy of inviting or allowing Africans to come here to clean. You know, the Africans which are here to clean are ... here through a variety of routes: some of which are legal, some of which are not, some of which are somewhere in between. But none of them are here because we gave them a work permit to be a cleaner. So, you know, the fact they came here is not policy-driven in that sense.
>
> ...
>
> Q: *So you're saying that the fact that we found all these Africans doing these jobs was – it was under the radar of policy in a sense? It was just quietly happening?*
>
> Yes.

Yet, although there was no overt attempt by the British government to recruit overseas workers to low-paid jobs, other aspects of government policy were clearly important in shaping the emergence of a new migrant division of labour in London during this period. Most importantly, and as we outlined in the previous chapter, a relaxation of immigration policy in the late 1990s opened the doors to a growing supply of potential workers. At the same time, the labour-market policies of both Conservative and New Labour governments in the 1980s and 1990s created the conditions in which such workers were very likely to find work.

As Doreen Massey (2007: 54–5) has argued, the growing divide in London's labour market – between an increasing number of highly paid managers and professionals on the one hand, and growing numbers of low-paid workers and the economically inactive on the other – is no 'paradox' (for exactly this claim, see Hamnett 2003: 19, Hill 2003: 5). Rather, it is a result of the shift from manufacturing to service-sector employment traced in the opening part of this chapter. This shift is itself best understood not as the result only of some abstract force – a restructuring world economy – over which national policy actors have little or no control (as both politicians and proponents of the 'global cities hypothesis' alike too often claim), but as the product of a complex raft of policies and practices that helped to reconfigure London's and the wider global economy in this period.

London's position at the centre of this new global economy is no accident. Rather, it has grown on the back of its position as a centre of world trade and of imperial power in an earlier era (Eade 2000, King 1990). More recently, far from simply reaping the benefits of a restructured global economy, London's financial institutions have played a leading role in the development and promotion of that economy. Whether opening up the eurodollar market in the 1960s, or promoting policies of financial deregulation and privatisation around the globe in the 1980s and 1990s, as Doreen Massey has put it:

It is not only that certain parts of the London economy function, now, as a command and control centre of the reworked international economy, it is also that the City was in at the beginning, inventing and taking the lead in developing that very reworking. (Massey 2007: 44)

The seminal moment in this 'reinvention' of London as a global financial centre, and in the explosive growth of its financial, property and business services industries, is often held to be the deregulation of the London Stock Exchange and the shift to a new electronic trading system in October 1986 (Marks 2006, Treanor 2006). Yet, although what became known as the 'Big Bang' was undoubtedly important, it was only part of a more complex set of processes behind London's reinvention, with government policy also critical in facilitating changes to London's economy in this period. Most obviously, even as the then Conservative government pumped millions of pounds of government subsidies into the creation of a new financial and business services quarter in London's Docklands through the 1980s (Smith 1989), the deregulation of mortgage lending and the privatisation and marketisation of the public sector fuelled the growth of these industries, and of a new private-sector managerial and professional elite (Buck et al. 2002, Perkin 1996). While privatisation (especially of steel, telecommunications and the gas industries) had a catastrophic effect on blue-collar employment across the UK (Martin and Parker 1997, Mohan 1999), the expansion of London's business and financial industries also had a more direct effect on traditional sources of employment in London – with escalating land prices in London's Docklands contributing to the decline of the area's small-scale manufacturing and related activities (Ogden 1992).

As we have shown, the expansion of these industries and of a new professional and managerial elite not only hastened the decline of traditional sources of manufacturing employment, it also fuelled the growth of new sources of low-paid work, with new jobs in retail, catering and hospitality, security work and cleaning, personal services and care work. Importantly, however, the terms and conditions of these new jobs were quite different to those that preceded them. Even as government subsidies underwrote the expansion of London's business and financial services industries, a number of policies – including the assault on trade unions, the abolition of the Wages Councils, the introduction of the market through competitive tendering in local authorities, and market-testing in the National Health Service – all encouraged a growth in out-sourcing that initiated a steady decline in the pay and conditions of employment, along with growing casualisation, of many low-paid jobs in Britain (Allen and Henry 1997, Reimer 1998, Wills 2004).

Seen in this way, far from being the product of forces operating beyond the reach of individual firms, politicians and policy-makers, London's financial institutions and government policy have played a very significant role in shaping the emergence of a new and more polarised labour market in London. Policy has been much less effective, however, in securing the new and more flexible labour force required by employers. Indeed, notwithstanding the introduction by the New Labour government of a national minimum (though hardly living) wage, and of working tax credits in an effort to 'make work pay', these new low-paid jobs have remained unattractive to many 'native' workers. Even the increased compulsion introduced into the benefits system under New Labour's New Deal (Peck 2001) has not had much success in shifting people off benefits and into (low-paid) work. As we have seen, levels of economic inactivity in London have remained high, and they have risen among those with no qualifications, even as the economy has grown (HM Treasury 2007).

Changes to the rules on benefit eligibility applying to those subject to immigration control have been much more effective in influencing labour supply. Introduced by New Labour in April 2000, the new rules determine that neither overseas students, tourists, work-permit holders nor asylum-seekers are eligible for anything other than contributory benefits (with even the latter withheld from those residing in Britain on an irregular basis) (Representative of the Child Poverty Action Group). Once again, it seems unlikely that these changes represented a deliberate attempt to manage the low-wage economy by managing the supply of low-paid migrant labour. Rather, they are most likely better understood as an attempt by government to manage a growing backlash against rising immigration by tackling public perceptions of migrant 'benefit scroungers' (ibid.). But, whether by design or accident, the effect of such changes has been to help secure a remarkably 'flexible' and 'motivated' workforce – one perfectly suited to the demands of London's new and more 'flexible' labour market. As we show in the following chapter, without Jobseeker's Allowance or Income Support to fall back on when out of work, and without access to the working tax credits designed to boost the earnings of the lowest-paid when they are working, many of London's new migrants have been left with little choice but to take any job they can if they are to secure the income necessary to survive in the city.

Making and Remaking London's Migrant Division of Labour

Even if it is not possible to point to the kind of overt shifts in immigration policy understood by Piore and others as signalling an attempt by the state to construct and deploy a new labour reserve, it is clear that previous and current government policies – across a range of arenas, rather than only in the field of immigration – have played a significant role in shaping the emergence of London's new migrant division of labour. The differential benefits system introduced in April 2000, especially, goes some way in explaining both why migrants may be willing to take on the work that native workers are reluctant to do, and why employers may apparently 'favour' migrants even in a situation of surplus 'local' labour supply. But government policy is not the only factor shaping these dynamics. Gaining a fuller understanding of exactly why employers may favour migrants over native workers, and how and why migrants are drawn to such work, is clearly also important.

While, as we have noted, research into the relationships between immigration and employment slipped off the research agenda in Britain during the 1980s, research in this field remained buoyant in North America. Spurred on by a continuing rise in levels of immigration to the US and Canada throughout the 1980s and 1990s, a group of researchers responded to the critiques made of the Marxist-inspired work of the 1970s with new work exploring the agency of migrant workers (Guarnizo 2002, Massey et al. 1998, Theodore et al. 2006) and the role of employer demand (Portes and Rumbaut 2006, Waldinger and Lichter 2003) in determining the role of migrant workers in urban labour markets. From the point of view of contemporary developments in London, this research is particularly important in capturing the motivations of migrant workers and employers in the context of changing government policy and economic reform.

In seeking to explain migrant divisions of labour in Los Angeles, for example, Waldinger and Lichter introduced the notion of the 'dual frame of reference' through which migrants compare the wages on offer 'back home' with those on offer in their new place of residence. As they suggest,

> The foreign-born comprise the preferred labor force, but not because employers have suddenly developed a soft spot for immigrants, immigration or the broader cultural or social changes wrought by large-scale immigration. Rather employers perceive the newcomers as workers who assess the situation relative to the conditions and options encountered 'back home' [and] the immigrants' dual frame of reference puts America's low-wage sector in a remarkably favourable perspective. (Waldinger and Lichter 2003: 179)

Such findings are echoed on this side of the Atlantic, with employers reporting that their foreign-born workers are particularly willing to work (S. Dench et al. 2006).

But employers may also prefer to employ foreigners as a way to distance themselves from the moral economy of the labour being done. Whereas they might baulk at employing 'their own kind' to do dirty, dangerous and difficult work for very low rates of pay, it can be easier to employ those who are coded as 'other' (Waldinger and Lichter 2003: 40). This might be particularly true in relation to intimate work, and Bridget Anderson (2007) has found that parents who accommodate au pairs at home are able to feel better about themselves if they re-code the work as charity – as help for someone from a poorer part of the world – rather than work.

Employers thus recruit migrants *because* they are migrants, with different qualities to the 'native' labour supply. Yet, when faced with an over-supply of would-be workers, employers have the opportunity to exercise further preferences in a 'hiring queue'. In low-wage labour markets, firms are reluctant to invest in lengthy and costly recruitment screening, and employers tend to adopt national and racialised stereotypes to determine the reliability of potential recruits. As Suzanne Model explains,

> Queuing theorists believe that, as long as the supply lasts, employers will hire into the best jobs workers of the heritage that employers rank most desirable. As the supply of such workers declines and/or the job opportunity becomes less attractive, employers will consider applicants with less desirable ancestries. And they will hire members of the least desirable heritage only when the supply of more favourably ranked groups is exhausted. By the same logic, when the workforce must be reduced, members of the least desirable heritage are the first to be made redundant. (Model 2002: 85)

In her multivariate data analysis of these trends in London, New York and Toronto, Model found a 'relatively stable cross-national hierarchy of discrimination' which reflected established prejudices and stereotypes, as well as the impact of employers' ethnicity and the availability of different streams of labour supply (ibid.: 132). Given the opportunity, employers' preferences in all three cities were for foreign-born whites, followed by East African Asians, Indians and Chinese. These workers were found to fare at least as well as native-born whites (especially men) in each geographic location. In contrast, however, employers would choose to employ Africans, Pakistanis and Bangladeshis only in the absence of the more highly-ranked groups. In the US, African-American men were found to be the least favoured group, selected only when there were no migrants left in the queue.

As employers compete for the most desirable workers, those with the least desirable jobs are likely to have less choice over who to employ. Hence, in London, we would expect that the employers with the poorest-paying and least desirable jobs would be dependent upon the 'least desirable' workers, who have the fewest alternative sources of income and work. However, the volume of potential workers looking for work will also play a big part in shaping any migrant division of labour. In London, as elsewhere, recent changes in government policy and the wider immigration regime have reconfigured the balance between different streams of the labour supply. In our case, changes in the regulation of irregular migration and the decision to open Britain's borders to the wider EU have been particularly significant in reconfiguring employers' hiring queues, with workers from the EU often privileged over those from further afield.

During our research interviews, employers and their representatives argued that migrant workers provided a critical source of labour to London. In care, construction, cleaning, hospitality and food processing, employers felt that they would be unable to provide an acceptable level of service without migrant workers. A number of employers also had a clear sense of what we are calling the 'hiring queue'. Employers in the cleaning sector, in particular, had a strong preference for particular nationalities of workers – Portuguese, Filipino and eastern European workers were mentioned positively a number of times. As one respondent put it: 'I'd die for a Portuguese. You hang on to them, you ask for their sisters, their mothers, their brothers, marvellous! Filipinos, fantastic! Poles, very good!'

More generally, however, employers argued that they preferred to employ migrants because they were better than the 'native' labour supply (see S. Dench et al. 2006, Stenning and Dawley 2009). As one respondent explained in relation to construction, 'The major reason we use immigrant workers is because they are better than the people who are available locally.' Likewise, the human resources manager at a food processing factory said that the migrant workers they employed, who were largely from eastern Europe, were more disciplined than the 'native' labour supply. Some employers expanded on this by contrasting the commitment of migrant workers to the 'work-shy' 'natives'. As one manager in the cleaning industry put it, the role of the benefits system meant that those who were entitled – and especially those with young children at home – would be better off staying at home:

> Let's look at it this way. The English are used to a social security system ... they're used to having that, whereas the immigrants don't have that in their country. We've always had something to fall back on, so those English that are not educated – that, you know, didn't go out and get themselves great jobs – could come out and do cleaning, but they won't do it for a lower wage because they might as well sit indoors and get paid to look after the kids ... To motivate them you'd need ten pounds an hour, definitely.

Given that most of the migrant workers we encountered were not entitled to claim benefits due to their immigration status, they were more willing to work than the 'native' population.

In this regard, a number of respondents from refugee communities made related arguments highlighting the fact that irregular migrants were more likely to work than regular ones. When migrants had failed in their claims for asylum and/or were trying to regularise their immigration status in the country, they had no recourse to benefits and had little choice but to work, and tended to find themselves in low-paying, low-status jobs at the bottom end of the labour market. A number of interviewees from community organisations highlighted the paradox that, once such individuals secured leave to remain and/or became British citizens, they were less likely to take up employment. Once they were able to claim benefits, and particularly Housing Benefit, migrants had less financial incentive to work and, in many respects, started to behave more like those who were born or naturalised within the UK (see Legrain 2007, Piore 1979, Portes and Rumbaut 2001). As one interviewee from the Community for Congolese Refugees explained:

> Once you are authorised to remain in the country, you have the same right as British people, but the issue is low-paid employment which cannot allow [people] to pay into their own house and [if] they decide they want to remain legal ... the only way is not to be employed.

Calling housing a 'huge barrier for employment', this respondent went on to suggest that there was little incentive for migrant-citizens to work unless they could find well-paid and secure employment in London. As we explore further in Chapter 4, without proven experience of professional work in the UK, and in the context of real and perceived racial discrimination, such migrants were likely to get trapped. When irregular, they were trapped in low-paid employment; and after regularisation, they were trapped in unemployment. In tandem with 'natives' without qualifications or prospects for career development, this group of workers was condemned to low-paid work or benefits, neither of which allowed them full access to wider society. Furthermore, at the time of writing, these individuals were under greater pressure to take up employment, securing benefits only on the basis that they were looking for work.

From the point of view of low-paying employers, our research suggests that the most willing employees would be those without the legal status to work, or those who were unable to claim benefits, such as international students. As the government has increased surveillance and control over illegal labour supplies, those without papers are likely to be forced into more marginal and exploitative employment. As we highlight in Chapter 4, this has increased employer preference for available supplies of labour from eastern Europe over those from beyond the EU. The combination of legal changes and the new labour supply are allowing employers to reconfigure their hiring queues, and thus remake London's migrant division of labour.

Reflecting on these changes, interviewees from groups of migrants from the global South argued that their communities would lose out compared to the eastern European arrivals. As one interviewee from Carila, a Latin American community association in London, put it: 'Polish competition. Yes. They're whiter and better educated, and all of them, even if they speak little English, they always speak more English than a Latin American.' Likewise, a representative of the Central Association of Nigerians in the United Kingdom (CANUK) argued that his community was bound to lose out 'once an employer has an alternative' that 'doesn't expose them to risk'. Given the unprecedented arrival of eastern

Europeans, employers of low-paid labour had greater choice about who to employ, and hiring queues were now reflecting this increase in choice.

In this context, the workers who quietly arrived during the 1980s and 1990s and filled the gaps in London's low-paid economy are now in danger of being squeezed out by new arrivals, and by the added weight of the law. For many of those representing these 'unacknowledged' communities of workers in London, this reflects the 'false morality' of the British. As a Brazilian community leader put it, 'the [British] excess of tolerance only works ... when it is convenient to them'. While they were needed, workers from the global South were employed, but not fully acknowledged. Now that their labour is no longer needed, these communities are being very publicly rejected. As one interviewee from the Ghana Black Stars Network explained: 'They've taken your train ticket, they've looked after your sick family member, but you haven't really seen them or noticed that they're there.' As we outlined in the previous chapter, and explore further in Chapter 4, the new immigration regime is focused on sending many of these workers back home.

In this chapter we have charted the emergence of a new migrant division of labour at the bottom end of London's labour market. In attempting to explain the emergence of this divide, we have dusted off – but also polished up – some familiar concepts, developing work by Piore and others that focused on the role of employer demand in shaping state immigration policies and resultant divisions of labour, to point instead to the variety of forces shaping state immigration policies, and to the relative roles of government, employers and migrants themselves in shaping a migrant division of labour.

Indeed, in contrast to earlier analyses, our reading of British immigration policy suggests that the emergence of London's migrant division of labour was hardly the result of some kind of conspiracy between employers and the state. State policy was obviously important, and the emergence of new trends was clearly related to conscious political decision-making; but there was no clear plan that created a new migrant division of labour. Rather, the emergence of large numbers of foreign-born workers at the bottom end of London's labour market is better understood as an unintended consequence of labour-market policies implemented by both Conservative and New Labour administrations during the 1980s and 1990s, and of the relatively lax immigration regime in the early years of New Labour government. These policies created the conditions within which a migrant division of labour was able to take root and flourish. Thus, while others have pointed to the significant role that policies of privatisation and labour-market deregulation played in the restructuring of the London economy in the 1980s and 1990s – policies which we would argue helped to produce the more polarised, more 'flexible' labour market that we see in London today – we also need to consider new immigrant labour supplies. Denied recourse to public funds, those entering Britain as visitors, students or spouses, those on temporary sector-based employment schemes, and those arriving illegally generally had to find some employment. Immigration ensured that the demands of a more 'flexible' labour market were met with an equally 'flexible' labour supply.

As the next chapter will discuss, the membership of London's new migrant division of labour is also dynamic and 'rotating' (Castles and Kosack 1973: 463). Such dynamism has obvious costs for those who find themselves being pushed down the hiring queue. It may also have costs for employers and consumers if labour demand is not met. While our research has highlighted the increasing role of central and eastern European workers in London, there are strong indications that, as the economy moves into recession and as other countries open up their labour markets to these migrant flows, the UK is becoming less attractive to these particular groups. This raises issues of economic sustainability for the future. More importantly, our research also highlights the injustice at the heart of our economy. While the migrants who find themselves in low-paid jobs often suffer very poor terms and conditions of work, struggling to survive in the city, those Londoners (many of them settled migrants or second-generation citizens) who are priced out of employment are also living in precarious circumstances, forced to rely on low levels of state benefits. In the next chapter we turn our attention to the working experiences of migrant workers, exploring the dynamics of London's changing migrant division of labour through the words of these workers themselves.

3

LONDON'S LOW-PAID FOREIGN-BORN WORKERS

I was scared how I am going to be accepted in London. Then I realised quite quickly that as much as I might be a foreigner, I was not more a foreigner than anybody else in London. London is full of foreigners. They did not look at me through the picture of a foreigner, as I had pictured myself. I ... began to feel [good with] all other millions of people who are originally from somewhere else.

Bojan, a Polish hotel worker

In this chapter we provide an overview of the men and women working in care, cleaning, construction, hospitality and food-processing whom we met between 2005 and 2007. Our research allowed us to talk to more than 400 individuals – almost half of them women – outside their places of work, in cafes, community centres and also their homes. We asked people to tell us their stories and were rewarded with rich accounts of when and why they had come to London, how they had made their way into the labour market, the nature of their jobs, the challenges they faced in supporting their families both in London and in their 'home' countries, and their hopes for the future. While we had 429 conversations that flowed around a questionnaire, we were also fortunate to have longer encounters with just over 100 migrant workers. Here we draw on both sets of data to people the story of London's migrant division of labour. We begin by providing a broad overview of this labour force, highlighting the geographies of origin and residence in London. We then move on to look at work in more detail, exploring people's routes into work, their terms and conditions of employment, and their experiences of work. This latter part focuses in more detail on the accounts provided by workers employed in care, cleaning and hospitality. In the final section, we provide an overview of workers' more general responses to London's migrant division of labour. We highlight workers' structural location in relation to the labour market, taking up the consequences of this position in more detail in the following chapter.

As will become clear, our research highlighted the extraordinary diversity of London's low-paid workforce. Indeed, while social networks – often based on nationality – were found to play a key part in helping potential workers to access the labour market, this did not mean that most migrants were working only with co-nationals. Most of our respondents were living and working alongside a diversity of other national groups, and many found this a positive aspect of their experience in London. We also found extraordinarily high rates of labour turnover – most people had been in their present job for less than a year – and people moved between employers, and even sectors, in an attempt to improve their conditions of work. This mobility facilitated rapid change within any particular workplace, and our respondents reported frequent shifts in the national origins of the people working alongside them. Given the poor pay and conditions of work – less than 10 per cent of our sample were earning above the London living wage[1] – labour-market mobility represented the best option for improving socio-economic status and prospects. Our respondents were eager to 'move on', and did so largely through labour-market mobility.

In subsequent chapters we add to the picture presented here by looking at processes of segmentation within this labour force, highlighting the palimpsest of new and old cleavages associated with legal status, nationality, ethnicity, race and gender (Chapter 4); the challenges of survival (Chapter 5); the wider impact of the situation in London on family, community and nation back home (Chapter 6); and the consequences for political voice and collective organisation in London (Chapter 7). For now, however, we start with the basics. We illuminate the hidden corners of London's economy, exploring the lives of the people who are working in low-paid employment.

Inhabiting London's Low-Wage Economy: Who's Doing the Work and Why

London's low-wage economy is populated by a remarkably diverse group of workers. We encountered people from as many as 63 different countries of origin, excluding the UK. While many were the sole representative of their national group (including countries such as Burundi, Estonia, Libya, Syria and Togo), we also found larger concentrations of workers from countries in eastern Europe, Latin America and Africa. Indeed, we found unexpectedly large numbers of workers

1. The London living wage (LLW) is the 'low-cost but acceptable' income calculated for the city. This figure was first generated for the London Living Wage campaign (see Chapter 7), but, following pressure by the campaign, its calculation has been adopted by the Greater London Authority (GLA). A team of independent economists uses a recognised methodology to calculate the costs of a basic standard of living for different family types, and this is compared to 60 per cent of median income, adjusted for family types in London, and assuming full benefit take-up. An annual figure is then agreed and published (see GLA 2008).

from sub-Saharan Africa. Despite the absence of any official immigration channels beyond family reunification and the opportunity for temporary residence as a student, as many as *half* of all the workers we encountered were born in Africa, the majority coming from Ghana and Nigeria. As outlined in Table 3.1 and Fig. 3.1, Africans far outnumbered those originating in either Latin America and the Caribbean, Europe, or Asia. While our data are obviously dependent upon the economic sectors we studied, as well as the leads that we followed, they nonetheless point to the ingenuity of this labour supply. African workers had found their way around the British immigration system, arriving as asylum-seekers, tourists and students. Some had since managed to regularise themselves, and a small minority of longer-term residents had become British citizens. However, many had been working irregularly for at least some of their time in the UK, and our research thus highlights the limits of immigration control, at least in the run-up to the period when it was carried out (see Castles 2004; and for the US, Cornelius 2005).

Table 3.1   Regions and countries of origin

Region	Geographical distribution	Number	%
Africa		224	52
Key countries	Ghana (72 – 18%), Nigeria (68 – 16%), Congo (19 – 4%), Mauritius (9 – 2%), Kenya and Uganda (7 – 2%), Sierra Leone (6 – 1%)		
Minor countries	Burundi, Cameroon, Gambia, Guinea-Bissau, Ivory Coast, Libya, Morocco, Senegal, Somalia, South Africa, Tanzania, Togo, Tunisia, Zambia, Zimbabwe		
Latin America and the Caribbean		76	18
Key countries	Brazil (23 – 5%), Colombia (17 – 4%), Jamaica (14 – 3%), Ecuador (5 – 1%)		
Minor countries	Argentina, Barbados, Chile, Dominican Republic, Guinea, Honduras, Nicaragua, St Lucia, Trinidad and Tobago, Venezuela, 'West Indies'		
Western Europe		55	13
Key countries	Portugal (18 – 4%), Spain (8 – 2%),* Ireland (4 – 1%)		
Minor countries	France, Italy		
Eastern Europe		44	10
Key countries	Poland (31 – 7%), Bulgaria (11 – 3%), Lithuania (10 – 2%)		
Minor countries	Bosnia, Croatia, Estonia, Latvia, Slovakia, Slovenia, Ukraine		
Asia	India (8 – 2%), Sri Lanka (5 – 1%), Pakistan, Philippines, Thailand	23	5
Other	St Helena, South Yemen	3	1
No response		4	1
Total		429	

Source: Analysis of authors' questionnaire survey. Please note that the number of respondents is only given in relation to countries which represented more than 1 per cent of the total sample (5 or more people); see also Appendix 1.

* There is strong anecdotal evidence, backed up in our interviews, suggesting that many workers with Portuguese and Spanish passports actually originated in Latin America (see also McIlwaine 2007b).

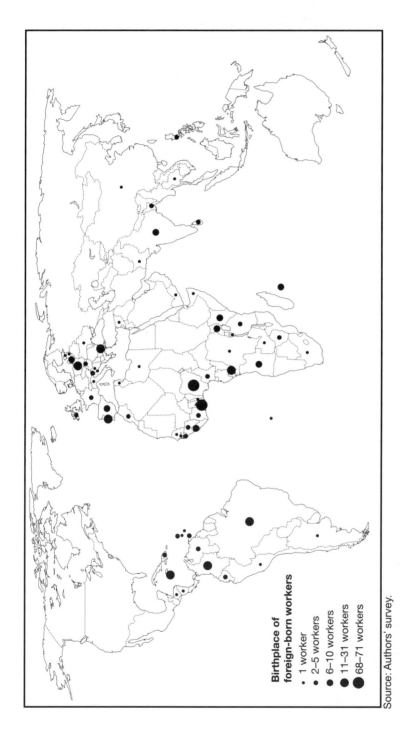

**Birthplace of
foreign-born workers**

· 1 worker

• 2–5 workers

● 6–10 workers

● 11–31 workers

● 68–71 workers

Source: Authors' survey.

Figure 3.1 The geographical origins of London's low-paid workers

About a third of the 429 workers we surveyed appeared to lack the papers to work. While some refused to answer the question about immigration status (14 per cent), a very small group admitted not having the papers to work (3 per cent) and a further group reported other rather ambiguous arrangements, such as having a work permit (despite their unavailability for low-paid employment). In addition, a further 11 per cent described themselves as students, and our interviews revealed that student registration was commonly practised as a means to secure legal employment, with or without the intention to study. This was particularly important among communities that had no access to the asylum system, and in a related study of one Brazilian community in London we found that 16 per cent of this population of 423 people were working on student visas (see Box 3.1). As we saw in the previous chapter, such students would not be legally entitled to claim welfare benefits and, while more secure than their paperless colleagues, these international students could only secure long-term residence or citizenship by gaining a work permit for a particular post or through marriage. As many as 40 per cent of those we surveyed therefore represented a classic reserve army of labour. These were mostly individuals who had come to the UK expressly to do low-paid work (sometimes in conjunction with being a student) without any alternative means of survival.

Box 3.1 **The Brazilian Community in London**

The last decade and a half has seen a remarkable growth in the number of Brazilians arriving in the UK. Given the lack of historical links with Britain that might exempt them from immigration restrictions – particularly those against taking up paid employment – Brazilians have commonly entered the UK on tourist or student visas, with the expectation of staying on. And as they have stayed on, they have helped the Brazilian community to expand into a sizeable new immigrant community. Estimates suggest that there are something like 200,000 Brazilians now living in the UK, the majority based in London. Brazilians represent a particularly interesting case, as a population that has not had any chance to secure residence using the asylum system, and with little historic connection to the country. Brazilians therefore represent a good example of a community that has grown due to economic and educational immigration, and much of the population comprises irregular migrants.

One indication of this spectacular growth is the equally impressive number of formal and informal businesses that have appeared in the last decade or so. They are mostly provided by Brazilians for Brazilians, and include personal care, domestic cleaning, money transfer, removal and transport, and legal and counselling services. A good number of cafés, restaurants and shops offering Brazilian food and goods now

▶

also operate in London. Their services are advertised in the dozen or so Brazilian publications that circulate widely in this thriving community.

However, the ghost of irregularity haunts many Brazilians, and this was brought to national attention on the occasion of the death of Jean Charles de Menezes at the hands of police, after he was mistaken for one of the terrorist bombers responsible for the July 2005 bombings in London. Soon after he was shot, the press reported that Jean Charles had overstayed his visa, seemingly implying that his irregular status somehow justified his tragic death.

This issue has been at the forefront of a campaign organised by London Citizens called 'Strangers into Citizens', which calls for the regularisation of some half a million immigrants who are thought to be in the UK without authorisation (see also Chapter 7). To help bolster the campaign, a team of activists based at a Brazilian church in London conducted a questionnaire survey of Brazilians in the autumn of 2006. The survey produced a total of 423 returns, and the results were reported in 2007 (see Evans et al. 2007b). Here, we reproduce some of the key findings of this research.

Brazilians in London

Slightly more men (52 per cent) than women participated in the survey. Over four-fifths of respondents were aged 18–40, with an average age of 33.5 years. Women dominated the 18–30 age group, while more men than women were aged 41–50.

As with many other immigrants, the key rationale leading Brazilians to emigrate was the prospect of earning higher wages and being able to save money. Often their savings were to be spent or invested in Brazil. Remittances were sent to support family members, to clear debts, to buy land or property, and to set up and run small businesses. Nearly half of the respondents reported coming to the UK either for economic reasons alone, or in combination with other aims. For instance, nearly a quarter had come with the aim of working to earn and save, whereas a further quarter intended to work and study.

The findings also showed that over half of the sample (54 per cent) had attended secondary school, with one-third continuing up to first degree level. As education can be taken as an indication of class membership, it is clear that the majority of the Brazilians surveyed came from a middle-class background.

Regarding immigration status, the findings confirmed what has always been an open secret: that many Brazilians eventually become irregular migrants. Over one-half of Brazilians in the London study (53 per cent) had overstayed their visas. Of those who held valid visas, 16 per cent were on student visas and one in ten held a tourist visa. In addition, one in ten held a European passport – often obtained as a result of eligibility due to recent European ancestry, mostly deriving from Italy and Germany.

▶

Confirming an observed increase in flows of Brazilians to the UK over the last decade, more than two-thirds of the Brazilians surveyed (69 per cent) were relatively recent arrivals, having been in the UK for a period ranging between one and five years, with an average stay of 2.8 years.

Brazilians at work in London

In tandem with the other migrant communities documented in this book, Brazilians in London are commonly found to be doing unskilled and low-paid jobs which usually have little, if anything, to do with the kinds of jobs they used to do at home. Their immigration status, which may limit their ability to work, tends to combine with their lack of knowledge of English to restrict their labour-market options.

The results of the London survey showed that Brazilians took up jobs in two main sectors of the economy. Nearly one-third of the sample reported working in cleaning (of both offices and private homes). Of these, the large majority were women (80 per cent of all cleaners). Over one-quarter of all respondents worked in the hotel and catering industries, and most of these were men (70 per cent), who generally took up jobs as kitchen hands or waiters. Men also worked as couriers and drivers (10 per cent), and as labourers in construction (9 per cent). Finally, 13 per cent of respondents were working in various other jobs in retail, office work, education and customer services. The only jobs undertaken solely by women were those of au pair and nanny, although these made up a very small proportion of the sample (3 per cent).

Contrary to findings produced by other studies of migrant workers, the overwhelming majority of the Brazilians surveyed held only one job. Over two-thirds were working full-time (35 hours a week or longer). On average, they worked 42 hours per week, but the gender split revealed that men were working longer average hours than women (46 compared to 37 hours).

The national minimum wage (NMW) and the London living wage (LLW) were used as yardsticks to categorise the survey data on wage levels. The results show a degree of variability with the largest group – 38 per cent – earning between the NMW and the LLW, a further 11 per cent being confined to the NMW, and as many as 17 per cent earning less than this rate (and nearly three-quarters of these were irregular migrants). Although as many as 15 per cent did not answer the question about wages, the remaining 19 per cent were earning at least the LLW .

Finally, the survey showed that about one-half of Brazilians were looking to the middle- to long-term to fulfil their objectives in the UK, expecting to remain for a number of years. Whatever the expectation, however, for many the decision to stay invariably entails becoming an irregular migrant and living in constant fear of deportation. This has provided motivation to engage in London Citizens' campaign to turn 'Strangers into Citizens' (see Chapter 7).

Source: Authors' analysis of survey data (further information in Appendix 1); see also Evans et al. (2007b).

In addition, however, a further 20 per cent of survey respondents were also in a fairly insecure position within the UK. While very small numbers described themselves as being asylum-seekers or refugees (3 per cent), a much larger group described themselves as having Indefinite Leave to Remain (ILR) (18 per cent). ILR is generally granted to those who secure residence following family reunification or refugee status, and in many cases it does not entitle the individual to welfare support. In these cases, the words 'no official recourse to public funds' will generally be stamped in the passport. While it is possible to accumulate benefits on the basis of employment and the payment of National Insurance contributions, including Jobseeker's Allowance and the State Pension, these individuals are not entitled to Child Benefit, Income Support, tax credits, Housing Benefit or housing provision (Home Office, n.d.). ILR is thus also likely to push individuals into employment, and it is only when or if they become full British citizens that they will have the guarantee of alternative means of support. In addition, however, access to British citizenship can take a long time to acquire, and it is now associated with passing both language and general knowledge assessments and face-to-face interviews, which may deter would-be applicants (Rutter et al. 2008). It is also very expensive, with costs set to increase further.

More than half of the low-paid migrant workers we encountered in London clearly had little, if any, access to the benefits system. Moreover, of the 40 per cent who reported having British or European citizenship, a sizeable minority had recently arrived from eastern Europe, and were not entitled to benefits until they had secured a 12-month period of uninterrupted employment while documented as being on the Worker Registration Scheme (WRS). As many as 50 per cent of the 44 workers we encountered from the countries of eastern Europe had been in the UK for less than a year, making them ineligible. It is also likely that some of their colleagues were similarly ineligible due to their failure to register with the WRS, not least because of the fees and paperwork involved (see Anderson et al. 2006).

An interview conducted with a representative of the Child Poverty Action Group (CPAG) revealed that many such European workers were found to be falling into a 'benefit hole'. From 1994 to 2004, the Habitual Residence test determined that means-tested benefits were only available to those who had been resident in Britain and looking for work for at least three months. However, in 2004, this was augmented by the Right to Reside test, which requires those from eastern Europe to work without interruption for at least 12 months while registered on the WRS before being able to claim. All European workers who become unable to work can fall foul of one of these rules. The CPAG interviewee recalled the case of a Polish woman who had two children, aged 12 and 18, living with her in the UK. She had undertaken registered work for ten months before being diagnosed with cancer, and then found that she had 'no benefits, nothing at all. She is undergoing treatment, chemotherapy, and sleeping on somebody's sofa because they can't pay for the rent.' This same interviewee also argued that EU nationals were similarly affected, as permanent illness prevented them from looking for work, which meant that they lost their right to reside. Highlighting the role played by the Red Cross in supporting increasing numbers of non-WRS-eligible and sick Europeans, failed asylum-seekers and irregular migrants who were effectively destitute, the CPAG interviewee argued that 'it's a sort of underclass ... we have this group of people that nobody feeds and nobody's aware of. How they are surviving, I just don't know.'

Our research suggests that immigration status – and its relationship to benefit entitlement – has been critical in creating London's new migrant division of labour. Although some 90 per cent of respondents reported paying income tax and National Insurance contributions, only 15 per cent (65 people) of those surveyed reported being in receipt of one or more forms of state benefit – with about a third of these in receipt of Child Benefit and/or Working Tax Credit and/or Child Tax Credit. As might be expected, British citizens were more likely to be claiming than their non-citizen colleagues (30 per cent compared to 15 per cent), and rates increased sharply with time spent within the UK (40 per cent of all those claiming had been in the country for more than a decade). Despite the fact that as many as a third of respondents (33 per cent, or 142 people) were responsible for children aged 16 or under living in the UK, only half this number were claiming. Thus, while many migrants have children, and their low wages and lack of benefit entitlement will be contributing to child poverty in the city today, the tax credit regime is not reaching these workers. Moreover, while the low take-up of benefits is likely to reflect a lack of entitlement, it could also be due to the complicated process of making a claim. Data for the city as a whole suggest that as many as 150,000 children are living in low-income working households that do not receive tax credits. It is clear that the government's flagship policies to make work pay and end child poverty are less effective in London than elsewhere in the UK (MacInnes and Kenway 2009).

But our research clearly found that the migrants working in London's low-wage economy were motivated by the prospect of employment (as well as by educational and social factors that are outlined further below) rather than by benefits. People reported coming to London because they had heard it was easy to find work, and because they knew that the rates of pay were better than those on offer at home. In a particularly stark example, one young Congolese man who had lived in Sweden with his parents from the age of seven described how he had completed his studies there only to find that he could not secure work: 'As a European, my friends in the UK advised me to travel to the UK where more opportunities for work are available. In Sweden the labour market is too tight, it is really difficult to find a job.' At the time of the interview, Lord had been in the UK for more than five years, working as a cleaner in Bolton, Manchester and London.

At the broadest level of analysis, a good 40 per cent of those surveyed said that they had moved for economic advantage. Moreover, although a further 25 per cent reported coming to join family and wider social networks, many of these individuals incorporated economic interests as part of their decision to move. Respondents had a strong sense of the 'dual framework' that we identified in the previous chapter: while they knew the job was low-paid by local standards, they evaluated it in relation to the wages and costs of living 'at home'. As Janet, a carer from Jamaica, explained:

> Money-wise, you know, here is better. If you compare the pay scale here to back home, it's better being paid here. In terms of all the opportunities and the benefits ... even being a healthcare assistant, the money you get, someone back home would not get that money. So I feel I'm better off here.

Likewise, Vijay, a carer from Mauritius, said, 'When you compare [the job in London] to my money, Mauritian money, it's still better ... Otherwise, we wouldn't be here.'

In the same vein, a number of respondents argued that being in London allowed them to 'speed up' the acquisition of the goods they desired. As Luis, a Brazilian cleaner, put it: 'What I managed to achieve here in one year, I would achieve there in five or six. It sped things up a lot.' Similarly, Brygida, a 30-year-old Polish carer, emphasised the greater spending power that came with working in London: 'I bought a computer with one, two months' savings ... in Poland, maybe I would buy in a year or two years of saving ... Put it this way, I save money for a shorter period of time [here] than in Poland.'

Other respondents saw working in London as a route to their long-term financial independence and security. Jaime, a young man from Venezuela, argued that his cleaning job allowed him to live on his own for the first time: 'Even though I don't like to do this kind of job, I pay for everything myself.' Similarly, Adanya, a Nigerian cleaner on the London Underground argued that low-paid work in London had allowed her to learn to be independent. As she explained: 'Back home I've got uncles and friends that I can go to and say "give me some money for my shopping", but here there's no-one to give. You have to work hard. You have to be independent. I'm focused on doing something on my own.' A number of workers from the Democratic Republic of Congo said similar things, as one young man, Mamputu, explained: 'In Congo I was not independent but here I am. Now I am able to help financially those who helped me while in Congo. Here I get my wages and other benefits. That helps me to send money to my parents.'

We also found that many respondents were from countries without welfare systems, and some of them argued that they needed their jobs in London to sustain themselves in old age. As Pedro, a Brazilian cleaner in his fifties explained:

> If I hadn't come here I would probably be in Brazil without any prospects, with no pension. I would have to wait for the state pension based on my age ... only a minimum wage and I wouldn't even have enough to eat. I would depend on my children. The way I am planning [now he's in London], I won't depend on my children. Of course, when I get to a very advanced age, I might need them but if I have a place to live and a little money here and there, I can manage myself. I will live here and in Brazil.

In addition to the opportunities for employment, respondents also emphasised their desire to study in London. Almost 20 per cent of those surveyed (69 people) reported coming to London to study; respondents were taking language courses and vocational training as well as higher education degrees. People also appreciated having the opportunity to learn from the workplace, and many emphasised the role of the city in giving them a 'new perspective on life'. As Vijay, the Mauritian carer, explained:

> You get a lot of experience in London. You know people from around the world. You have an idea of how the world is ... Perhaps you don't realise that when you come from another country like Mauritius, a small island, but the fact that it is small gives you ... a narrow perspective of life ... When you come to London you see the world as it is, large, big, and [while] the difficulties are big, the prospects are also big. You get a new perspective on life.

Many of the migrant workers we spoke to described their excitement in 'meeting the world' as part of their new life in London. They were generally living and working alongside a wide array of other nationalities and, despite tensions between national groups (which we explore more fully in the following chapter), our respondents regularly reported this as a key benefit of working in London. As Luis, the Brazilian man, put it: 'The amount of different ethnic groups is large and I have met many people from all over the world – Japanese, Chinese, Angolan, Ecuadorian. People from all over the world are mixing with each other.' One Congolese woman similarly commented: 'I have learned working with people from different horizons, which is a rewarding experience.'

Indeed, as the quotation that opens this chapter suggests, migrants tended to live their lives alongside other migrants, and many reported that their biggest disappointment was having few chances to get to know English or British people while staying in the UK (see also Herbert et al. 2008). This lack of integration between migrants and 'natives' can be partly explained by the extent to which London's low-paid economy now depends on the foreign-born, so that the 'natives' people encountered at work were likely to be their employer. However, this situation was also due to the fact that new arrivals have tended to settle in the areas of cheapest housing, which already accommodate significant numbers of foreigners. Indeed, Fig. 3.2 shows the percentage of residents earning less than £7.50 per hour in 2008, and the areas with the highest percentage are those known to accommodate large numbers of migrants. We found that the majority of new Londoners were living in just eight of the city's 32 boroughs, concentrated in the south and east of the city. The boroughs of Croydon, Hackney, Haringey, Lambeth, Lewisham, Newham, Southwark and Tower Hamlets had the largest number of respondents (each with at least 6 per cent of the total sample, or more than 25 people, as illustrated in Fig. 3.3). But it is also important to acknowledge that migrant workers were found to be dispersed across the capital, and we encountered people living in as many as 27 different boroughs in total. While patterns of agglomeration tended to reflect historical concentrations of minority ethnic communities, due partly to the landscape of housing costs and provision, the new migration had also permeated the wider city, not least because low-paid jobs were also widely dispersed.

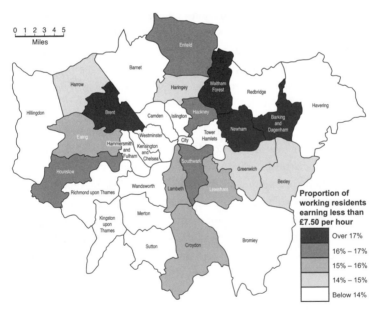

Source: Annual Survey of Hours and Earnings (ASHE), 2008, MacInnes and Kenway (2009: 54).

Figure 3.2   The geography of employees earning less than £7.50 per hour, in London, by place of residence, 2008

Source: Authors' survey, data missing from 73 respondents.

Figure 3.3   The geography of foreign-born workers' residence in London

Getting a Job

Our interviews revealed the extraordinary energy that people had put in to the search for work. Arguing that their poor English made it difficult to find a job over the phone, many suggested it was easier to try to find employment through face-to-face contact. As Piotyr, a young Polish man, put it:

> I didn't speak English very well so I couldn't speak on the phone, and I had to go to a place and talk to someone face-to-face. I packed my sandwiches and went to Bow, knowing that there are many industrial buildings. I was walking from business to business [for] something like six hours, and finally I found this removal business ... they needed drivers. In the evening they called me and said to come to work next day at 7am.

Berenik, a Polish chambermaid, recalled a similar experience when she first arrived, saying that, after registering with a language school,

> I prepared cover letter and CV and began to visit hotel after hotel leaving my CV in each of them ... I was lucky, after having left I think something between 15 to 20 CVs ... in one hotel I was asked to come to the interview the next day. On Saturday I got a phone call that I am to come to work the following Monday to work as a receptionist.

Despite these cold-calling strategies, the vast majority of workers secured their employment through personal contacts. Very few went through official channels by looking at advertisements and complying with formal application procedures. Indeed, when asked how they secured their current position, as many as 68 per cent of respondents (256 people) said that they had relied on a personal contact, dwarfing the numbers who had answered an advert (8 per cent), performed their own search (11 per cent) or used an agency (9 per cent). Many workers reported that it was relatively easy to find work; once employed, people were constantly using their contacts to move between jobs. Indeed, our survey showed that about half of all workers had been in their present position for less than a year (ranging from 43 per cent of those in cleaning to 54 per cent of those in the hospitality sector).

When describing how they found work, people mentioned a wide range of such contacts – including aunts, uncles, cousins, friends, house-mates and colleagues. As Rita, a young Chilean cleaner, told us, she found her first job

> through a Chilean woman who had worked here in the mornings ... she came and spoke with the manager. They gave me a phone number and I called every day to find out if there was work. As I spoke Spanish, it was easier of course.

Likewise, João, a Brazilian man who was working in construction when we interviewed him, reported finding his second job as a cleaner in Liverpool Street through a friend:

> She told me that there was a place available and that the supervisor was a Colombian. She said 'Here is her phone number, you can call her, she is a friend and likes me very much, I always introduce people to her. Call her.' So I did [and] she asked me to start the day after.

Such contacts were often fairly extended. As João commented, telling us about a subsequent job, there was a

> Portuguese girl that lived in the same house as I lived. She had a friend of a friend, who had a friend who did part-time work in this bakery and learned that there was a vacancy there. She took me, because I didn't know how to get there.

In some cases, contacts were also valuable as a way of avoiding immigration control. As Ptchens, a Congolese worker, explained:

> An old acquaintance of my 'foster' family helped me find the job that I am still doing till now. As he was working there and was well appreciated, they didn't require seeing my papers.

A number of respondents also used various more formal labour intermediaries in an effort to secure employment, including recruitment agencies in their home country (in the case of Poland), labour agencies in London, unofficial job brokers, and hiring corners in the city – as well as 'job sellers', who would sell their job for a fee. Marcelo, a Brazilian man, told us how he bought a job for £400, explaining:

> If you work in cleaning and you earn £100 a week, and if I start working on the same job to replace you, I will have to pay you £400 to have the job. So I will pay you one month to have the right to carry on in that job. I will carry on working there for two, three months or longer, but I have to pay the first month to you.

A number of workers told us how a friend or contact would get paid for introducing new staff at work. Describing his experience in Ireland, Eafeu, a Ghanaian man, told us that he had found work through a contact who spoke good English and had connections to a local labour agency:

> The Irish men would come from the agency and talk to this Brazilian guy who speaks English, and it was this Brazilian who got me the job ... He earns to do that, because the Irish guy paid him to find people. I think he earned £50 for each person he introduced.

Similarly, one Polish woman told us she had had to pay £250 to a contact for the opportunity to secure a job at a London hotel.

Other unofficial practices included the use of hiring corners in the city, where construction workers would go to find jobs. Darek, a 29-year-old Polish man, told us how he had found construction work at a

> kind of meeting point. I went there three days. The guy who was coming to take people for work saw me, and asked if I speak English. On my third visit, he took me and so I began to work for him. As it turned out, my foreman was a Pole.

Many construction workers also reported being self-employed, even though they were working directly for an agency or employer. As Paulo – a Brazilian man in his forties who had moved through a number of low-paid jobs in London before ending up in construction – explained:

> They don't give you a contract. I mean, if I give you a contract and you come to work but then you don't work, I have to pay you. If you are self-employed, then you have to get to work and get the work done. That's how it works!

More commonly, however, and particularly in care and hospitality, workers used various agencies to find low-paid jobs in the city. As Alena, a Polish woman, explained, her brother had given her 'the address of this agency, so I went there and said that I am looking for a job. She said to come on Tuesday and that I could go and do the training.' Likewise, Cewe, a young Slovakian woman, reported finding a carer employment agency through a friend of mine. This agency did not require any particular qualifications, and I got a job as a carer through them. The only requirement was that I had to be flexible regarding my time and place of assignment. I had to go everywhere they sent me.

Another respondent described being approached speculatively by an Albanian man on a train. As Orszula put it: 'He asked if we wanted a job and at first we thought, "Yeah, we know what kind of work that would be", but he gave us a telephone number and it turned out to be a normal job. It was a cleaning agency.' Workers reported that agencies tended to specialise in particular kinds of work, and in some cases particular kinds of worker. We interviewed one Bulgarian cleaner on the London Underground, working with a business visa, who had found his first job through a Bulgarian agency that advertised in London's only Bulgarian newspaper. His first job was to clean photocopying machines in Camden, before he made the contacts he needed to secure alternative work.

In contrast to most of our respondents, who had turned up in London before looking for work, a number of workers from Poland had actually been recruited at home before they travelled to the UK. As Berenik, a Polish woman who arrived in 2004, recalled:

Once Poland joined the EU, many [agencies] appeared in Poland, as there was money to be made. One of them is [name of agency] that employs people to work on ships, but recently they began to select people for work in England in the hospitality sector ... I arranged a meeting and went to this agency. They told me that very soon someone from England would come to hold interviews with candidates. There was a chance that soon I could have a job in England. I began to study harder in order to finish my dissertation, and I was lucky because as soon as I finished writing it up – it was December – I got an invitation for the interview. They said that my English was adequate, yet I was told that at the moment there would be nothing except [a] hotel maid position. Cleaning rooms ... I had no choice. I had to get out of these debts.

Some Polish recruitment agencies have reportedly exaggerated the quality and benefits of employment in the UK prior to workers' arrival, and the more open immigration regime provides these agencies with considerable power in selecting workers at home. In contrast, most of the workers from outside the EU had to seek opportunities once they arrived. As we have seen, most used personal contacts, unofficial intermediaries, agencies and their own energy as a route into employment. Over time, these workers often sought to better themselves by moving into alternative work: whereas they might start by delivering leaflets or working as a kitchen porter, they could then improve their language skills and contacts sufficiently to secure better work with the same or a different employer. As an example of this, we interviewed José, a 30-year-old Brazilian man who had moved from car-washing to a restaurant, then cleaning, and finally construction. Recalling his employment history, he told us that he always looked to move on:

A friend of mine got a job in a restaurant where they also needed a washing-up person. He told me about it. It was in Piccadilly. I worked for a month as a washer-up but, as I told you, I was always paying attention because I wanted to learn. When I start in a job I don't want to stay at the bottom, I want to move up. Another friend, who I met there, he was going back to Brazil and so they would need another person. He taught me it all, writing down the names of everything on a piece of paper to learn ... to assist a chef, working with fish. Two months later the head chef, having seen my performance, promoted me to chef.

Our research thus exposed the extraordinary degree of flexibility in London's labour force, which involves migrant workers moving between jobs and between sectors in the low-wage economy. We encountered workers who had moved from hospitality to care, from cleaning to construction, from a factory to the London Underground. These jobs were all characterised by low barriers to entry and the presence of personal contacts – themselves often related to nationality – which were generally more important than official qualifications and skills in getting the job. Particular jobs tended to become associated with particular kinds of worker, and the combination of social networks and employer preferences created new configurations of the hiring queue, which then had an impact on the wider distribution of jobs, income and prospects.

Multinationalism at Work

As might be expected, the importance of social networks meant that some of our respondents were predominantly working with their national compatriots. As Angela, a young Portuguese woman who worked in cleaning, said in relation to her workplace: 'The majority are Portuguese and from Madeira. The manageress, the supervisor, all from Madeira.' Similarly, a cleaner from Guinea-Bissau reported that his team were all Portuguese-speakers because the supervisor was Portuguese. Reflecting the colonial legacy of the Portuguese nation, this meant a workforce of five people included two from Guinea-Bissau, an Angolan and a Brazilian, along with a new arrival from Poland who was not a Portuguese-speaker. In places where supervisors, rather than more senior staff, had a role in recruitment – most often the case in office cleaning – it was common to find very significant numbers of co-nationals, and/or those sharing a common language, working together. As Tahir, an Angolan office cleaner, explained: 'Three or four are from Sierra Leone – they are mostly from Sierra Leone because Donald, the manager when I started, he was from Sierra Leone.' Similar patterns have been documented in North American cities where social networks among co-nationals from Mexico and the Caribbean are particularly well established in low-wage employment (Rouse 1992, Waldinger and Lichter 2003).

However, our research also revealed that levels of labour turnover and the impact of new arrivals could quickly change this pattern of co-national employment. As Brazilian Luis told us in relation to his job: 'It was me who started to introduce the Brazilians. Myself and my girlfriend. After we started there, now you'll see the hotel is full of Brazilians.' Indeed, once a new person was employed it was relatively easy for new social networks to become established at work. As June, a Caribbean office cleaner, recalled:

> When I first went there, the majority were Ecuadorian and Colombian. Then a lot of them left because they never had proper documents [and were threatened with an immigration raid]; 95 per cent of them left. Then we had a lot of Ghanaians and a few of them left. At the moment, we've got a huge number of Polish and Lithuanian, we've got a bit of Portuguese, a few Nigerian and a few Ghanaian.

As we have shown, London's low-wage labour market is particularly dependent on an immigrant labour force that is differentiated from locals through immigration control. Once they are available and looking for work, migrant workers reported that employers would take the best of the workers on offer. Moreover, in doing so they tended to adopt short-hand routes to finding employees. If they had a good experience with one worker, they would be more likely to employ their friends or their national compatriots. While this process could create national 'employment ghettos' in a stable environment, the mobility of the workforce, in combination with a steady stream of new arrivals, created the dynamism we reported above. Indeed, the vast majority of our respondents told us that they worked alongside a multinational workforce.

Describing his work in a restaurant, Paulo, a Brazilian man, was joined in the kitchen by '[a] Bolivian, a Muslim [*sic*], an American – who is the sub-chef – a Spaniard and one from Nepal'. When asked to describe the geographical origins of the waiting staff, he added: 'Brazilians, Mexicans, Irish, Poles, people from all over, all over.' Likewise, Eafeu, who worked in construction and care, told us about his co-workers, who were 'the Polish, the Congolese and the Romanians ... and other people from central America'. Hotel workers described a multinational workforce that included increasing numbers of people from eastern Europe, including Kosovans, Romanians and Ukrainians. As Portuguese worker Rosana put it, there were people 'from Poland, Romania, Russia; we have some from Africa and some Mongolians'. Matshuda, a 39-year-old Congolese respondent, described his kitchen as having 'two Congolese, one Togolese, one Angolan and one Polish'. Many respondents valued this experience of working across difference; as Abam, a Ghanaian office cleaner, put it:

There's a Filipino, one from Colombia, one from Brazil, people from Ghana – including me, it's four – and I think Nigeria ... we are a mix. The most interesting thing is when we go on break and people bring food, we get together ... we've got a mutual life here.

We believe this diversity epitomises London's migrant division of labour. While there have long been clear patterns of ethnic and gender segmentation in the labour market, contemporary circumstances are recasting divisions around two new axes. The first is immigration itself, particularly as it divides those who are able to claim benefits from those who must find alternative means of support; and the second is legality, which divides regular from irregular migrants. As we outline further in Chapter 4, these new cleavages cast a long shadow over existing patterns of ethnic and gender segmentation, and they help to explain the multinational nature of the workforces in London's low-wage economy.

Conditions of Work

Despite the importance of the dual frame of reference that makes London's low-paid economy so attractive to many foreign-born workers, our research also revealed uniformly poor employment conditions in care, cleaning, construction (labouring), hospitality and food-processing. At the broadest level of analysis, we captured a labour market that was characterised by minimal employment standards. While a quarter of the workers we surveyed were paid the national minimum wage (NMW) or less, just 7 per cent were paid anything like the London living wage (LLW) or above (see Table 3.2). While employers generally respected the law, and most had found it necessary to increase wages slightly above the NMW, the wages paid were still below the level recognised as the minimal standard to live (now benchmarked by the LLW) – with an average annual wage of only £10,200 a year (before deductions), less than half national average earnings (£22,412) and just a third of London's average annual salary (£28,912) (Office for National Statistics 2005, GLA 2008).

Table 3.2   The wages of low-paid migrants in London

Wages	*Number*	*%*
Up to and including the NMW	105	25
Between the NMW and the LLW	289	68
Above the LLW	30	7
Total responses	424	

Source: Analysis of authors' questionnaire survey.

Note: The data have been adjusted to reflect changes in the NMW and LLW during the period of data collection (see also Appendices 1 and 4).

In addition, however, our research revealed the almost complete absence of any social wage. Holiday entitlement was generally at the legally agreed minimum of 20 days' paid leave, including eight bank holidays. Most staff had no sick pay beyond government-funded Statutory Sick Pay, and this in turn required that workers earn more than £90 a week and were able to provide documentary evidence of their illness for absences of more than four days in succession. Most workers reported having no annually agreed date for a pay rise – some working at the same rate for as long as five years – and most worked overtime and on bank holidays at the standard rate of pay. Just 45 people (11 per cent of those who responded) had access to a company pension.

While many valued the chance to work, to earn money, to meet people, and to have new experiences (see Table 3.3), workers were also acutely aware of the low status of their work within the UK. Indeed, when asked what they liked about their job, as many as one in five said 'nothing'. Moreover, respondents tended to have many more 'dislikes' than 'likes' about their work. Given the option to tell us up to three things that they disliked, for example, many complained about their employers, about working practices, and about the nature of the job and the pay and benefits provided (see Table 3.4). Contrary to expectations, however,

Table 3.3   Likes about the job

Likes	Number	% of all respondents
The work itself	134	31
Nothing (it's just a job)	90	21
Social contact	85	20
The opportunity for an income	67	16
Caring for people	32	7
Other	61	14

Source: Analysis of authors' questionnaire survey.

Note: Respondents were invited to give up to three responses to an open question that were later recoded into these categories (see also Appendix 1).

Table 3.4   Dislikes about the job

Dislikes	Number	% of all respondents
Employer's treatment and work practices	205	48
The nature of the work itself	150	35
Pay and/or lack of benefits	142	33
Treatment by customers, clients and public	15	4
I have no complaints	27	7
Other	60	14

Source: Analysis of authors' questionnaire survey.

Note: Respondents were invited to give up to three responses to an open question that were later recoded into these categories (see also Appendix 1).

pay was not the main concern – and as discussed below in relation to each sector of employment – workers tended to be more exercised about the nature of their work, their workload, and the way they were treated at work than they were about the actual level of pay.

Getting Down to the Job

Many of the comments made by workers during our interviews were specific to the particular sector in which the respondent was working, and it therefore makes most sense to unpack this further by looking at each sector in turn. As outlined in Table 3.5, the three sectors for which we had most respondents (care, cleaning and hospitality) had much in common. However, workers in hospitality reported the lowest wages, including a small number who were paid less than the NMW due to a piece-work system for room-cleaning. In contrast, the average wage was more than a pound higher in the care sector, and all the better-paid workers (those receiving the LLW or more) were working in care. In addition, the care sector had slightly more workers who were guaranteed an annual pay rise and access to a pension through work. This partly reflected the influence of the public sector, with some of our respondents being covered by the Transfer of Undertakings (Protection of Employment) regulations (TUPE) after having been transferred into private-sector employment; but it also reflected the demand for some qualifications and experience for at least some of these jobs. Most care workers had undertaken at least minimal (one- or two-day, generally unpaid) training prior to taking up employment, and others had considerable experience that afforded them some leverage in the labour market. A number of workers told us that they had been able to study for National Vocational Qualifications while working in care.

Other striking differences concerned the national, ethnic and gender make-up of the workers in these sectors of the economy. For example, whereas Ghanaians and Nigerians were the largest single national groups in cleaning and care, Poles were the most significant group in the hospitality sector. Similarly, men and women were often found doing quite different jobs. While women typically worked in quasi-private spaces such as in hotels and, in the case of care work, the houses of clients, men were more likely to do work in quasi-public spaces – such as cleaning in offices or on the Underground. Such differences are further explored in the following chapter. Here, however, we look at the experiences of work in each of these sectors, before going on to explore the wider impact of this kind of work for the workers involved.

Table 3.5   Wages, conditions and the characteristics of labour supply in care, cleaning and hospitality

Selected variables	Employment sector		
	Care	*Cleaning*	*Hospitality*
Sectoral split (%)	14	65	21
Gender split			
Male (%)	14.5	61.4	41.5
Female (%)	85.5	38.6	58.5
Age			
Range (years)	18–58	19–67	20–62
Mean (years)	34	36	34
Median (years)	33	35	32
18–34 (%)	59	45	51
35–44 (%)	26	31	29
Countries (total sample N = 64)			
Countries with largest contingents			
Ghana (%)	31	19	5
Nigeria (%)	20	21	7
Poland (%)	4	0	26
Region of origin			
Africa (%)	70	61	31
Europe (%)	7	9	26
Eastern Europe (%)	4	8	24
Latin America and the Caribbean (%)	11	19	12
Ethnicity			
Black African (%)	62	57	28
White (other) (%)	6	19	48
Black Caribbean (%)	9	6	2
Time with current employer			
Range	1 month–23 yrs	1 month–12 yrs	1 month–29 yrs
Mean (years)	2.8	2.0	3.5
Median (years)	1.0	1.4	1.0
12 months or less (%)	52	43	54
Working week (number of hours)			
Range (hours)	4–62	2–69	7–55
Mean (hours)	30	36	35
Median (hours)	30	40	39
Between 35 and 48 hours (%)	33	65	71
Between 16 and 35 hours (%)	51	15	18
Wages			
Range (£)	£4.00–£9.00	£3.50–£8.00	£2.00–£9.80
Mean	£6.29	£5.46	£5.13
Median	£6.30	£5.25	£5.05
Up to and including NMW (%)	3.8	22	41
> NMW and < LLW (%)	69	75	51
Above LLW (%)	27	2.4	8.6

Note: Sample Size = 389
Source: Analysis of authors' questionnaire survey (see also Appendix 1).

Working in Care

As intimated in the previous chapter, official data suggest that about 80 per cent of home-care services in the UK are now provided by independent providers. What used to be relatively secure, albeit low-paid, in-house jobs have become less secure jobs, with even lower pay (Wills 2003). In the process, the labour market for care work has changed, and turnover has increased as wages have fallen. As a representative from the Home Care Association put it to us:

> The pattern that we see emerging now is that you have a cohort of people who have been in home care for some time, particularly people who worked for the local authority in the past, but [since] 2004 ... a larger proportion of the workforce have been in the sector for less than three years ... suggesting high turnover and a drop in the number of recruits staying in the sector.

In London, increasing numbers of migrant workers have been attracted into work in both residential and domestic homes. As our data in Chapter 2 indicated, the sector now relies very heavily on workers born abroad, and our representative from the industry went so far as to declare that 'migrants are essential to even maintain[ing] the same level of service today' (see Datta et al. 2011; and for wider arguments in relation to care, see Anderson 2000, Dyer et al. 2008, Ehrenreich and Hochschild 2002, McGregor 2007, Parrenas 2001).

Although Criminal Record Bureau checks might act as a barrier to irregular workers, our respondents reported finding it relatively easy to secure work in care, with most holding no prior qualifications. Indeed, workers reported that, having registered with an agency – most often through personal contacts – they then faced few obstacles in securing work. Those in domiciliary care were paid by the hour for their work on 'zero-hour' contracts – with no guaranteed hours of work – and those in care homes were often hired to work for the day. Home care workers were under pressure to move quickly from one client to another, not least because they were not paid for travelling time. In addition, these workers had little security in their long-term employment. Care workers would often lose work because of the death or hospitalisation of regular clients, and there was no certainty of finding replacements. As a woman from the Caribbean working as a carer, but who also had two cleaning jobs explained:

> That one [the caring job] is like an agency. Today you can have like ten people, tomorrow you have none. They can all die, they can all go into hospital. You won't be getting paid. With this agency, today she give you five and tomorrow she took them away from you.

In contrast, those working in residential care reported difficulties with their status at work. Some felt that agency workers were given the least desirable tasks, with little chance for negotiation. As Ajua, a Ghanaian woman, put it: 'When you are agency, they will give you the hard, the heavy patients ... because they know you are agency, you have no choice, you have to do it.'

Despite such employment conditions, carers reported being engaged in a remarkable range of tasks. Indeed, the research highlighted the extent to which domiciliary carers were doing tasks that were once carried out only by the NHS: dressing wounds, managing feeding tubes, and administering medication. As the representative from the Home Care Association put it, this represented a significant 'migration of tasks': 'Fifteen years ago home help would do a bit of dusting and making the client a sandwich, now their roles are merging to some extent with qualified nurses working in community settings, district nurses.' Indeed, Zelu, a migrant carer who had trained as a doctor in Bangladesh, reported that he necessarily drew on his medical training in doing his job. When he arrived in the UK and found that his qualifications were not recognised by the General Medical Council, Zelu secured work in domiciliary care instead, drawing on his medical training from home. Despite being paid little more than the national minimum wage, he described his work with one of his clients as follows:

> One of my clients, with whom I do 45 hours, is totally disabled. Young chap, 24 years of age. He can't speak, can't take food, he has urinary incontinence, bowel incontinence, he has a gastro-stromal tube that is back-feeding and there is a tracheal stomach tube. When I saw him first time, I thought everything is known to me, it's not a problem for me – [my medical training means] I feel comfortable with them, doing this caring job.

Likewise, Brygida, a Polish woman with a degree, described the range of tasks that she performed:

> In care you have to be just a little bit the nurse, just a little bit psychiatrist – you have to be like a support worker as well, and you have to be someone like a friend ... a bit of each to be a good carer. You have to be even sometimes like the GP, give advice.

Care work extended to providing emotional support for clients; Malani, a young woman from Mauritius, told us:

> Sometimes you feel happy when you see somebody who doesn't have any children and you do something for them. And even when they have children, they don't even bother to come to see them. You can speak to them and they will tell you what's in their heart.

Despite an average wage of £6.30 per hour, paid on the basis of a zero-hour contract, and with only minimal training, these care workers were fulfilling critically important work in the community that would once have been done by healthcare professionals.

Yet, rather than complaining, many of the carers we interviewed valued the opportunity to learn new skills and overcome the challenges of doing such work. As a Ghanaian carer, Ajua, put it: 'I've really learned about people, especially older people, I've really learned about them. I've gained how to handle people ... I've learned to be very, very tactful.' While we met one or two carers who did the job just for the money, these were the exceptions. Indeed, most carers expressed a strong sense of moral commitment to the work they did, with many disapproving of those who worked only for the wages. For example, Ajua, who worked in a residential home, told us:

> I know some people who are doing the job for the money ... the way they talk to patients, the way they treat patients. Oh my God! You feel like slapping somebody in the hospital, you know? I would say to people: If you want to do nursing or you want to be a healthcare person, you want to enter care, is it because of the money? If it is because of the money you better do something else ... one thing I've noticed is those who are money-conscious, they just leave the job. They can't stand it.

As might be expected, many of the women we spoke to saw caring as an extension of their traditional role in the family, and the gendering of the work helps to explain the low status and pay of the labour involved (Dyer et al. 2008, McKie et al. 2001, McDowell 2004b). However we encountered a high number of men who spoke about the work in similar terms (see also Chapter 4, and Datta et al. 2009). A surprising number of workers used the word 'love' to describe their work and their clients. In some cases this was a reflection of religious belief (which we explore further in Chapter 7); but respondents also reported wanting to show a 'human' love for their clients. As Ajua put it: 'I love caring for people. I love to look after vulnerable people. Last year, I left college to look after my mum and my grandma back home.' Likewise, June, from the Caribbean, told us: 'I enjoy [care work] because I cared for my godmother until she died. I [think of] everybody as my grandmother. That is a job I really enjoy most of all.'

Many workers valued the work that they did and the time that they spent with their clients. As a result, our research highlighted the extent to which migrant care workers had a stronger professional ethic than those we encountered in other sectors of London's low-wage economy. Even though the job was often insecure, mediated through employment agencies, and associated with relatively low rates of pay, many workers clearly enjoyed the work that they did. While they complained about the pay and conditions of work, they did so less often – and less vigorously – than those working in other kinds of employment. Where workers were more vociferous, it was often about the perceived failure to provide their clients with the care they felt they needed. For workers, this failure to provide adequate care was understood as a result of growing intensification within the sector (such that workers typically had less and less time for individual visits), as well as reflecting wider differences between the ethics of care evident in London and those in their countries of origin (see Datta et al.

2011). As Mary, a 51-year-old care worker from Ghana who had four children of her own, said of her first care job:

> I started with home care, and as I said before, back home, when you are old, you are respected. What I found was, it was something like a culture shock ... somebody had eight children and you can't find any of the children. This person is old for God's sake – where are the children? Back home, even if you don't have a child, once you are old, you are the responsibility of the community, the extended family, so there is no way that you have a child and you grow old and your children will not be there, no way.

Our findings would suggest that workers valued the personal relationships they were able to forge with their clients, and the sense of moral worth that came from the work. Whereas workers in others sectors complained about a perceived lack of recognition and appreciation from their employers, carers had the opportunity to develop personal relationships with their clients, and this gave them a feeling of worth. As we show below, this occupational moral economy was unique to those working in care.

Cleaning Up

We interviewed 260 migrants who were working as cleaners in workplaces such as hospitals, offices and schools, as well as in underground stations and trains. These workers were all employed by cleaning contractors, some of which were large multinational companies in their own right. Particularly significant groups of respondents worked for Blue Diamond (19) and GBM (14) on the underground, and KGB (15), Initial (34), ISS (45), Lancaster (62) and Mowlem Pall Mall (12) in jobs across the city. In contrast to other areas of low-paid employment in London, cleaning was characterised by a significant number of relatively large employers. There has been considerable amalgamation in the industry since the 1980s, and while small companies still exist, the largest players have taken an ever-increasing share of the market. These companies are in regular competition with each other for contracts across the public and private sectors, and as a result profit margins have fallen: they were reported to be as low as 5 per cent by a representative of one employer in the sector. Competition for contracts has ensured that the cleaning industry provides whatever the clients want, whenever they want it – and for the lowest possible cost. This has created an inevitable pressure on staffing levels, training and support, as well as on the wages and conditions of work – not least because labour in this sector represents at least 80 per cent of industry costs (Herod and Aguiar 2006).

In this context, cleaning companies are struggling to make a return; as a representative from the employers' association explained, the industry desperately needs to find ways to compete on the basis of quality and productivity, rather than price (see Wills 2008). As cleaning companies struggle to provide the services demanded at the required standard of cleanliness, cleaners themselves, not surprisingly, have experienced this as increased pressure placed on them. Many workers told us that staffing levels had fallen over time, that materials were often missing or of poor quality, and that labour turnover had risen. Staff turnover and shortages worsened the situation for those who were left, as they had to spend time 'training' new starters, as well as covering for absent colleagues when they left for other employment.

Migrant workers have long had a role in cleaning the city (Rowbotham 2006); as we saw in the previous chapter, the sector is now almost wholly reliant on foreign-born workers. High rates of labour turnover ensure the regular transformation of the cohort of workers doing the jobs, as one wave of immigrants is replaced by another. As one manager of a contract at Canary Wharf put it when reflecting on the changes she had seen during her career in the industry:

> [I]n 1991 it was predominantly Jamaicans cleaning. That has gone ... I see it as ... they educated themselves and they stopped cleaning. Now you've got the South Americans and the eastern Europeans coming in. It's just a wave. Now the South Americans have settled here, their children won't clean. You watch, they won't – they'll get educated and then they'll do other things.

Although it is not mentioned in this quotation, most of the workers we interviewed on this contract, and many others – particularly those on London Underground – were from sub-Saharan Africa (see Table 3.5). While increasing numbers of eastern Europeans were coming into the sector, migrants from Ghana and Nigeria still played a very significant role.

Respondents told us that cleaning was a job for 'new arrivals', as it was relatively easy to get a job in the sector. Cleaning demanded no qualifications or prior experience, and high rates of labour turnover meant that contractors were often looking for staff. Most reported that they learned to clean 'on the job'. They would be given a uniform, a duster, or a mop, and be assigned to a colleague and left to get on with it. As Nivaldo, a 22-year-old Brazilian man with a university degree, explained: 'The first day I collected the cleaner T-shirt, the guy gave me a mop and said: "That's your job." I had a laughing fit, I thought: "Gee, I'm a cleaner now!"'

Cleaners reported doing relentless physical work for long periods of time – emptying bins, picking up rubbish, vacuuming, dusting, cleaning toilets, and buffing floors. Cleaners working on the Underground typically spent up to eight hours at a time away from fresh air and natural light in the dirt, dust and noise of London's underground system – conditions that were clearly bad for their health. As one worker commented:

Sometimes, if you use like cotton, white cotton ... you see there is a black carbon deposit because of the electricity down here ... put your hand on the wall, or use some glove to clean it, before you know it, it's black. It's no good for our health.

Most workers were assigned to do the same task across a very large area, and often worked on their own. For example, cleaners in hospitals were often assigned to work on a ward on their own, serving the patients their food, washing up, tidying, and deep-cleaning the facilities; cleaners on the transport system would collect rubbish from the same trains and platforms every day; those in offices would be given one task (such as the bins, the toilets, the desks, the rubbish compaction, or the floors) on one or more floors of a building to clean on every shift. Fausto, a Spanish man who worked on the night shift at Canary Wharf, described his work as follows:

> There were two people doing the bins and two people hoovering. The bins were too much – it was over 1,000 each ... some of the bins are very full, and the amount of time you have to bend ... Some floors, especially the trading floors, these people don't do other than eating. Eating, eating, eating ... when you see the amount of rubbish, it's unbelievable. You think: What are these people doing!

Likewise, Benedito, an office-cleaner from Guinea-Bissau, reported:

> I have two floors to do. One floor is huge and the other normal size. I first collect the cups and the rubbish from the tables and then I clean them with water. Once I finish I start to vacuum clean; on the biggest floor I do it in almost five hours, but I have to do it in a rush because, to do this work in only one night, I don't have time to do one floor, [and] I have to rush to do the other floor as well.

Many respondents told us that they had to cover for absent colleagues who regularly failed to show up at work, as well as working long hours of overtime as a means of survival. Adanya, a Nigerian who worked as a cleaner on the Underground, told us:

> Sometimes, when we're short-staffed we are asked to do cover for 14 hours. From 7am to 11pm, and we're not paid for the break. We go for one hour break [and] we have to stand all day ... you're not allowed to sit down. Even if there is no train, you are not allowed to sit down.

Most of our respondents described their labour as tiring, but those removing rubbish and delivering supplies also complained about the physical demands of the job. Pedro, an office-cleaner from Brazil in his fifties, told us:

> The workload is heavy, too heavy. Many people don't show up for work because it is too much work. I have a problem in my arm, both arms, because of the workload ... I spend too much time cleaning. It is a nerve swelling ... the pain will only stop the day I quit doing this job.

Many cleaners also complained about the low pay and poor conditions of the job. None of the 260 cleaners we interviewed were paid more than the London living wage, and most were paid just above the minimum wage. In addition, many cleaners were concerned about the low status of the work, and what they perceived as a lack of recognition and respect for the work they did. In the words of Sally, a Nigerian woman working as a cleaner on the Underground: 'It takes a courageous person to say yes, I am a cleaner ... In the street I will say nothing to you because I don't know you.' Indeed, the cleaning contract manager we interviewed at Canary Wharf suggested that men often found it particularly difficult to come to terms with the social status of being a cleaner – 'They don't like admitting to their latest girlfriend that they're a cleaner' – and went on to suggest that many men would prefer to do a security job.

As in the other sectors we looked at, many workers in cleaning had prior experience in more professional jobs in their countries of birth. It was not uncommon to find people with university degrees working in cleaning, and for many this drop in social status, and the stigma associated with cleaning, was as big a problem as the pay and conditions of work. Akelo, a Ghanaian man, told us:

> I've been a classroom teacher before. How come now I am holding a mop? Mopping the floor with the machine, buffing the floor, when I've got a profession ... My certificate from Ghana which is highly, highly recommended was not regarded here.

Likewise, Alena, from Poland, said: 'I can't deny that it was embarrassing for me. In Poland I worked as a sales representative for a good company and here I do cleaning. I dropped in this social hierarchy ... we are only cleaners.' Those who had once had professional autonomy were being subjected to close managerial supervision and discipline, with little recognition or respect for the work they did. A number of workers objected to the use of security cameras to watch them working at night, and others reported the humiliation of being searched when they left the building each morning.

There was thus an emotional vacuum at the heart of this type of work. As Kojo, an Underground cleaner from Ghana, told us:

> This [cleaning] is not a job you can work for life ... there is no future for you to be there because they only look at numbers, they don't care what you do. They don't appreciate what you do – you're just there as a person to make up the numbers, you see ... they get their money, that is what matters to them.

Similarly Daniel, another Ghanaian who was cleaning a university while studying for his MBA, told us: '[The managers] don't recognise you. I would say you are there to do the job and they're okay with that, but if you encounter any slight problems, then no ... then it's your own problem.' And Fausto, the Spanish cleaner working at Canary Wharf, described this transactional economy by saying: 'The company doesn't care about anyone, only profit. Not only this company, it's every company.'

We found that cleaners were doing important jobs, keeping public and private spaces functioning for others to use and abuse; and yet they felt overlooked by their employers as well as by the wider community. Esi, a Ghanaian hospital cleaner, remarked:

> I'm a domestic ... they don't respect us. [People] drop things on the floor because the donkey domestics will clean it. We have to work hard; then, at the end of the day, who gets the low wages? I think there should be due respect to each and everybody.

One Sierra Leonean cleaner described himself and his colleagues as 'ghost workers': 'The job has to be done. But who are the people? They don't want to know. They just want to come and see that it has been done.' London's cleaners

Photo 3.1   Migrant woman cleaning offices (photo by Chris Clunn).

are largely taken for granted, and the workers doing the jobs are acutely aware of this fact.

Hospitality

As befits a capital city with a leading role in the global economy, London has a very large number of restaurants and hotels. This includes all the leading luxury hotel and restaurant chains, alongside standalone small and family-run businesses. The sector has always been the lowest-paying and least unionised in the country, and it has proved remarkably difficult to implant trade union organisation even in the largest hotels (Dutton et al. 2008, Lucas 1996, Wills 2005). Our survey results show that hospitality workers were paid less than others in low-paid jobs in the city, and that the majority of workers are now foreign-born. This ethnic and national diversity is often seen as a great asset to the industry. As a representative of the British Hospitality Association put it during interview: '[Our staff] come from all over the world, and that's one of the selling points of London for the Olympics. Wherever you come from in the world, you'll probably find your national cuisine here somewhere' (for similar arguments, in relation to the role of hospitality workers welcoming participants at sports events in Canada, see Tufts 2004, 2006).

In the past, most hotel staff were directly employed by the establishment, and even if they were low-paid they had relative security in their employment. Today, however, we found that an increasing proportion of hospitality workers, particularly those in room-cleaning and restaurant services, were being bought in through specialist agencies catering to the sector. These workers were being hired – often long-term – to fulfil key roles in room-cleaning, restaurant services and bar work. We found that it was increasingly common for establishments to leave staff vacancies unfilled, and then to use agency staff as required. This 'subcontracting-by-stealth' gradually served to alter the terms and conditions of employment for staff (see Evans et al. 2007a). Indeed, our survey revealed a cohort of agency workers who were paid on a piece-rate system according to how many rooms they cleaned, with only those capable of cleaning more than 15 rooms a day being able to reach the national minimum wage. The survey also showed that non-TUPE-covered agency workers had significantly less holiday entitlement, and few had access to occupational sick pay. Not surprisingly, labour turnover was much higher among those working for agencies than among those working in-house.

Echoing the reports of those working in cleaning, respondents highlighted the repetitive – and exposed – nature of the work they did. Those cleaning rooms generally worked on their own and, despite having to meet exacting standards, were also under pressure to work very fast – either because of the pressure of the piece-rate system or because of the managerial allocation of tasks. As Zofia, a 22-year-old Polish woman, told us: 'They gave this list of rooms that one has to clean. Every morning we have to go to the office and stand in the queue to get this list of rooms and the uniform. It made me feel like Cinderella.' In addition, the low rates of pay meant that workers often took on extra work to increase their income. This could mean working for exceptionally long periods of time, as Emilija, a Polish woman, reported: 'At the beginning, I was working only day shift, but the money was not enough so I did double shifts – one from 8am until 4pm and then from 5pm until 9 or 10pm.' For many, this had implications for their health and well-being. Another Polish woman, Berenik, told us:

> In the first three months I wanted to earn a bit more and was working six days a week. But I paid for it with my health. I injured my spine and could not move for two days from the floor. I was lying on the floor because it was hard and that would bring me a bit of comfort.

Indeed, the physical demands and long hours of work pushed some of our respondents close to the edge. Zytka, a young Polish chambermaid reported:

> [A]fter my first period here ... I was near a nervous breakdown. People couldn't talk to me. I just couldn't communicate with anyone ... That was after working at 4am until 7am cleaning restaurant and front of house ... reception, public areas and bar ... Then, at 8am, I began cleaning rooms and I was doing, as I said, 15 rooms. Then I had a one-hour break and started the so-called evenings, 4pm until 10pm ... I was again cleaning rooms ... dealing with various requests by guests such as bringing towels to a room, sugar ... all sorts of things.

Even those who ostensibly had scope for greater variety, autonomy and collegiality at work in the sector bemoaned the physical demands of the job. One Spanish chef told us:

> It was very heavy ... I had to get the dough from a machine, which would be turning, and place it on the table. Then I had to cut it and place it in a 40-to-50 degree hot oven. The heat was straight on your face. It was not doing me any good at all! I can't remember all the times I burned my hands by holding the hot baking tray.

Like those working in cleaning, hospitality workers reported that they had little, if any, voice at work. Many felt they were part of a faceless machine, and they were acutely aware that they were easily replaceable. As Elvir, a Bosnian woman, said, the pressure of the labour supply eroded the space to complain:

> The thing is that in hospitality here, and maybe it's everywhere ... you don't have the possibility to complain. It's better to be quiet than to complain. If you can do your job, do the job. If you can't, then the best thing is to leave. There are lots of people who are

looking for work and [employers] have such a big choice. If I am doing the job or somebody else is doing it, doesn't matter [to them].

This situation was particularly problematic for those without the papers to work. Given that they had fewer opportunities to find alternative work, irregular migrants had even less scope to complain. Talking about his job in a restaurant where he was paid just £20 a day for washing up, Roberto, a Brazilian man, said: 'These guys prefer the illegal people. They prefer that we are illegal because we work cheaply.' Such irregular workers also argued that their employers would be protected by the terms of the law. While their employers had a duty to check employee papers to the best of their ability, workers told us that they, not the employer, had to carry the risk. As Marcelo, another Brazilian man, put it:

Restaurant people know that when we go there with the Portuguese ID we are using fake cards. What do they do? They hire us, and if anything happens [such as a raid by immigration] they'll say that they couldn't guess that it was false. That is, they run the risk, but if there is a problem they'll pass the hot potato to the worker.

More than any others, hospitality workers complained about their terms and conditions of work. The work was often more physically demanding than cleaning and less rewarding than care. Many argued that their employers had little interest in them, so that they too adopted a largely instrumental approach to their work, seeing it as solely a means to earn money – both to survive and, if possible, to remit some back home to their families (for further details on the moral economy of low-paid employment, see Sayer 2005).

Living London's Migrant Division of Labour

While we have highlighted the extent to which workers' experiences of employment depended upon the sector in which they were working, our research found a number of common features across London's low-wage economy. Most obviously, these reflected the structural position of migrant workers who arrived in the country without access to the benefits system and needed to work to survive. Given that their qualifications were often not recognised, and that many had language difficulties and/or lacked the legal status to work, they were forced to do entry-level jobs like those being done by their compatriots who had already arrived. This situation created a particular disposition towards the labour market. Migrants regularly spoke about having to work, needing money, and doing their best to survive. As Danilo, a young Brazilian labourer, put it:

I only work because of the money. You can't live here without a job. You have to pay rent, or there is nowhere to live. You must pay for food otherwise you go hungry ... I go to school to learn and I go to work to get the money to support myself.

Likewise, Christina, a Nigerian carer, told us: 'If you don't earn money, you can't eat, you can't pay your rent. We have to work, it's compulsory. It's just everything about the country, just money, money, money. You have to work.'

Many workers thus spoke about their jobs in terms of compulsion. They were compelled to work to survive, and yet in so doing were almost always looking for something much better in future. Sally, a Nigerian cleaner, told us: 'The job is a dirty job. I don't like it much but I haven't got any choice for now.' Jeanette, a woman from Lesotho who was cleaning to support her young sons, said:

> I'm still praying to get a better job because I think I'm more than this job. In this country you can't stay home for nothing. At the end of the day you got bills to pay so you can't just leave a job whilst you have nothing to do … I'm hoping and I've applied for jobs and I'm looking for whatever I can.

Most of the workers we spoke to were acutely aware of their limited options in London, and a number of the Europeans in particular were surprised at the labour-market conditions that confronted them when they arrived. Jernej, a Slovenian cook, compared the relaxed and better-supported conditions at home with the 'sweated' nature of labour in London:

> In Slovenia, when you are employed you get paid transport; you also get paid lunch as well as paid lunch time; you get paid sick leave – and here you don't get any of these things … Work is much more 'hard core' and much more stressful here than in Slovenia. Here, they make good use of you – they squeeze you out; and in Slovenia I have not seen this kind of exploitation so much.

While the wages were better in London, employment conditions were generally thought to be worse. Miguel, a Spanish man working as a labourer in the construction industry, reported:

> I thought that here the working conditions would be a little better than in Spain. That is what I thought. I knew that the trade unions were born here; I thought trade unions were a powerful force in all that has to do with work in London. When I get here and see what the picture is like, I think: 'Just see how behind they are here, in this country, or in this city' … it was all very surprising.

A number of respondents also complained about the impact of agency working and the fact that they had no job security. Darek, a Polish labourer, explained:

> One can lose [a] job fairly quickly. I never know how long I am going to work there. I can lose my job any time. I can get a call from my boss saying, 'Darek, do not come to work tomorrow.' Just now, half of labourers were fired, but luckily, I was spared.

Our research thus highlighted the extent to which migrant workers were on the frontline of London's deregulated labour market and that, given the deepening recession, many are likely to be losing their jobs.

Migrants' structural position as relatively new arrivals looking for work at the bottom end of a largely deregulated labour market meant that they had to deal with the challenges of low pay, poor conditions and low social status. Inevitably, this was mediated by individual personality, expectations and prior experience. Nationality, ethnicity, class, gender, religion, age and legality all shaped workers' opportunities, as well as the ways in which they made sense of their position at work. Workers were differentially able to draw upon ideological explanations and resources to bolster, or at least rationalise, their position at work. Discourses of race and religion were particularly important in this regard. We explore the former in the following chapter, and the latter in Chapter 7. Broadly, however, migrant workers frequently told us that they wanted greater respect for the work they did. As one domestic worker from Ghana put it in relation to her experience in an East London hospital: 'People are human beings and they have to be respected. We take dog and cat and put them in the house and treat them like human beings. Yet not other people!' Such comments were common, and they reflected the structural position of migrant workers in London's low-wage economy.

4

LIVING AND REMAKING LONDON'S ETHNIC AND GENDER DIVISIONS

What is the heavy footfall on the cold damp pavement before the rest of the world is awake? What is the freezing figure fumbling through the fog, feeling its way to the bus stop, or clattering down the steps of the sleepy underground at this unearthly hour?

It is the black man. He is the first passenger of the day. He is the harbinger who will put the kettle on to boil. He holds the keys of the city, and he will unlock the doors and tidy the papers on the desk, flush the loo, straighten the chairs, hoover the carpet. He will press switches and start motors. He will empty dustbins and ashtrays and stack boxes. He will peel the spuds. He will sweep the halls and grease the engines.

Sam Selvon (1975: 6)

You're portrayed as all these criminals and yet we actually hold the keys to all of these buildings, 'cause we're the cleaners. We're the guards. We lock up and we close down. And we're so untrustworthy? [LAUGHS] And we've got, oh, we've got everything.... If Africans went on strike, there'd be no security men, there'd be no ... trained nurses on the wards, there'd be no cleaners, there'd be no ... traffic wardens. All the jobs nobody else wants to do.

Representative of the Central Association of Nigerians in the UK

From nine till five London belongs to the mainstream, but from five till nine it belongs to us.

Representative of Ghana Black Stars Network

Writing a few years before Piore's seminal study (1979) of the role of migrant labour in 'advanced' industrial societies, Sam Selvon's novel *Moses Ascending* (1975) set out the experiences of those who had come to London from the New Commonwealth countries during the 1960s and 1970s. The quotations from interviews we conducted with Nigerian and Ghanaian community groups in 2007 reveal how these experiences are echoed in the contemporary situation. For example, Selvon's account illustrates a workforce hidden and divided from the rest of the city's population, one that started work early and prepared the city for the working day – vacuuming the carpets and straightening the chairs for those above them in the occupational hierarchy, people whom they would often never even encounter at work. Selvon's novel revealed the racialised nature of London's labour market in the 1970s, with those coming to Britain from poorer parts of the world tending to fill the ranks of the lowest-paid jobs, taking on the dirtiest, most dangerous or difficult jobs that London's 'native' workers were no longer willing to do.

Of course, Selvon's novel also documented the extent to which many of the men coming to London from these parts of the world found that they had to take on lower-status jobs, including what is traditionally seen as women's work, if they were to find work in the city. In migrating, they had to take on jobs that offered significant challenges to their sense of masculinity. This historical context makes the riposte from the members of London's contemporary Ghanaian and Nigerian communities outlined above especially interesting. These community leaders told us that they literally 'hold the keys to the city', and that during the night London belongs to them. Their comments partly reflect ongoing efforts to revalorise the work that they do, which is still so widely devalued. Such comments also reiterate London's dependence on an army of workers who are widely ignored, and even denigrated, despite the work they do.

Thirty years after Selvon's observations, this chapter seeks to explore the continuities and changes over the intervening period, examining what has happened to longstanding patterns of ethnic and gender divisions in London's labour market. As we have already outlined, there have been profound changes in patterns of migration to the UK, as well as to Britain's labour market, over the last 30 years. While migration has been complicated by what has been characterised as 'super-diversity' (Vertovec 2007b), the London labour market has been restructured away from manufacturing towards services, and increasingly deregulated. There have also been profound changes in the traditional gender division of labour (McDowell 1991, 2001). While some women have taken up professional employment, most remain in poorly paid work and a wide gender pay gap remains (McDowell 2001).

As the bourgeoning literature on 'intersectionality' has shown, ethnicity, gender and other facets of differentiation are not experienced in isolation, but intersect in different temporal and spatial contexts to create specific configurations of power, privilege and inequality that shape people's lives (see McDowell 2008 for a recent review). As might be expected, patterns of ethnic segmentation in London have come to reflect subtle differences between different groups of migrants – groups that are further differentiated by immigration status, by gender and by geography. Indeed, today's migrants are much more sharply differentiated by the immigration system than their counterparts of 30 years ago, so that immigration status now interlocks with ethnic and gender divisions to remake complex patterns of disadvantage within the low-wage economy (for similar arguments on the US, see Hudson 2006).

Developing the arguments advanced in Chapter 2 (where we traced the changing preferences of London employers), here we show that a growing divide is now emerging between EU and non-EU workers, with the preferential access to low-paid work enjoyed by EU workers reinforcing existing ethnic divisions of labour (see also May et al. 2008). We then highlight the ways in which increasing numbers of migrant men are moving into feminised jobs, such as cleaning and care. We contrast men's experiences with those of their female colleagues, who have not had to confront the same challenges to their gendered identities and who often articulate a far more positive view of their experiences of living and working in London (see also Datta et al. 2009). But we begin by providing a brief overview of the processes by which labour markets are segmented along cleavages of nationality, ethnicity and gender, highlighting the spatialisation of these processes and the need to integrate a sharper focus on immigration status itself.

Labour Market Segmentation: Nationality, Ethnicity, Gender, Immigration Status and the Importance of Place

Early theories of labour-market segmentation were based on the principle that labour markets can be divided into two segments (Doeringer and Piore 1971). The first, or primary segment is characterised by better-paid and higher-valued, permanent jobs with good working conditions and opportunities for career development and progression. Conversely, the secondary sector consists of temporary jobs, which are low-paid, low-status, have poor working conditions, and lack job security and career prospects. Importantly, while the primary sector tends to be dominated by men from the dominant ethnic group, the secondary sector tends to be composed mostly of women, migrants and ethnic minorities who are deemed temporary, and therefore receive minimal investment in terms of training and career development, as well as wages and conditions of work (Dale et al. 2002, Evans and Bowlby 2000). According to labour-market segmentation theories, movement between the segments is severely limited and, in particular, secondary workers are unable to secure work in the primary sector. Moreover, once segmented in this way, workers are generally restricted to particular jobs, with little opportunity for further advancement. Regardless of their human capital, members of minority ethnic communities, women and migrants are found to be restricted to particular forms of work.

Such analysis is clearly borne out in relation to both ethnicity and gendered employment in London. As Fig. 4.1 shows, there are dramatic variations in average pay rates for different ethnic groups in the capital: almost half of all Bangladeshis earned less than £7.50 per hour in 2005–07, compared to just over 10 per cent of the white British population. Such trends are replicated and exceeded in relation to household income: more than 60 per cent of the Bangladeshi population had below-average income in the period 2004/05–2006/07, compared to about 20 per cent of white British households (see Fig. 4.2). Each ethnic group is further divided by gender, and the gender pay gap for the whole of London is wider than for Britain in general (GLA 2005b). Indeed, in 2003, female hourly pay rates were just 76 per cent of male rates for full-time workers in London – 7 percentage points behind the level for Britain as a whole (see Fig. 4.3).

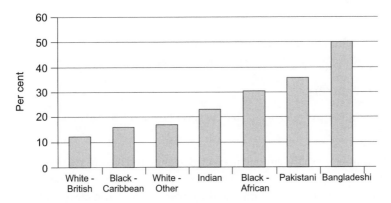

Source: Labour Force Survey, ONS; the data is the average for 2005 to 2007, MacInnes and Kenway (2009: 65).

Figure 4.1   The proportion of workers in London earning less than £7.50 an hour, by ethnicity, 2005–2007

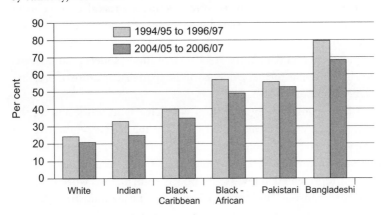

Source: Households Below Average Income, Dept. for Work and Pensions, MacInnes and Kenway (2009: 61).

Figure 4.2   The proportion of the population on below-average income, by ethnicity, 1994/95–1996/97 and 2004/05–2006/07

Source: GLA (2005: 42).

Figure 4.3   The gender pay ratio in London and Great Britain, 1974–2003 (full-time workers)

In practice, of course, the labour market is segmented into more than two parts. Moreover, there are different dynamics at work in the segmentation of migrants, minority ethnic communities and women. There is also clear evidence that such processes are spatially uneven, sedimented in regard to the relations that already exist (McDowell and Massey 1984, Massey 1995). In his pioneering work in this field, Jamie Peck (1989: 51) has argued that scholars need to pay attention to 'the ways in which the particular local intersections of labour supply, labour demand and the state's regulatory infrastructure are revealed in the form of concrete outcomes'. The differentiated geography of gender relations, race relations and labour migration across the UK has shaped the development of local patterns of employment and the nature of local institutions. Indeed, our analysis of the situation in London is further evidence of the spatialised nature of ongoing processes of labour-market reform.

Processes of labour-market segmentation were clearly at work among the minority ethnic groups who arrived in the UK from the New Commonwealth countries in the years after the Second World War. These individuals faced serious racial disadvantage in the British labour market and, as a result, they became disproportionately represented in low-status, poorly paid, manual work – mainly in the service sector, transport and traditional manufacturing industries (Brown 1984, Smith 1976). As we argued in Chapter 2 in relation to the hiring queue, employers will use a 'short-hand' technique to determine a potential worker's suitability for employment; and, in the context of the post-war labour shortage, racialised immigrants were slotted into low-wage jobs that were often classed as unskilled, and that white, British-born workers were reluctant to do. Scholars at the time began to explain such patterns in relation to race, rather than to immigration per se. And while white, low-skilled immigrants were similarly slotted into particular kinds of employment – and there are excellent studies of Irish workers and migrants from the Baltic States that explore this position (see McDowell 2005) – the issue of immigration was largely eclipsed by that of race. Thus, a number of important studies focused on the experiences of black and minority ethnic workers in the labour market in relation to ethnicity – and discrimination – rather than to immigration history and status themselves (see Brown 1984, Daniel 1968, Jones 1993, Modood et al. 1997, Smith 1977).

It is only since the emergence of increased rates of immigration in the context of the new immigration regime that scholars have begun to re-address the legal aspects of labour supply, providing an opportunity to explore how this situation may change employment patterns in relation to nationality, ethnicity, race and gender. For some groups, patterns of early disadvantage persisted, and even worsened, as the industries in which many were employed shed workers in the later 1970s and early 1980s with the restructuring of Britain's economy (Dustmann et al. 2003, Iganski and Payne 1996, Virdee 2006). In contrast, others – most notably, perhaps, Gujarati South Asians and East African Asians – fared much better, moving up into higher-status work, including managerial and professional employment (Ballard 2003a, Vertovec 1994).

There are further complications in relation to gender. The processes of racial discrimination and labour-market disadvantage faced by New Commonwealth migrants were, and continue to be, cross-cut by gender. Thus, a number of scholars have argued that minority ethnic women suffer a 'double jeopardy' in the British labour market (Parmar 1982, Phizacklea 1983). For example, research has revealed that African-Caribbean women are not only disadvantaged in relation to white British workers – tending to become located in low-paid manual jobs – but are often confined to domestic roles 'befitting' their gender, such as cleaning and catering work (Jayaweera 1993). Furthermore, even within jobs that have traditionally been gendered as 'women's work', there are significant differences between labour-market outcomes and experiences for minority ethnic women and their white counterparts, the former being more likely to be concentrated in lower-status specialisations such as geriatric and mental healthcare (Doyal et al. 1980).

While subsequent accounts of labour-market segmentation have drawn a more nuanced picture of the labour market, with divisions stretching beyond a basic distinction between primary and secondary segments (Lee and Wrench 1987), scholars have also begun to move beyond a simplistic view that migrants will necessarily find themselves in poor-quality employment (Piore 1979). Indeed, researchers have begun to chart the ways in which migrants are not necessarily projected into the low-wage economy at all (Jayaweera 1993, Model 2002). Instead, given that migrants are now differentiated by skill when they enter the UK, it is increasingly likely that they are 'sorted' into the labour market before they arrive. This is certainly the case for those arriving as highly skilled migrants, or with employment agreed, who are now covered by Tier 1 and 2 in the UK's points-based immigration regime. While these top-tier migrants will often be from wealthier economies, and many will be white, this is not always the case. In the past, these migrants have included both women and men, and we find significant concentrations of black and Asian women in professional jobs, most notably working as doctors and consultants in the National Health Service, as well as taking on business roles in the City of London (Winkleman-Gleed 2006).

Immigration law is now playing a very significant part in differentiating between groups of migrants both before and after they come to live and work in the UK. While migrants from Europe have clear advantages in the entry hierarchy, the focus on skills has also restricted access for those characterised as lower-skilled from the rest of the world (see also Chapter 1). Immigration law is itself reconfiguring the employment possibilities and prospects of individuals who come to live and work within the UK. While the new points-based system differentiates between high-skilled and low-skilled workers, it also determines the access of these workers to the benefits system and to citizenship. It also further widens the gap between low-skilled workers from the A8 countries, who have recently been granted the de facto right to work and reside indefinitely in Britain, and those from beyond the EU, whose rights to work and residence have remained restricted. In the remainder of this chapter we chart the complex experiences of London's new migrants as they negotiate these new and old trajectories of ethnicity, gender and legal status in London's low-wage labour market.

'Some of Us Don't Have the Papers': (Ir)regularity and the Labour Market in London

As we intimated at the end of Chapter 3, our research has exposed the extent to which London's low-wage migrant workers are acutely aware of their position in what Piore (1979) would call a 'labour reserve'. For Berenik, from Poland, for example, the reason that the English managers failed even to acknowledge her presence or to greet her in the mornings was clear:

> We are the cheap labour that is to be exploited to achieve their targets ... here we would never be at the same position we would be in Poland ... at the very bottom of this social ladder and work as hotel maid.

We found such workers had a keen appreciation that they were easily replaceable; as Potyr, also from Poland, recalled: '[the head chef] rushes me around the kitchen like a dog, as if I was a slave ... but I can't say too much because there are a hundred other Polish to replace me'.

As we have seen, many migrants worked alongside other new migrants; if they were present at all, 'native' workers tended to be confined to more senior positions. As Felipe, a chef from Colombia, told us during his interview, his colleagues were 'all immigrants' because

> [t]he European[s] do not like to do low-grade, menial jobs ... fortunately us in Colombia or in all of Latin America will work in anything, there is no problem with working in any job. Unfortunately, the Europeans, the English, they don't like to do this, so logically, we are all immigrants at work, the only one, the head chef, he is English, all the other ones in the kitchen are immigrants.

Yet, while being an immigrant was part of the story, we also encountered more subtle differences between and within the sectors and workplaces of London's low-wage economy, with very clear vertical and horizontal segmentation at work. As we saw in the previous chapter, Africans were more concentrated in cleaning and care than in hospitality, which relied more heavily on eastern Europeans, while women were more likely to be working in care than in cleaning. Such patterns reflected inherited patterns of labour-market segmentation along divisions of nationality, ethnicity, race and gender.

But our research also highlighted the extent to which such patterns are subject to change. We found that London's employers were beginning to reconfigure their hiring queues, and eastern Europeans, rather than workers from beyond the EU, were emerging as the favoured workforce today. One reason for such a shift is the increased risk of fines now facing those found to be employing people in contravention of their immigration status. As we outlined in Chapter 1, the introduction of the civic penalty regime (Sections 15–25 of the Immigration, Asylum and Nationality Act 2006, introduced in February 2008) has prompted a significant increase in workplace raids (or 'compliance visits') by British immigration officials. Between February and September 2008, 91 penalty fines were issued to employers, up from just 37 in the nine years between 1997 and 2006 (Migrants' Rights Network 2008: 4). This new legal regime requires that employers inspect and record immigration documentation, acting as another arm of immigration control. Given the ambiguity about the legal status of low-skilled workers from beyond the EU, European workers from the A8 countries have become increasingly attractive, because they are known to be legitimate workers. Moreover, given the racial heritage of European workers as white, this legal regime has also provided further grist to the mill of racism, with black workers being pushed down the employment hierarchy by the arrival of whites. Employers have been able and willing to reconfigure their hiring queues to the disadvantage of workers from countries in Africa and Latin America, who have been doing low-paid jobs in London for a number of years.

Such changes have made it far more difficult for those from outside the EU to find low-paid employment in London. But in addition – as Adesola, a London Underground cleaner from Nigeria awaiting the outcome of his application for asylum, argued – the situation can also provide unscrupulous employers with much greater control over those without the papers required to work:

> Now they introduce people from Romania, Bulgaria, they brought them in. What they do is when they bring them in, they remove some of these Africans, they tell them these people are Europeans and they have better right to work than you.... Some of us don't have the papers. So you can subdue us, you can do anything. Make us lick the floor; we will do it because if [we] don't do it, we are sacked; and when they say you are sacked, it gives you fear. How do you survive? You can't go elsewhere to work, because if you go elsewhere they'll tell you: 'Where is your [papers]?' You know?

As an asylum-seeker, Adesola's situation was especially precarious. In the early stages of the application process he was not allowed to work; but even after six months, when work was possible, he was known to be vulnerable because he did not yet know the outcome of his application. If he was unsuccessful, he would have little choice but to work illegally, with the constant threat of administrative detention and deportation if later discovered.

Of course, this level of vulnerability extended far beyond those applying for asylum itself, encompassing all those working without papers, as well as those who had restrictions on their hours of work and access to the benefits system. As we have seen, workers from the global South are now poorly positioned in relation to those from the enlarged EU – and although the international students we met had the right to work, they had no right to settle, and could only work legally for 20 hours per week during term-time. With no route to settlement, any of these migrants who intended to stay longer typically ended up breaching the conditions attached to their visas by overstaying, and thus becoming undocumented and irregular. This, in turn, pushed them further down the hiring queue, or into greater vulnerability in their employment.

As a result, workers holding student visas often expressed feelings of being trapped in low-paid employment. These workers typically described a triple-bind, whereby they found it difficult to complete their studies or attend lectures because they were either too tired from work, or simply needed to work longer hours to meet the costs of living in London. But working longer hours put them in breach of their visa, making them semi-compliant (Ruhs and Anderson 2006). At the same time, the lack of qualifications further limited their chances of securing a work permit, and so gaining the opportunity to become legally resident in the long term. We met one worker who had been a teacher in Ghana only to find himself employed as a security guard in a cleaning firm while he studied in London:

> I appreciate the development in this country; it's a very good stepping-stone to develop your life to be able to achieve something better, but it's very difficult if you happen to start from scratch because you haven't got your 'indefinite' and you're restricted ... Every time, even if you qualify in a work, they will ask you if you have work permits – 'No I'm a student', 'We can't employ you' – which is a big setback for anybody who wants to advance in this country. If you happen to be a student you're only entitled for 20 hours per week – it's very good, you can concentrate on your studies, but at the other side because you haven't got a sponsorship or sometimes it is difficult to send money from Ghana to this place, you find it difficult to cope with the situation; and if you don't study here you're going to fail your exams, and if you fail your exams the Home Office will send you away without you completing your goal, and it makes the life very, very challenging and very, very difficult.

The additional pressure to remit money home often placed greater demand on such workers, and these pressures were compounded by the need to pay for their studies within the UK. In Akelo's case, his fees were £6,000 for one year of an accountancy course. Such pressures were by no means uncommon, and another respondent explained that he had to fit his studies around three part-time jobs. Similarly, a woman from the Democratic Republic of Congo who was working in cleaning told us: 'I was very happy to come over. It was a good occasion to do my accountancy [studies] but I quickly realised that my dream was destroyed, as the studies are expensive and I couldn't afford to pay.' Indeed, we found that many of those who came to Britain in an attempt to further their education and/or earn more money to support their families at home simply had to give up. Gladys, an international student from Ghana, explained:

> If you don't become determined you can't go to school here. You know, we don't get any help so you have to be very determined. The situation here will make you lose focus on what you came here to do, so things get very tough especially for the foreigners – very, very tough. If you don't pay your rent then they say you'll find yourself outside there, so you have to struggle and work alongside with your education – you have to do that, and some people can't cope, literally. They end up with no education. They just pack it in.

In contrast to earlier eras of labour migration, the introduction of a managed migration regime has therefore introduced an important line of demarcation within London's migrant workforce. The new regime has created a divide between those with the legal right to work and reside in Britain (many of whom hope that, in time, they will progress beyond their current position) and those for whom the opportunities for progression are severely curtailed by their immigration status. As we have seen, international students struggle to hold down a job and to complete the studies that might provide them with a route out of low-paid employment; those waiting for an asylum claim to be processed are left in limbo, often for years; and those without legal status remain in fear of the law (Ruhs and Anderson 2006, Whitewell 2002).

Competition and Race in London's Low-Wage Economy

Clearly, immigration status creates important lines of differentiation within a national and/or ethnic group, and there are new forms of polarisation and exclusion between those who can at least attempt to establish a career path in Britain and those whose progression beyond being a pool of cheap labour is blocked (Ruhs and Anderson 2006, Whitewell 2002). In effect, the hierarchical immigration regime has created a corresponding hierarchy of migrant labour supply. As we have seen, Europeans are firmly favoured over non-Europeans in the hiring queue, and tensions have greatly increased between migrant groups.

A number of non-EU workers bemoaned the new arrivals from Eastern Europe for their perceived willingness to undercut the going rate of pay. As Marcelo from Brazil explained:

> I was working in this restaurant and there was this guy working there as well. A Polish guy came in trying to take his job. The Polish guy went to the manager and said, 'How much does this guy earn to do this work?' The manager answered, '£4.85' [per hour]. It was the minimum wage, which is now £5.05. The Pole said, 'I will do the same work for £3'. Why? Do you know how much a pound is worth in their currency? It is [worth eight times as much]. For us [it is worth just four times as much]. It is a big difference. They are coming over and taking our jobs. They have the additional advantage of being allowed to work.

Other workers highlighted the renewed racialisation of the migrant hierarchy within the UK. As one Brazilian man working in the construction industry observed, the supervisors were 'all white', and this included not only white British people, but white South Africans and Zimbabweans as well. Likewise, a cleaner employed at Canary Wharf explained that he felt that the black Africans were being kept on the night shift, when no one would see them, while their white European colleagues were being hired to work during the day:

> What I mean is like there's a lot of eastern Europeans there now, especially in the day, and I've mentioned that to the management, and I said: Look, we were struggling in here for years, and ... now the day staff ... most of them used to be black in the day, now it's the eastern Europeans [who have] overtaken the black people there.... I've said there's a policy to get rid of us, yeah, so you can bring in the eastern Europeans. Not that I have anything against the eastern Europeans, I mean, everybody wants to earn a crust, yeah,

I haven't got no problem with [that]; but if it means I'm going to get kicked out because you want to bring them in, then sorry, I'm not happy with that …

Interviewer: *So why do you think this is, because they want white workers there when the client is around?*

Yeah, in the day, in the daytime, we don't fit in too well, this is how they're looking at it…. It looks better for the business or what have you. So slowly but surely they're manoeuvring us out and bringing in the eastern Europeans.

Such sentiments were echoed by Julia, a cleaner from Ghana, who told us: 'the night supervisors are blacks, the nights we are mostly blacks'. Such claims clearly echo research conducted over 20 years ago showing that African-Caribbean women experienced barriers to employment that involved contact with the white British public (Jayaweera 1993; see also Webster 1998).

Consequently, racism was a key theme in the narratives of the African workers we met. Many felt that their race prevented them from receiving the respect they deserved, just as it also prevented them from moving up into more professional jobs. As Sachin, who had moved to London from the Caribbean, remarked: 'Well when you're going for jobs, because of your colour sometimes they don't give it to you.' We also spoke to Sally, from Nigeria, who said: 'The most job offer the black person [can get] is a cleaner job.' Moreover, workers felt that their qualifications and experiences did not guarantee improved employment prospects within the UK. Joshua, for example, had worked as a manager for Unilever in Ghana, and he spoke to us at length about his credentials and the skills he had acquired through studying for an MBA at London Metropolitan University, none of which were sufficient to get the job he deserved:

You are the person who has done the MBA, at the managerial level … so you know how to handle people very well, how to deal with cases, how to solve cases and the like … leadership, personal development and the like – we've been taught all this in the MBA.

Yet, despite having this educational and experiential capital, he could not transform it into any economic advantage in London. As he observed, when someone like him goes for interview,

You will not be taken … the racism, we don't see it but it is happening. Because I've been in a lot of interviews; you finish, they will tell you they can't understand you. I know your accent cannot be my accent. I can't speak like you do.

Joshua's experience and qualifications were disregarded due to his pronunciation, which acted as a marker of difference. For him, London's labour market was 'more than frustration, more than frustration'.

This sense of frustration was also evident in other interviews. Another worker, Antobam, emphasised the statistical skills, knowledge and status associated with her previous job at a port inspection company in Ghana. In Britain she had decided to work in the housing sector and completed a relevant course. But she found, like Joshua, that this did not serve as a route into employment: 'What I have is a certificate. I have never worked at it, it is just a bit frustrating sometimes. You know I feel like going [back to Ghana] because I'd spent £400 on it.' Like Joshua, she felt that the costs embodied in the certificate – the investment of her time, labour and money – had not culminated in any tangible value. While Joshua's lack of success was explained as a matter of his communication difficulties, Antobam's experience was couched in terms of her 'lack of experience'. Yet both held a strong conviction that their situation was actually a matter of race. Moreover, this conviction was further reinforced by the stories of migrants who had tried to get professional employment in London. As Antobam explained:

> When we were on campus in this school, in the university, some of my friends came here for holidays, and when they came back [they said blacks don't] get the kind of job you want to do or be qualified [in]; [the employers] would prefer to give it to a white person or to the person who is not qualified [and then] train [the] person to do the job ... This is your country, you prefer to work with people that you know [rather] than working with a foreigner, although the foreigner might be competent. I listened to those things and friends like this, and they said when you come here, you just come to [do a] cleaning job, some to do care, jobs that English people don't like doing. Those are the jobs that you get.

Our research has thus clearly exposed the extent to which many workers from non-European countries have encountered a tacit hierarchy within the labour market that automatically situates them as inferior to whites and Europeans. Despite their qualifications and experiences, their legal situation, coupled with racial discrimination, has served to exclude them from professional and white-collar jobs (Vasta and Kandilige 2007).

Moreover, this analysis is borne out by interviews with employers that echo the stories of workers. Thus, our research exposed employer preferences for workers from the countries of eastern Europe over those from Africa, in particular. For example, one manager from the Canary Wharf cleaning contractor argued that he preferred the enthusiasm and energy exhibited by eastern Europeans to the attitude of Africans, who were often 'difficult to motivate'. While this may have been more complicated than simple racism – not least because he cited the personal circumstances of some of the African workers, who tended to be older and more 'encumbered' with family than the newer arrivals – he explained:

A lot of them [Africans] have other jobs, a lot of them are up during the day either collecting the children from school or they've got a young one that keeps them awake and they can't sleep, so they come tired to work, and that makes them look lazy [especially] compared to the east Europeans that come in buzzing. They come in buzzing.

Of course, the use of stereotypes such as the 'lazy African' and the 'mañana Latin' have a long tradition in Europe (Whitehead 2001; see also Anderson 2007, Cox and Narula 2003, Glenn 1992, Stiell and England 1999 on this racialised division of labour in relation to domestic work). As we suggested in Chapter 2, ethnic stereotypes also play an important part in the employment hierarchy of migrants, and other researchers have likewise exposed the deployment of stereotypes such as 'the hard-working Pole', 'the deferent South Asian' and 'the obedient and subservient Filipino' (Batnitzky et al. 2008, McKay 2007, Matthews and Ruhs 2007).

Moreover, while national groups of migrants were clearly compared by employers, migrants were themselves also acutely aware of the extent to which their fortunes diverged. As we have seen, this was most obvious in the queue for employment, but it was also evident in the scope for upward mobility once within a firm's employment. A number of non-European respondents commented that eastern European workers had achieved more rapid upward mobility within their workplace than was open to them. Alvro, from Brazil, described this situation within the construction industry:

> The labourers are all Brazilians, but other workers are from Europe. There are a lot of people from Armenia, Albania; there are also lots of Polish tradesmen – they'll come for one week, or for one month, and they'll come back to do some more work later.
>
> Interviewer: *What do they do?*
>
> They do the electrical work and the plumbing.
>
> *They do the more specialised work, then?*
>
> Yes, they are professionals [tradesmen], but the labourers are all Brazilians. Europeans don't like to work as labourers; at least, as far as I can see, they don't like it.

For Alvro, the demarcation of eastern European workers as 'European' differentiated them from the non-Europeans, who were confined to the lower-status work. While eastern Europeans were able to secure some of the more skilled positions, Brazilians were restricted to the less desirable jobs. Reflecting the strength of the labour supply, many of our respondents felt intense competition from Polish workers, in particular. The combination of immigration law and institutional discrimination located non-Europeans at the bottom of the low-wage labour market and – as far as these workers were concerned – Polish workers had been

given an unfair advantage. Their legal status, race and geographical origins gave
the Poles a clear advantage in the hierarchical hiring queue.

Identity-making at work

It is very significant that many of the eastern Europeans we talked with (most of
whom were Poles) were very conscious of the advantages conferred on them by
their white European identity within Britain's labour market. In a mirror-image
of the complaints about the employment hierarchy made by non-Europeans,
eastern Europeans articulated a sense of superiority over their non-European
colleagues on the basis of a 'European' identity constructed around an extended
European Union, and underpinned by issues of race. Thus, some Polish workers
positioned themselves in direct opposition to non-EU workers, drawing this
distinction according to a legal differentiation. In the words of Sylwia, a Polish
woman working in a hotel: 'Since we joined the EU I have the right to be here.
I did not come here when I was unwanted.' Likewise Mirek, a construction
worker, declared: 'I am coming here to work and I can work legally as a citizen
of a member-state of the European Union, while others often are here because of
persecution or had to escape war.' At a time when asylum-seekers were popularly
seen as a public policy problem and a drain on public resources (Berkeley et al.
2006, Saggar 2003), a number of Polish workers also stressed their entitlement to
travel, settle and work in Britain, and were keen to distinguish themselves from
other migrants who did not share the same rights.

For others, the distinction between EU and non-EU workers was more obviously
drawn on racial grounds, with respondents deploying a mixture of the 'old' and
'new' racism; that is, constructions that revolved around issues of both skin-colour
and cultural identification (Gilroy 1987). Mirek claimed that Poland would not
accept non-European migrants as Britain had done, because although he believed
in 'the idea of united Europe [the] Bangladeshi or Kenyan somehow do not fit,
they do not assimilate well'. Similarly, Tobiasz, a construction worker, said: 'I
think that I deserve more to be here because I am white and Britain has always
been white [more] than someone from, let's say, Pakistan.' Moreover, while such
workers were responding to their position within the labour market in London,
they were also able to draw on the racist discourse of their home countries to
reinforce their claim to be here, which fostered further resentments. For one
hospitality worker, for example, 'If you live in Poland ... we think of black as
lesser people, and if you come here [it is] they who are appreciated and we not.'
According to Zytka, her supervisor in the hotel where she worked was African and
favoured other African workers over Polish workers. Arguably, working alongside
other migrants in low-paid work threatened her sense of superiority, which as a
white person she was socialised to expect (see Bonnett 2000, Frankenberg 1993,
1997, Hage 1998, Hartigan 1999, Herbert 2008a). Although Zytka found that

her white identity did not confer the privileges she expected, and working for an African person clearly undermined her status within the racial hierarchy, she still expressed a sense of superiority and injustice in relation to race.

Our interviews thus exposed the extent to which new migrants from eastern Europe deployed racist discourse in relation to their fellow migrants. By constructing a white identity, they naturalised and reified whiteness, in contra-distinction to an inferior 'blackness' associated with workers who were variously argued to be 'aggressive', 'lazy', 'criminal', and even 'animal'. Many claimed that the British preferred Europeans, for their whiteness, to African employees; Mirek, the construction worker, claimed: 'Black people ... see us as a threat. We are white, usually better educated. [The] English who, I think, are not officially racist, but are rather open, would prefer to employ Polish, who work harder than a black person.' Similarly Brygida, another worker from Poland, described the delight of her client on seeing that he was to have a white carer:

'Oh, yes, yes, please come, please come, please come.' ... 'It's nice to meet you, very nice, because ... You know what, the Africans, they don't do... they don't do their job very properly.' I say, 'No, that's right' ... No, no, no ... they are very rough, even when they provide, you know, personalised care and they don't care. I mean they're always in rush, always in rush. ... It happened once, I had one English, white English, who asked only for white carers.

Interviewer: *Really?*

If they send black, she was very, very rude. Because of, you know, racism and prejudice.

These findings resonate with Roediger's (1991) research on the history of migrant identities in the US, in which Irish and Italians constructed a white identity for themselves by positioning themselves in opposition to African-Americans. Such findings also chime with work that has explored the wider politics of identity-making (Wetherell 2009). Indeed, whereas many African migrants emphasised the value of their diasporic identity as a vital source of support and belonging, Polish workers tended to play down their national identity. In fact, they tended to 'scale up' their identity, making claims to be members of an extended European, rather than Polish, community in London. When Anna, a care worker, was asked about her relationship to the wider Polish community, she claimed:

I have no contact with the Polish community.

Interviewer: *There aren't any cultural things?*

No, thank you very much. [LAUGHS] I had enough when I was in Poland.

Really?

No, honestly, I don't need for this kind of community, if I want to drink Polish beer, I go to the shop, they sell everywhere, if I miss for something, miss something which is Polish, they will sell.

Similarly Matyja, a Polish construction worker, claimed he had no interest in a Polish diasporic culture, or in maintaining links with his country of origin. He told us that he avoided watching Polish television and preferred English TV because

I know that I have to learn English and TV can be very useful ... watching it can help in better understanding, and Polish TV I had watched it for the past 26 years. But I lost interest in events in Poland ... Earlier on I would buy Polish *Newsweek*, but reading it I only got annoyed so I stopped buying it ... I don't need it [as I] am not interested in Polish politics.

Arguably, these sentiments reflect the ambitions of an urban middle-class Polish community that subscribes to individualism and success in a British meritocracy (Garapich 2008); or they can be seen as an attempt by immigrants to avoid becoming the object of possible public anxieties about the 'Polish invasion' (Foggo and Habershon 2006). Yet they can also be read as part of a wider strategy that recognises the benefits of being European and white. According to Garapich, Poles in Britain have historically played down their ethnicity in order to distance themselves from other ethnic minorities: 'Emphasizing ethnicity too much would mean having to share the multicultural pie with others on an equal footing' (Garapich 2008: 140; see also Eade et al. 2007). Moreover, the immigration regime determines that Poles are free to travel home whenever they want, and thus able to dabble in their home culture whenever they choose. In contrast, those without the ability to traverse borders with ease – and particularly irregular migrants – are often never able to visit their home countries. This increases the imperative to retain and defend a sense of culture, tradition and identity while living in difficult conditions in London (see Chapter 6).

Some respondents also intimated that the desire of Poles to distance themselves from co-nationals was related to the fiercely competitive environment in which migrants found themselves when living in London. Other Poles were sometimes seen – like with other migrants – as a threat in a context of limited resources such as housing and jobs (see Chapter 5). As Ewa – a chambermaid – explained: 'Poles very seldom help, and are hostile to other Poles coming here. Simply ... it is very strange for me, but that's how Polish behave.' This respondent went on to make a distinction between those who were well-established and had lived in Britain for a few years, who were generally friendly, and newcomers who 'were afraid that one wants [to] take something from them ... work or something else'. Similarly, Zytka claimed:

In Poland I had more time for friends and would spend more time with them. Here I have friends, but not many. I have also learnt that Polish are very jealous nation and the worst I have come across ... even black people would also keep together, but Polish would never help each other, and would stab you in the back. I have seen it here – we are so afraid that someone would do better than [we] do.

Emilija, a chambermaid from Poland, also claimed that relations between managers and maids in her hotel had recently deteriorated since Polish people had been promoted to management positions: 'Polish would just exploit you; here, one Pole is the enemy of another Pole. That is what I think.' It is important to note that these internal divisions were also evident among other ethnic and nationality groups, with several migrants complaining about their own people (see McIlwaine 2005). Angela, a Portuguese cleaner, for example, said that the Portuguese were 'gossipers' in the workplace, and that you had to maintain your distance in order to gain respect from them.

Competition could also be intense between different national and ethnic groups, stereotypes often being applied on the basis of nationality, ethnicity, race and gender to further particular ends. For instance, some Ghanaian women working as care workers typically emphasised how their national attributes were more suited to caring than those of other nationalities. Abina, a female Ghanaian care worker, for instance, felt that Ghanaians were better suited to care work than Nigerians, because they were more patient and composed:

Oh, Ghanaians are calm, calmer than the Nigerians, you see ... you can see [the] difference. Nigerians are always hard like, they ... want you to like things to be done the way they want it. Ghanaians are calm, they try to take their time to do things.

Another care worker from Ghana similarly claimed that Nigerian workers were less diligent, more domineering, and thoughtless towards their clients:

We have a problem working with [Nigerians] because their way of working is different. Normally they are lazy. They want the money but they don't want to do the work properly. That's one thing about them. Secondly, they are a bit bossy.... When we are working, we have been told to use English language as official language, but they speak their local language – sometimes with the residents. They speak their language with residents – you know, when somebody is speaking and you can't understand, you feel they are discussing you or something. That's why I also don't like ... them.

Workers thus valued their own group over others as a means of competing in the labour market, and workers also used gender in this way. Many women argued that their experiences as women made them particularly suitable for jobs in care, just as men working in construction asserted that they were intrinsically hard-working and strong. Indeed, as we explore in the following section, gender ideologies and identities were used as a resource in the competition for jobs. But, as we also show, these gender positions were complicated by the fact of migration itself, which sometimes disrupted more traditional gender identities and expectations.

Remaking Gendered Employment

Gender can itself be deployed to reinforce the ethnic and national stereotypes used to compete against other groups of migrants, and to buttress both self- and group identity in a situation of low-wage employment. For example, Brazilian construction worker Eduardo claimed:

> They [the bosses] never give the heaviest work to [English or Indian workers]. They know the Brazilians have energy. If you compare the Brazilian army with the North American army, there is no comparison; they only have the technology, they are not as fit as us.

Eduardo's physical strength was also illustrated by the ease with which he completed the work:

> That bag of red brick is very heavy – it tires you out to get that onto your back! You have to carry more than 50 bags like those in a day. You feel the difference. But I still manage to go training after [work].

Men would frequently emphasise the notion that their work was 'men's work', describing it as tough, hard, and requiring physical brawn in hostile and tricky terrain (see Johnston and McIvor 2007 for similar constructions of masculinity in the heavy industries in Glasgow). Uniform was also important in this image of work; for Nivaldo, from Brazil, a uniform reinforced his sense of being a tough man at work. He told us: 'You look at yourself with the boots and the guy gives you a helmet and safety jacket, so you think: That is it! I am labourer.' Steel-capped boots and hard hats were necessary because of the hazardous nature of their employment, and this reinforced men's sense of the risks of their work.

These comments reveal how workers often found themselves working in a context that reinforced traditional gender norms. In these cases, workers' experiences tended to reinforce gender ideologies by aligning with ascribed notions of femininity or masculinity in wider circulation. However, our research also revealed that some migrant men were now working in 'feminised' sectors. In the previous chapter we showed that as many as 60 per cent of the workers we encountered in cleaning, almost half of those in hospitality, and 15 per cent of those in care, were men. In particular, black African men were concentrated in the feminised cleaning and care sectors, comprising 80 per cent of all the male workers cleaning on the London Underground, over half (57 per cent) of all male care workers and just under half (47 per cent) of all general cleaners.[1] This can be seen as a direct consequence of employer options and preferences, as well as of immigration status itself. Moreover, the movement of these men into female-dominated and low-paid sectors revealed how immigration had strengthened the segmentation between the primary and secondary sector for non-EU men. These men found that it was easier to move into 'women's work' than to secure career progression in more traditional roles (Schrover et al. 2007).

As is well known, work is central to the construction of masculine identities (Jackson 1999, McDowell 2004a), and the men we interviewed responded to the challenge that undertaking 'women's work' in cleaning, hospitality or care posed for them in a number of ways. Most obviously, few of these men explicitly acknowledged that their work was traditionally associated with women (see also Rouse 1992 on Mexican migrants in the US). Instead, workers spoke about the unfamiliar nature of these jobs, and the opportunities such work provided to learn new skills – thus re-evaluating what might otherwise be seen as 'women's work' as in fact more highly skilled, and as presenting a challenge they had been able to master. Carlos, a cleaner from Honduras, noted:

It was very difficult for me because I had never held a vacuum cleaner in my life, a hoover – never. And cleaning, I had never cleaned in my life. It's true ... it was difficult, but you have to learn everything in this life.

In the same way, Abiodun, an Underground cleaner from Nigeria, said that his job was the worst thing he had ever done in his life: 'I've never done cleaning job in my life, never. It's either a teacher, or the office managing ... never done it before. It's a new experience and ... one never stop learning.'

A second strategy deployed by these respondents was to highlight the physically challenging nature of these jobs, even in relation to masculinised occupations like construction. Thus Paulo, a Brazilian construction worker who had moved in and out of construction jobs, described his time washing up in a restaurant as 'worse than building work': 'When I left this washing up job they had to employ two men to replace me.... You'd wash about 2,000 to 3,000 plates per day, and 300 to 400 large pans.' Furthermore, he would not 'advise any woman to do that, only if it is to pay for the ticket [back home].' Rather than dwelling on a loss of status through de-skilling, which is usually understood in terms of class, men thus tended to stress the 'hard' nature of the work, highlighting their manliness and thus restoring some value to the labour itself (see Herbert 2008b, Jackson 1999, Simpson 2004).

1. Of the 68 interviews that were conducted with migrant men, almost half (31) worked as cleaners (23 in general office cleaning and eight on the London Underground). A further four worked as carers, while 24 worked in the construction industry, mostly as labourers.

It is little surprise to find that men and women often had very different perceptions about the same kinds of work. For instance, Kwame, a male Underground cleaner from Ghana, complained: 'The work is very hard, especially picking train [collecting rubbish]. It's not my job at all. You're working the platform and the train ... the trains are tips.' Yet Daisy, from Zimbabwe and also an Underground cleaner, said that the work was relatively easy (although she was in a minority in this regard):

> There's a lot of work to do but the conditions, they are good, they are good conditions, they are very good. If you do your work you can rest, but if you don't do your work they keep on coming telling you to do your work; but if you do everything perfect, no problem. (See also Lupton 2000)

Male respondents also sometimes sought to justify their work in the service sector in terms of the roles they had performed in their home countries. Zelu – who we met in the previous chapter – had worked as a doctor in Bangladesh, and claimed that this prepared him very well for his new job in London:

> I am a medical graduate, I know what is tracheal-stomach tube, I know what is back feeding, and what ... goes inside catheter, everything. But one of my colleague, he is just simple ... he has completed A level or O level [and] he has no idea what it is, and when he give the suction, though they are given the training ... they don't feel comfortable sometimes. I feel comfortable, because everything is known to me, that is why. That is why, I think, that for me, it's best ... this caring job is very suitable.

He further reflected:

> I thought that actually, really, it was perfect for me, this job. Many other students who come here, they are doing in supermarket, in restaurant, but ... I think that this is best job in my view, caring job, if you can do it.

Rather then emphasising the intense emotional labour involved in care work (Dyer et al. 2008), Zelu highlighted how his previous technical skills and knowledge suited his current job. Other men claimed that they had previously taken on caring work in their country of origin, even if it was unremunerated and not widely acknowledged (see Datta et al. 2009). For example, Joshua, a care worker from Ghana, justified his work as a carer in Britain in exactly these terms: 'For the care work, I had a passion; that passion is with [the clients], because when I was back home I was looking for my granddad and the like, so I had a passion, that was fine.' Similarly, Eafeu, also a carer from Ghana, spoke about the fact that caring for the elderly came naturally to him, as it was the same as looking after his own elderly relatives:

The work that you do for them is more greater than the reward that you get for such work. So you've got to be sympathetic, like maybe you helping your own old dad or your own old mum – to me, that's how I think of it.

Thus, although these men often stressed the complexity of their work, their strategy was to reconstruct popular discourses about their jobs in order to highlight the more masculine elements of the work, and to emphasise their previous experience in similar roles. Like their female colleagues, they often located this experience in their own national traditions, as demonstrated by a culture of supporting the extended family, respecting elders, and having a duty of care for each other. In these cases, men working in typically 'female' occupations would sometimes present themselves in feminised terms, and with strong parallels to the women carers introduced in the previous chapter (Kofman et al. 2000; see also Batnitzky et al. 2008 on South Asian men who emphasised their servility and deference in the hotel industry).

Moreover, as we saw in the previous chapter, many migrants could justify their currently poor employment circumstances – irrespective of whether their jobs were characterised as 'men's' or 'women's' work – by reiterating their compulsion to take any kind of work that was on offer to them as a means to survive. Anzelm migrated from Bulgaria and worked as a cleaner on the Underground on a self-employed visa, and argued: 'The job is a dirty job; I mean, I don't like it much but I haven't got much choice for now.' Likewise, Kwame, from Ghana, who also worked as a cleaner on the Underground, explained:

I have to cope with the situation. There's nothing I can do. In my life I never steal or do something like that. I always try to work, do something that's of benefit to me. So ... I can't go to the street, do some pickpockets, do something like that, I have to have work. Whether the work is cleaning job or washing cars, I have to do it to survive.

Significantly, Kwame added that he had dependants to feed back in Ghana; as we will see in further detail in Chapter 6, the need to remit money home played a key part in workers' rationalisation of the jobs they did. Indeed, many men felt that it was acceptable to do jobs that were beneath them, and that were associated with women's labour at home, in order to fulfil their traditional role as the family provider. Ryan, for example – an Underground cleaner from Nigeria – told us that he hated his job, and that only uneducated 'riff-raffs' would do it in his country; but he was doing it in order to be able to return to Nigeria and to be a success: 'Because my vision is to be a successful man, a chartered accountant. That's why I'm here, that's my aim.' For Ryan, work was a means to an end, and being 'out of place' made it easier to tolerate his social decline.

As others have noted (see McKay 2007), one of the strategies to cope with this suffering and emasculation is to prioritise 'delayed gratification': male migrants are able to put up with the restricted employment opportunities and ethnic and racial discrimination that they face in their host country by drawing upon the validation that will come on their return home as successful migrants – valued over and above other family and community members. It would therefore seem that male migrants may operate a 'double masculine consciousness' (McKay 2007: 630): subordinated in one gender regime, but hegemonic in another.

But it is important to note that life-course location and class were also important dimensions in these men's experiences, and, in particular, some middle-class men from Brazil who worked in construction and did not have a family to support claimed that their job instilled a newfound sense of responsibility in them. Danilo, aged 20, claimed:

> I think I will go back with another way of thinking. I will earn my own living. In Brazil I didn't care because I have my father. But now it's time to earn my own money, be independent, stop being dependent on my parents.

Marcelo, aged 25, claimed: 'In terms of the experience, it was worth 100 per cent.' He added, 'I learned to value money more. In Brazil I didn't value money much. I used to spend too quickly. Here I value it more because I have to sweat to earn it.' For this particular group of men, working in construction was seen as part of their personal development in London (see Jordan and Düvell 2002).

Conversely, the women we interviewed did not experience the same challenges to their gender identities through their employment. As we saw in relation to care in the previous chapter, women often described their occupations in relation to hegemonic notions of the 'natural' caring and nurturing roles of women that have their origins in the private and reproductive spheres of the home (Dyer et al. 2008, Laurie et al. 1999, McDowell 2004b). For example, Barbara, from St Lucia, told us that the reason she went into care work was to learn how to care for her relatives later in life:

> I think of my mum, and if any of my relatives are sick, how ... will I have the courage, you know, to help them, give a bath, how will I do it, you know? ... Most other people, they don't like exposing their dignity, how will they go about doing such things, you know? I always ask that question, how will I give my mum a bath? ... I would feel it's embarrassing, yes, so I wanted to at least learn to do such things.

Other women emphasised that they only struggled to learn the technical elements of their jobs, as the rest was simply innate. A care worker from Ghana explained: 'There's a saying that as a woman, you have to care for somebody – it was in me, though I didn't have any theoretical knowledge in care.' Women migrants tended to reiterate that their jobs reflected their roles in the home. A cleaner on the Underground from Zimbabwe noted that her job was: 'Cleaning.

Photo 4.1   Migrant man cleaning offices (photo by Chris Clunn).

Like domestic. Like you are doing in the house, cleaning, wiping everywhere, yeah that's the job I'm doing.'

In fact, in contrast to the men – particularly those employed in cleaning and care work – who evaluated their job in terms of necessity, the lack of alternatives, and economic survival, women often viewed their jobs in more positive terms. Many women emphasised that their migration and work in London, albeit low-paid, had enabled them to feel more independent (see Gamburd 2000, Hirsch 1999, Mahler and Pessar 2001, McIlwaine forthcoming). Adanya reflected on her move to Britain from Nigeria, explaining that, ultimately, she felt her situation had improved: 'You have to work hard, have to be independent; I'm focused to do something on my own. I really like it here in a way.'

Other women typically emphasised that the fact that they could no longer rely on relatives for help was a benefit to them in the long term. Patricia, a care worker, stated that, in Jamaica, there was always money on the table from her father, and taking employment outside the home was a choice rather than a necessity: 'If you don't want to work you don't have to work, you know what I mean? Here it's like you've got to work, you want to be independent – so I've got to do it.'

This newfound sense of independence also involved a determination to succeed. Ellen who was working in care, claimed: 'I really want to move up; I don't want to be stuck. 'Cause I've seen people who have been qualified for years and years still at the same place – that's not me. I want to climb up there.' Similarly, Antobam, also a care worker, claimed: 'I just want to set up. I feel hungry now.'

Moreover, some women claimed that their independence had created a greater sense of equality within their relationships. As Ajua, from Ghana, explained:

Back home, like, if you're in a relationship ... when you go out for a meal, the boy has to pay; going to cinema, the boy has to pay; everything you do, the boy has to pay it. But here, the girl has to do a lot of things, and it's both of you even when you are married – when bills come sometimes you have to pay some, husband has to pay some. Back home, it's the man's job ... Back home, the women, they seem to think of babies and stuff; even though the woman is still working gaining her income, the man has to pay the bills and everything ... so here [there's] equality in roles, that's why I say my life has changed, because the way I used to rely on people, I don't do that any more.

This emphasis on equality sometimes extended to roles within the household. As Rita, from Chile, claimed:

I've met very sexist Latin men here – like, these two guys whom I share with, they are sexists, so of course, in the beginning, maybe they thought I was going to move in to become the 'housewife'; but no, to an extent I am, but we are all equals: I am working, you are working, you're studying, so we all have the same rights.

She added: 'I cook at the weekends, but, for instance, during the week if he is in, he cooks. I arrive at night and he'll have cooked and is waiting for me with food ready, and we both eat then.' Influenced by Western norms associated with dual-earner households and women's role in the workplace and wider society, some migrant women told us that the division of labour within their households had altered quite significantly with the move to Britain, with men being accorded much greater responsibility for household tasks.

Some women also suggested that their paid employment outside the home had granted them the self-confidence to challenge the traditional gender roles they had grown up with. As Emilija, a chambermaid from Poland, explained:

I was brought up in this very old-fashioned way ... I had this idea stacked in the head that a man is ruling a woman ... like in middle ages ... so when I got married, whatever my husband said, it was the end of discussion. It meant that this is how it should be and there is nothing to argue about. So that is how it was in Poland ... he stood somewhere higher than I did. Since I came here, I have learnt self-reliance and that I can make decisions on my own. When he came here we argued a lot. He wasn't prepared for it – for the changes that I have undergone. He couldn't give in and I didn't want to go back to the old way.

Emilija went on to explain that decisions were now made together, and reflected that her experience in London had given her

more self-esteem ... I was able to cope here on my own. I came without knowing language, having £200 in my pocket only, and I still did manage to find work and organised my life here ... perhaps for an English person, it wouldn't be anything special but for me ... I think I did well here.

Even though Emilija was engaged in low-paid work, it was nevertheless valued because it granted her a sense of autonomy and empowerment that had an impact on her personal relationships and her sense of self. While, for Emilija, migration had been a route to economic advancement, it had also changed her in very positive ways.

This chapter has revealed how London's low-wage labour market continues to be characterised by national, ethnic, racial and gender divisions, and how these divisions are experienced by the workers themselves. It has also shown how immigration law has created new lines of segmentation that are now a key factor in allocating workers to jobs. Most notably, there is a fundamental divide between EU and non-EU workers in relation to low-paid employment. Those who had migrated from the global South felt considerable and growing disadvantage within the labour market, due to their often precarious immigration status and a renewed racialisation of the hiring queue. They argued that there was a tendency for eastern European workers to undercut their wages, block their entry into employment and their socio-economic advancement into professional jobs. Many also argued that their qualifications and experiences were ignored in their quest for new and better employment.

Corresponding with this, the eastern European workers were acutely aware of the benefits of being white Europeans, and often played down their national identity as a result. Yet, while their whiteness conferred privileges, in reality they often found themselves positioned alongside other migrant workers from the global South, intensifying their desire for 'distance'. In competition with their black and minority-ethnic rivals for work, these workers would often emphasise their sense of entitlement and freedom to work within the EU. Such boundary-drawing and identity-fixing were further complicated by divisions between national groups, so that Poles and Lithuanians would stereotype each other, just as Nigerians and Ghanaians did. Indeed, many workers emphasised how their innate national and gender characteristics complemented their particular occupations: Ghanaian women argued that they were particularly suited to care, and Brazilian men saw themselves as particularly strong, and thus good for construction. Workers attempted to position themselves or their group as superior within an intensely competitive labour market, and this was further reinforced by employer preferences in the hiring queue. Thus, while we are aware that communities are heterogeneous and internally differentiated, this chapter has highlighted how groups draw boundaries between themselves and others to boost their own collective identity.

Our data illustrate the ways in which new migrants came to inhabit London's labour market, reinforcing and/or challenging inherited norms. Indeed, we found that some gender divisions were being remade as migrant men took up work in traditionally female occupations, such as cleaning and care. Men responded to this potential threat to their masculinity in a number of ways – highlighting the unfamiliar yet physically demanding nature of the job; justifying the work in relation to their previous experience in their country of origin; or arguing that they were compelled to work to survive. Common notions of masculinity have long been tied to conceptions of men as breadwinners, and ultimately their job, albeit low-paid, enabled them to fulfil this role by supporting their families in the UK and further afield. Men thus carried out women's work, and thereby challenged social norms about gender and work without necessarily rethinking their own sense of manhood. However, the men who were engaged in the traditional male sector of construction tended to stress the more positive elements of their move – particularly those from a middle-class background who did not need to support families in their country of origin. This shows how their transnational class and life-course positions were important dimensions in shaping their experiences.

Conversely, women's jobs did not represent the same threat to gendered identities, and their experience of paid employment was generally viewed as more beneficial. Yet this work often served to challenge their own views and attitudes about women, work and wider society. Some women argued that their low-paid job had granted them self-confidence and independence, as well as a greater sense of equality within their relationships. These women claimed a sense of achievement that they had survived the difficulties of their low-paid jobs in London, and that they had emerged stronger and more independent as a result.

5

TACTICS OF SURVIVAL AMONG MIGRANT WORKERS IN LONDON

The cost of living here is very high. But people think they will come here and save money. You may even be able to save, but you would have to eat scraps from McDonald's, you would have to share a room with another six people, you would have to submit yourself to this kind of life, otherwise it's not possible. I cannot save money. There is no way!

Antonio, a construction worker from Brazil

As we have seen, global cities such as London provide migrant workers with sources of employment, but also with somewhere to live, the chance to interact with others, and the potential to contribute to the wider society (Benton-Short et al. 2005). As Antonio's comments illustrate, however, working in jobs with low levels of pay and the provision of very basic benefits means that many migrants struggle with the economic challenges of living in London. As a result, they have little choice but to develop complex practices, or what we call 'tactics', in order to respond to their situation. While some of these tactics relate to maximising income in the workplace, many are also developed in the household and the wider community. Moreover, while 'getting by' is the primary motivator, these tactics are also closely intertwined with efforts to ameliorate the impact of a range of exclusions. Taking a conceptual lead from research on livelihoods and coping strategies in the global South, this chapter draws on our research to explore how international migrants locate and mobilise the resources they need to address the disadvantages they face (see Datta et al. 2007a, Snel and Staring 2001). Although the bulk of the chapter focuses on various survival tactics, it also explores the implications of the current enthusiasm for fostering community cohesion in the UK. We argue that the structural inequalities faced by migrant workers who encounter multiple disadvantages in the workplace, home, community and nation will necessarily limit their opportunities to connect and cohere with wider communities within London and the UK.

Understanding the Strategies and Tactics of Migrant Survival

Migration has long been identified as a strategy for surviving and coping with the vagaries of life, especially when it entails moving from one country to another and from one side of the world to another. But moving across borders has rarely been the preserve of the poorest in society, and it is generally those with more resources who are able to move. Migration across borders can be seen as a 'calculated strategy' (Stark and Bloom 1985: 175) that involves sharing resources and risks within and between households (de Haas 2006). While the motivations and outcomes of migration are intermediated by a range of other factors such as age and gender, as well as geographical origins and destinations, it is clear that migrants move from one country to another in order to make improvements to their lives. Increasingly, however, it has also been recognised that, while migrants may certainly earn much higher incomes and be able to remit significant amounts of money to support their families at home, the challenges of living in foreign countries are often underestimated (Snel and Staring 2001).

For example, we met Adanya, from Nigeria, when she was working as a cleaner on the London Underground. At home she had worked in a professional job in human resources, earning £150 a month; but after a business trip in 2003 she decided to stay on in London, with the aim of earning enough money either to study or return home and set up a clothes shop. Although, when we met her, she was earning £600 per month from her job on the Underground (four times her income at home), she had to pay £300 in rent, leaving her only £300 to pay for travel and food, which in turn left her with very little to send to her three-year-old son in Nigeria (around £50 per month). As we have seen in previous chapters, these experiences are typical of the migrants we interviewed, many of whom struggled to survive in London today.

There is now a growing recognition that the ways in which international migrants in cities like London negotiate their survival converges closely with the types of mechanisms identified in the countries of the global South, as well as in the transitional economies of central and eastern Europe. Although debates about how people living in marginal situations survive have long been a subject of research across the globe (Stack 1974, Williams and Windebank 1999), research using a broadly conceived 'livelihoods approach' has been most developed in the context of the post-socialist and Southern economies. Research into the former has usefully explored the functioning of 'diverse economies', as people develop market and non-market mechanisms of survival, as well as highlighting the potentially cumulative nature of livelihood strategies among elites and the better-off (Smith and Stenning 2006). Such work overlaps with long-standing enquiries in the global South in which researchers have explored the livelihood strategies that disadvantaged people develop when faced with adversity. While early conceptualisations identified 'expenditure-minimising' or 'negative' strategies operating in tandem with 'income-generating' or 'positive' measures (Benería and Roldán 1987), these have since been reformulated to embrace the notion of assets or capitals, arguing that individuals and groups can mobilise a range of assets (such as education, skills, contacts, money, land and labour power) to secure themselves, their families and communities for the long term. Rakodi (1999) has posited four sets of intersecting strategies that she acknowledges are influenced by structural, household and individual-level factors (see also Wallace 2002). These include strategies to increase resources by intensifying the use of natural, physical or human capital (such as diversification of economic activities, or sending more household members out to work); changing the quantity of human capital (increasing household size to bring in more members either to work or provide childcare); drawing on social capital (developing extra-domestic links with extended family and friends); and mitigating or limiting consumption (cutting back on certain types of expenditures).

We found many of these practices being deployed by the migrant workers we spoke to in London. Reflecting Rakodi's typology, Afua, a care worker from Ghana, had previously had a range of jobs in her home town of Kumasi. Although her main job was buying and selling clothes in the local market, Afua was also trained as a caterer. She told us that selling clothes was not enough to live on: 'In our country, when you sell clothes and they don't buy it ... you don't get money to feed the children, and then it's hard.' In an effort to make ends meet, she made food for special occasions, such as *fufu* (boiled and ground plantain, cassava or rice), *omo tuo* (rice balls eaten with palm nut soup or groundnut-paste soup), and *banku* (fermented corn or cassava dough), which she sold to friends and relatives. Her decision to migrate to London in 1989 was an extension of this economic diversification: she was trying to maximise her income in transnational ways. After a visit to see some family members in London, she realised that she could earn much more than in Ghana, and, as she put it, she knew 'there [was] money here – if we send it to Ghana, it much more'. However, just as Adanya had found, Afua soon realised that life in London could be a real struggle. Despite her increase in earnings, her new life required even more intensive budgeting and careful management than her life in Ghana:

> What I learn [here] is economy. Because of the work ... and how the work is, you have to pay your rent, you have bills, send [money] to family, and do your shopping. So you have to put paper and pen, then you write every week what you use. In Ghana you don't – I don't do that, because when I buy something I just put my hands on the money then I use [it], but here I have to make plans.

Afua and Adyana's experiences reflect the challenges that international migrants face when living in expensive cities like London. As Snel and Staring (2001: 17) point out: 'Although international labor migration is generally perceived as a consequence of poverty, insecurity and income inequality and a strategy for escaping poverty, it does not necessarily put an end to the poverty of the immigrants.' Indeed, many of the migrant workers we met had often increased their social and financial obligations in order to move. Many had used a variety of resources, or what Nicholas Van Hear (1998: 51) refers to as 'migratory cultural capital', to facilitate their movement and settlement, and this had significant costs (see also Kelly and Lusis 2006, Nee and Sanders 2001).

At a minimum, migration usually involved friends and relatives of migrants providing initial accommodation and assistance in securing jobs, as well as the loans they needed to move (Portes 1998). While the Polish migrants in our study were among the least likely to have contacts in London before they moved – especially when compared with Ghanaians or Nigerians who often had many extended family members who were already settled (Vasta and Kandilige 2007) – Poles still depended on friends to provide them with initial help when they arrived. For example, Pavel, a construction worker from Bydgoszcz told us he had initially visited some friends in London for ten days, during which time he obtained a CIS card (the Construction Industry Scheme registers contractors and sub-contractors with the UK Treasury, allowing them to work) in order to facilitate his employment. Upon his later arrival, these same friends collected him from the train station and gave him a room in their flat. Furthermore, after Pavel tried in vain to find work in graphic design (his job in Poland), and later in cleaning and hotels, one of his friends managed to secure him a labouring job on the construction site where he worked. As we saw in Chapter 3, social capital is critical to securing a job.[1]

However, migrants drew on more than social capital, both in the process of moving and in their quest to survive. Indeed, as Zontini's (2004) cross-cultural research in Barcelona has shown, practices differ between and within groups of migrants even in the same place. While women migrants generally underpin the maintenance of survival mechanisms in every location, Zontini found that Filipina women concentrated their efforts on productive work while Moroccans focused on their caring roles (see also Duffy 2005). Such practices were created from a mixture of the expertise and resources developed at home, alongside the practices already developed by the diasporic community, in the face of the particular structural constraints encountered in Barcelona. Migrant communities were found to use different tactics, and this created variation within and between

1. Social capital refers broadly to the social relations generated as a result of participation in networks and organisations (Portes 1998). Such relations are often associated with the positive production of interpersonal trust and reciprocity (Putnam 1993, 2007), and these concepts have been widely used to assess the nature of networks among migrants in the UK and beyond (Cheong et al. 2007, Ryan et al. 2008).

TACTICS OF SURVIVAL AMONG MIGRANT WORKERS IN LONDON   125

groups of migrants. Such strategies inevitably engaged the whole household, but they were also developed in relationships to non-local people. Survival practices drew upon transnational resources and contacts, and were sometimes developed to engage with the state and a range of civil society groups within the host nation itself (Snel and Staring 2001).

It is clear that migrant communities are profoundly affected by their location in the wider socio-economy, where they invariably face discrimination and various sorts of exclusion. Since that exclusion refers to an inability to participate fully in a society on economic, social and/or political grounds, it includes but reaches beyond the issue of employment and poverty pay (de Haan and Maxwell 1998). Exclusion might involve poor quality employment opportunities and barriers to the benefits and welfare systems, as well as a lack of respect (Samers 1998: 126). Furthermore, certain types of migrants – women, those with irregular status, and those in countries where immigration regimes allow differential access to resources – are more likely to be excluded than others.

Our research exposed the extent to which migrant workers are themselves only too aware of the exclusions they face (see also Cheong 2006, McDowell 2008). Migrants' narratives about their lives in London illustrated a clear sense of economic exclusion compared to other workers, and an acute awareness that they do the jobs that British people won't do. For example, Antonio, from Brazil, was working as a construction worker at a large football stadium in London. He spoke about the lack of British people working on the site, arguing that it was only migrant workers who would put up with the harsh conditions of work – and that even they only stayed for short periods of time, moving on as soon as they could:

It's very demanding. It's very physical! These are jobs that the English people would not subject themselves to do. Usually people can't cope with the hard work ... Sometimes I feel like giving everything up and going back home. I have even cried, I sat down on the pallets and cried, thinking 'I am going home, I can't take it any longer.'

As we have established, London's migrant division of labour means that the foreign-born are now concentrated in low-paid jobs, without a social wage, because other workers are unwilling to do them. Yet the economic exclusions generated by the labour market are inevitably compounded by broader social exclusions. Many respondents articulated a perception that they were not treated as equal citizens with equal respect. Migrants' structural position in London's socio-economy had a strong emotional impact on them. Moreover, these workers often found themselves competing with other migrants for scarce resources and the right to respect (Kosic and Triandafyllidou 2003, Menjívar 2000). Most of the migrants discussed in Chapter 3 were living, working and socialising with other migrants in London, and the rivalries and hierarchies between migrants were often intense. Moreover, the arrival of new 'white' migrants from eastern Europe has tended to re-racialise migrant labour populations, adding to the complexity of the hiring queue.

The migrants doing low-paid jobs in London thus face a number of very significant challenges in relation to work and wider society. We sought to understand how they and their families survived, asking workers to tell us about the survival tactics they deployed in their everyday lives. Drawing on de Certeau's (1984) conceptualisation of tactics as the 'art of the weak', or what Scott (1985) has called 'weapons of the weak', we explored tactics as a way of articulating the everyday mechanisms that people develop in order to resist and cope in contexts of widespread injustice (see Williams 2006). Moreover, our use of the word 'tactics' rather than 'strategies' indicates our view that, although migrants have considerable agency to respond to the challenges facing them, such efforts are constantly undermined by poverty, poor working conditions, state policy, and community exclusions that frustrate their ability to develop longer-term or more 'strategic' goals. Indeed, although migrants' lives may include very careful planning and budgeting, these are often aimed only at coping with the immediate exigencies of their day-to-day lives.

While many migrants from the global South and central and eastern Europe bring a repertoire of coping mechanisms with them when they move into a city like London, they also have to develop new approaches once they arrive. Afua, the Ghanaian care worker, told us that she had to learn 'economy' when she moved to London. Her life shifted from a 'hand-to-mouth' existence in Ghana, where she was juggling two sources of income, to one that involved earning a higher income through a care job, but with the additional demands of living in London. For Afua, the economic opportunities that London provided were associated with particular penalties. She had to work very long hours (working a 12-hour day, seven days a week) and while she had more money, she faced greater problems and challenges:

> In Ghana, they help us and they protect us. What I see here is they don't care about us, especially us black people, they don't care about us. And [in] our country, the children are respectful; but here, no respect. When you go out on the bus, an old lady like me, I will stand there, and a small boy sitting down! ... In Ghana you can't see that a small boy [would do that], no, no, no. They respect you. That is better in my country ... So here, I'm going out [and] every morning I was going a bit afraid because maybe somebody will hit me or something, but in Ghana you go to work free.

In our research, London was often identified as an especially challenging city to live and work in, particularly compared to other cities in the UK and Europe. Goradz, from Croatia, worked as a kitchen assistant, and had previously lived and worked in Sheffield. He had moved to London in search of better-paid work, only to find that the cost of living was so high that the higher wages made little difference to him. Likewise, Akwusi, from Ghana, recounted that, when he had lived in The Hague in The Netherlands he had been much better off than he was now, living in London. He told us:

> There I could pay my rent, do everything, I was using a car, I could do everything, pay my MOT [Ministry of Transport certificate], everything you need. But when I came to England, you have to work more than eight hours before you can live.

Migrant workers were developing a mixture of 'reactive' tactics to respond to the challenges facing them, as well as more 'proactive' tactics to try and improve their future situation. In some cases, the latter involved sending money back home to establish business ventures, as we explore more fully in the following chapter. In addition, tactics occasionally involved the development of collective responses to improve pay, working conditions and immigration status in the host society (see Chapter 7). In the rest of this chapter, we explore the tactics used to negotiate migrants' everyday lives in London, focusing on practices associated with economic intensification, diversification and investment; on those involving the household economy; and on those intended to create and mobilise social capital. Each is considered in turn.

Economic Intensification, Diversification and Investment

Our research has highlighted the extent to which migrants in the lower echelons of London's labour market often had to intensify and diversify their primary jobs as a means of survival. The further use of their labour power was often the only option (see Rakodi 1999), and this was achieved by working overtime (43 per cent of our questionnaire sample) and/or taking on more than one job (18 per cent). Workers also moved frequently between jobs, with almost half (46 per cent) having been with their current employer for less than a year.

When he first arrived in the UK from Portugal, Mario worked as a waiter, in a 'live-in' position with his partner, in a hotel in Eastbourne. After three months, he moved on to work in two local glass and window factories, in pursuit of higher wages. With the aim of maximising their earnings, he and his partner then moved to London, where they both secured cleaning jobs with a contractor servicing a large city bank. Disappointed, Mario complained that this cleaning job paid only the minimum wage, and that the working conditions were highly exploitative: excessive workloads were accompanied by the arbitrary docking of pay. Mario was eventually sacked from this job for being absent more than twice a month (with a bad back), but he reported that he probably would have moved on in any case. Echoing our argument in Chapter 3, he told us that switching jobs was the only way to improve your situation or ensure any form of social mobility in London:

> Most people who got that job did it because they couldn't get anything else. Whoever manages to quit, does it as soon as they can. The ones who remain are the ones who have been working there for a long time and found ways of not working much and still earn their money.

After cleaning, Mario managed to find a job as a security guard, which paid more and which, in contrast to cleaning, he felt offered some route to advancement: 'My expectation is to progress within security. Or as a security officer, I could maybe try supervision or any other higher job with the firm. Or still as a body-guard. Security is something that generates a lot of money.' For Mario, switching jobs was a means of progress.

In addition to changing jobs, however, many migrants also sought to work longer hours in the job they did. Of those working overtime, more than half (61 per cent) worked an extra eight hours per week, with a further third doing up to 16 hours of overtime. In contrast to wider norms, however, only a minority of these workers (27 per cent) received a higher rate of pay for their overtime, and even then the premiums were relatively low (and much less than the time-and-a-half or double-time that are commonly paid), being paid at a rate of between £5 and £7 per hour. About one in five workers told us that they also took on an extra job to survive, and cleaning was the most common option (taken up by 51 per cent of those with a second job). A number of respondents also worked additional hours in hotel or catering jobs (15 per cent), retail (13 per cent) or in care and/or hospitals (6 per cent). In some cases, these second, and even third jobs were relatively time-intensive, and almost half (44 per cent) did these jobs for between 8 and 16 hours per week, with an additional 28 per cent working over 16 hours extra per week.

Most of our respondents were explicit that they had developed these tactics of intensification and diversification in order to try and earn enough money simply to make ends meet. Janet – originally from Jamaica, and working as a care worker and as a waitress at Kentucky Fried Chicken – stated that she had two jobs 'because of low pay'. Similarly, Pedro, an office cleaner from Brazil who already worked every night from 9pm until 6am, also worked at weekends selling football programmes at two south London football grounds. He was paid between £25 and £30 for this work, and he told us that he needed the money to pay for dentistry, as well as his pension back in Brazil. It was particularly telling that Pedro called his extra job his 'sacrifice', because it meant having to juggle night shifts and employment during the day. For him, and many others, sleep was 'sacrificed' on the altar of wages. Several migrant workers told us that they sometimes wouldn't go to bed at all, sleeping on buses and trains between their various jobs and courses. Such activities had potentially deleterious effects on people's ability to do their jobs. For Vijay, a male care worker from Mauritius, the long working hours had contributed to situations of negligence at work that the agencies largely ignored.

In addition to 'sweating' their own labour power, however, a number of migrant workers also sought to live in households with multiple earners (see Rakodi 1999). This was widespread, with 43 per cent of our respondents living in such domestic units. While this usually involved living with a partner or other family members who worked, migrants also shared accommodation with friends. In the majority of cases, this involved living with people from the same nationality or ethnic group, and working in the same types of jobs, such as cleaning (26 per cent) or other service occupations (29 per cent). Mary, who worked as a care assistant, lived with her husband and their two small children, as well as a friend and her husband from their home town in Ghana. Although her friend's husband had a job at a local DIY warehouse, she could not work because of childcare commitments, and she rented a room to Mary and her family in order to make up the shortfall in their household resources.

While the majority of migrant workers reported working hard to send money back to their families at home, a small minority were also investing in businesses with a view to returning. Unusually, we also met a couple of workers who were seeking to establish new businesses in London, using their transnational connections to do something new (see Andreotti 2006). One of these was Mary, who was developing a small retail business, purchasing goods in London and then sending them to sell in her home town in Ghana. Also transnational, but for survival rather than investment, were remittances sent in reverse, or across borders, from wealthier migrants. Rather than supporting families back home, some of the migrants we spoke with had to depend on family either at home or living elsewhere in the world when times got tough economically.

Our research also revealed some limited evidence of migrants mobilising their financial resources once they had earned them. A number of women from Kenya and Uganda had adopted the practice, known as *roscas* in East Africa, of establishing an informal savings scheme (Gugerty 2007). Jasmine, a care worker, described how her *rosca* had provided economic and social support, acting as a substitute family as well as helping her to save £50 a month that could also be used to help others in times of need. Other migrants reported using similar schemes to accumulate money to send to their local community at home.

The Negotiation of Household Economies

Many of the tactics of economic intensification, diversification and investment outlined above were not possible without rebalancing the work of the home.

Following Smith and Stenning (2006), we use the term 'household economies' to include the activities of all household members who contribute their labour and resources to the household unit. The micro-economic tactics identified at this scale involve manipulating household structures and living arrangements to maximise employment (as described above), to share childcare and other responsibilities, and to minimise consumption.

We found that migrants would seek to share their caring responsibilities, particularly in the case of childcare, in order to reduce household costs. Given the high costs of childcare in London (Jarvis 2005), migrants on low pay argued that formal childcare was completely beyond their reach. Those with dependent children in the UK (around 34 per cent) thus relied on a range of gendered tactics for support, both locally and transnationally. In some cases workers had left children at home, becoming transnational parents when they moved. This primarily entailed migrant mothers leaving their children in the care of grandmothers and aunts at home, although several men also identified themselves as transnational fathers (Datta et al. 2009, Hondagneu-Sotelo and Avila 1997, Pribilsky 2004). Many migrant mothers viewed transnational motherhood as an emotionally demanding tactic for economic survival. Adanya, from Nigeria, said that she bore the pain of her life in London by thinking about her son at home. She was currently trying to get a second job as a care worker (in addition to her job cleaning the Underground) in order to pay for his school fees in Nigeria. Similarly, migrant parents justified their decision to migrate and their suffering in London by reference to the longer-term benefits accruing to their children at home.

For migrants with dependent children in London, however, the challenges of childcare were also significant. Some migrants, like Antobam, a care worker from Ghana, increased their household size by bringing their mothers to London to look after their children (see Wall and José 2004, Zontini 2004). Others made do with local social networks, and the small minority who did pay for childcare relied on informal child-minding. Rosana, a Portuguese woman who worked as a chambermaid in a hotel, had a neighbour who dropped her children at school, from where Rosana was able to collect them later. Some women were able to use their partners to do more childcare than they would have been expected to do in their home countries (see McIlwaine 2008; see also Chapter 4). This was especially the case when parents worked alternative shifts so that they could take turns to care for their children. As Yoffi, a Ghanaian care worker, indicated, she arranged her shifts around her husband's, so that 'if it's the night by the time I'm about to leave, the Dad is in, so I just stay [at work] till the morning ... I'll be in before the Daddy leaves in the morning'. Such 'back-to-back' childcare was remarkably common, but it also reduced the time parents had to sleep and recover from work. Needless to say, those without partners were particularly penalised by their lack of household support. Some single mothers reported that their only option was to cut back on their hours of work, even if it increased their poverty and/or impaired their opportunity to move out of jobs such as cleaning (Wall and José 2004).

In relation to minimising consumption, a number of migrant workers shared their households with other non–family members to reduce household costs. Mirek, a construction worker from Poland, recalled that, when he had first arrived, his friend (from Poland) had taken him to live in his flat in east London, where 20 Poles were sharing a small four-bedroom flat. Most of the people who lived there had been in London for a short time, and once they found work they would try to move out. Mirek stayed there for a couple of months before moving to a three-bedroom flat, this time with five other Poles. In his most recent move, he had begun sharing with four other Poles in a three-bedroom place. With a wife and child to support in Poland, Mirek was keen to live as frugally as possible, and for him it made sense to live with other workers and share rent, food and other costs in order to be able to send money home. Our research found that it was very common for migrants to stay initially with family members and friends, until they found their feet in the city. For example, Portia moved from Zimbabwe to London with her husband and son, living with her mother for a number of months after their arrival. They subsequently found rented accommodation in a house with two other Zimbabwean women, sharing to keep the costs down.

Migrant men and women also described their efforts to minimise consumption and practise budgeting. They would also actively seek bargains and limit the purchase of luxury goods. Household budgets were often closely monitored and managed, down to the last penny. Ewa, a chambermaid from Poland, said that she limited her daily spending on food to £2, which fed three people (she would buy two chickens for £3 to make eight dinners, with salad and potatoes, as well as ham and bread for lunches). The majority of respondents told us that they 'shopped around' for bargains and special offers, with most saying that they favoured budget supermarkets and street markets as their main place to shop. As Mary, the care assistant from Ghana, recounted:

> If it's shoes, which I buy very occasionally, I go along the shops to see which one is the cheapest, but of relatively good quality. I don't just go there with open bags, and I know what I want. I buy most the ones when it's time for the sales, just to save some money.

A judicious combination of household management and expenditure control thus reduced costs.

The Mobilisation of Social Capital

So far we have explored workers' efforts at economic intensification, diversification and investment, as well as their creation of household economies designed to share responsibilities and reduce costs, as tactics of economic survival. Yet such tactics are themselves often dependent upon social capital: the personal networks that allowed people to find jobs, secure overtime, identify housemates and recruit childcare. But such social capital was not available to all, and did not always function to everyone's benefit (Portes 1998). Different types of migrants had varying stores of social capital, depending on their nationality, ethnicity, legal status, length of residence, gender and religion (for more on the latter, see Chapter 7). Migrant workers both created and used their social capital with different levels of success (Collyer 2005).

In some ways, social capital provided a buttress to assist migrants in coping with their new lives in London; yet it also led to further exclusions, as outsiders necessarily struggled to establish themselves and create connections to the wider host society. In London, the types of social capital mobilised by migrants primarily included 'bonding social capital', whereby strong ties with relatives, neighbours and close friends – usually with co-ethnics or co-nationals – provided important support and a 'launch pad' to some forms of 'bridging social capital', whereby weak ties linked individuals in a similar position in society. It is striking that there was little evidence of 'linking social capital', whereby poor workers could access those with influence in formal institutions, such as public bodies and government (see Putnam 1993, Woolcock 1998). Moreover, even the social capital that did exist within migrant society often generated further inequalities and exclusions (Cheong et al. 2007).

As we saw in Chapter 3, personal contacts – including both bonding and bridging, and to a lesser extent linking social capital – were critical in allowing migrants to access the labour market, and in some cases to secure accommodation, housemates and childcare. However, while such social networks helped those involved, they simultaneously limited access for others. Not surprisingly, supervisors who were able to make job appointments often selected and favoured their compatriots, generating complaints among those who were thereby excluded. Barbara, a care assistant from St Lucia, reported that her Ghanaian manager was more likely to employ other Ghanaians, and then favour them with extra shifts and easier work. Moreover, even those who secured their job through the deployment of social capital could then sometimes be expected to 'pay for it' by 'buying' the job or loyalty once at work (Cranford 2005, Soldatenko 1999; see also Chapter 3).

Invariably, social capital reflected nationality and ethnicity, and while this assisted the migrants involved, it could have the unintended consequence of reinforcing exclusion from British society. Most respondents told us that they had limited contact with British people – specifically 'white' British people – and that their friendships were largely with people from their home countries. Darek, a construction worker, described how he was living with people from the same housing estate in Poland, and said that his only other friends were a group from another estate in the same city: 'There are small groups – for instance we are from Kapuscinski estate, the other group is from Bartodzieja estate ... All those people have known each other from childhood.' Likewise, Carlos, a cleaner who was born in Honduras but raised in Colombia, spoke of his preference for maintaining only a few good friends from home: 'I'm very select with whom I can consider as my friends, or rather I only have a few people whom I consider to be my true friends – very few, very few; the rest are acquaintances.'

We were struck by the extent to which such selective friendships could act as a security barrier against other migrants from their own national group, as well as those from further afield. Indeed, Darek and Carlos spoke of their compatriots in disparaging terms, saying that it was often necessary to maintain distance from them and not to get too involved with co-nationals, who were not to be trusted. Carlos told us that his irregular immigration status made him particularly wary of strangers, who might potentially report him to the authorities (see McIlwaine 2005, 2007a). Likewise, Darek told us that Poles were selfish people who were reluctant to take responsibility for others, and that it was better to avoid them as much as possible, adding:

> Sadly, Polish sometimes have a very low self-esteem, forgetting often where they came from. I think that we Poles will never be able to stick together, and there is no solidarity between us. I think there is more of that among Bulgarians or Lithuanians; Polish are more [concerned] with his/her own pocket.

Such suspicions aside, however, even if migrants were open to forging new friendships while living in London, their position in the labour market and the consequences of low pay made it particularly difficult for them to do so. As we have seen, many migrants worked long and antisocial hours, and many reported their exhaustion after their work. As Mirek put it, the

> Life of a Pole in England looks more or less in the following way. I leave home for work at 6.45, take some over-time and am back home at 7.30. After 11 hours of hard physical work I do not have much desire for sociability.

Moreover, even if workers and their families were keen to socialise, cost presented a further barrier. In light of these challenges, it is not surprising that many migrants also developed psychological coping mechanisms to deal with the exclusions they faced. In tandem with other research into the psychological coping strategies of workers in low-status work, we found that respondents sought to 're-code' their labour as valuable to the wider society as well as themselves (Ashforth and Kreiner 1999). While high rates of labour turnover often prevented the creation of strong occupational and workplace cultures that might reproduce alternative cultures of value – as have been found among other groups – workers had developed individual-level responses to their work. As we saw in Chapter 4, it was not uncommon for men working in feminised jobs to develop a range of valorisation techniques that emphasised the difficulties and challenges of their work, or the fact that jobs such as caring were central to their cultural make-up, and were not just 'women's work' (see McIlwaine et al. 2006). A number of workers – particularly those working in care – also emphasised the intrinsic value of the work they did (often also citing their religious belief, as we explore more fully in Chapter 7). Still others focused on the benefits accruing to their families within the UK, as well as further afield.

Our research also highlighted the particular role of faith organisations in generating new social capital among migrant workers that could assist them while living in London. As we will see in Chapter 7, almost half of our respondents were involved in faith groups, which provided a safe, shared environment to forge relationships in. Given that many mosques and churches tended to be divided along ethnic and nationality lines – in the case of Ghanaian and Nigerian evangelical churches, even down to the specific area of the country where people came from – these institutions provided an important site for the creation of both bonding and bridging social capital, as well as a potential conduit to wider British society through linking social capital. We found that West Africans were the most active in developing and participating in faith societies in London, as well as in civil society organisations in their home countries (see Mohan 2006). However, large numbers of Latin Americans also participated in churches, and to a lesser extent in migrant organisations (see Evans et al. 2007b, McIlwaine 2007a; see also Photo 5.1).

Social capital, then, is not as straightforward or uniformly positive as Putnam and many policy-makers suggest (Spicer 2008, Zetter et al. 2006). As we have seen, bonding and bridging social capital are critical in supplying the information and initial contacts needed to survive in the city; but their use can also produce barriers to further integration – especially in light of limited linking social capital in the form of contact with wider British society. In addition, the structural constraints facing migrant workers in poorly-paid jobs with poor conditions, and without access to state resources, undermine their opportunities to create and mobilise social capital – particularly by forging links with the host society (Cheong et al. 2007). While migrant workers have certainly created a range of innovative tactics to deal with the consequences of this position, such tactics have generally been insufficient to overcome the barriers they have faced (at least in the short term). Furthermore, encouraging migrants to draw on their own social resources is neither morally nor practically defensible. Migrant workers were effectively left to fend for themselves, doing jobs that others would not do. Thus, whatever the view currently advocated by the government in the UK and beyond (Zetter et al. 2006), the building of social capital among migrant communities will always be insufficient to achieve social cohesion in Britain today.

Photo 5.1   Carila Latin American Welfare Group 30th anniversary meeting, London, July 2007 (photo by Cathy McIlwaine).

Migrant Survival and Social Cohesion

At the time of writing, there has been a shift in government and wider policy thinking in relation to the challenges posed by multicultural communities in Britain. Whereas migrants were once enveloped in the language and practices of multiculturalism, whereby self-organisation and cultural difference were encouraged and accepted, they are now expected to practise community cohesion (Back et al. 2002, Herbert et al. 2008, Joppke 2004, Muir 2008). The New Labour government has developed a range of new initiatives to foster community cohesion, illustrated by the Commission on Integration and Cohesion's 2007 report, *Our Shared Future* (see also Department for Communities and Local Government 2008). While still ostensibly 'valuing diversity', the government is now committed to building 'shared values' and a 'sense of belonging' among migrants and black and minority ethnic populations within the UK (see Cantle 2008).

Yet, along with concepts such as assimilation, integration and multiculturalism, cohesion has become another term associated with a range of meanings that can be manipulated according to circumstances (see Brubaker 2003, Spencer and Cooper 2006). Echoing the arguments about the limits of social capital outlined above, the focus on consensus-building through changing values tends to ignore the racism and structural inequalities that have often created a lack of social and community cohesion in the first place (Cheong et al. 2007, Zetter et al. 2006). Although 'making social injustice visible' is a core principle of *Our Shared Future*, for example, there is little consideration of how to do this. In turn, current conceptualisations assume a certain homogeneity within and between migrant groups that does not exist in reality. Indeed, Vasta (2007: 34) points out how inequalities are being ignored, so that non-economic solutions are proposed to address structural problems by shifting responsibility away from the state and on to individuals.

As we have seen, migrant workers from an extraordinary range of backgrounds are located at the bottom end of the labour market, where they have access to limited resources and experience enormous pressures on their time. Our findings therefore corroborate the argument that '[w]ork can be an obstacle to social cohesion and not, as is often assumed, an agent of integration' (Hickman et al. 2008: xi). Those without legal status are further compromised in their relationship to the wider society. Many of the migrant workers we interviewed did not have the immigration status and/or citizenship required to build stable lives in the country (see Rutter et al. 2008). Moreover, even if they had the desire and opportunity to become citizens, many were defeated by the conditions of their lives. For example, Pedro, an office cleaner from Brazil who was of Portuguese descent, who had the option of staying and becoming a citizen, told us:

> This is a country for work, especially for immigrants. Very few will settle here for good and this is because of the weather. Also, everything is too expensive here. A person will never settle here. Very few manage that. The income here is not enough to enable one to settle here. Many who are here have the idea of earning money and going back to Brazil … They save as much as they can, then they return to Brazil to set up a business.

Our research suggests that Britain's low-wage migrants often live what have been called 'parallel lives'; but we need to recognise that this is often not out of choice. Indeed, the creation of social and community networks among co-ethnics and co-nationals, however fragmented, often acts as a critical bulwark against exclusions and discrimination, being part of an arsenal of survival tactics in London. We found that conditions of work, coupled with the immigration regime, prevented social integration regardless of the ideas and desires of individuals. Migrants often had few avenues into mainstream British society: while they often wanted to integrate, their structural position prevented them from doing so. It is also significant that, while they were excluded and poorly integrated, many of the migrants we encountered lived very multicultural lives. This could be said to confound the expectations of those who suggest that multiculturalism is a public policy problem (see Herbert et al. 2008 on the contested meanings of multiculturalism).

Many workers told us they had learned to be more tolerant of difference through living and working in London. Teresa, a Polish chambermaid, spoke about the way in which London had opened her eyes to new ways of living. In stark contrast to her experience in Poland, she had learned to tolerate and even appreciate difference by living in London:

> I suppose people [here] do not judge and are very open-minded; [they] accept the differences ... When I came here – yes it was very surprising and even strange – there was so many cultures, different people. Often people do not want to become as everyone else – they want to preserve their own identity. I wear this or behave that way – I am a Muslim – so I will keep to my tradition.

The migrants we interviewed were already integrated into London life in terms of what Vertovec (2007a: 4) calls 'civil-integration'. By this, he means the 'acquisition and routinization of everyday practices for getting on with others in the inherently fleeting encounters that comprise city life'. This civil-integration was a necessary part of everyday life for migrants who lived and worked with other migrants in the city today. However, such individuals were also structurally and emotionally isolated from mainstream British society – and until this ends, pleas for community cohesion will have little effect.

This chapter has shown that an understanding of the lives of migrant workers in London must take into account the wider nexus of home and community in which they reside. Any exploration of the ways in which migrants 'get by' must incorporate the range of complex practices and tactics that people create to deal with the challenges of living in London. Our research highlighted the use of economic intensification, diversification and accumulation, and the renegotiation of household economies, including the sharing of domestic labour and the minimising of costs – all of which depended on the creation and mobilisation of social capital. We have argued that, while such tactics were immensely beneficial to those concerned, they were also insufficient to tackle the wider economic and social exclusions that arise from the structural location of migrant workers in London's low-wage labour market, coupled with the impact of the immigration regime. Despite pleas for cohesion, these structural issues remain critical in determining the socio-economic and political opportunities available to migrants living in London. Given these barriers, migrants are increasingly likely to favour collective and political organisation as a means of challenging their situation. At present, it is likely that many migrants are better integrated in their home countries than they are in London, and we explore this more fully in the following chapter.

6

RELATIONAL LIVES: MIGRANTS, LONDON AND THE REST OF THE WORLD

I love it here. I love the links with the world. London is the heart of the world. I can talk in this corner with a Nigerian and then round the corner with an Indian, over there I can talk to a Colombian, and so on. This is great! Brazil does not know the world. And the world doesn't know Brazil ... People talk about New York. Perhaps New York [is] a little bigger than London ... but it is more interesting here. London is more cosmopolitan.

Paulo, Brazilian construction worker

Certainly, in Western societies, there is a hegemonic geography of care and responsibility which takes the form of a nested set of Russian dolls. First there is 'home', then perhaps place or locality, then nation, and so on. There is a kind of accepted understanding that we care first for, and have our responsibilities towards, those nearest in. There are two qualities of this geography which stand out: it is utterly territorial, and it proceeds outwards from the small and near at hand.

Doreen Massey (2004: 9)

The arrival of new migrants in London is leading, in the opinion of some of the migrant men and women we interviewed, to the creation of a cosmopolitan city which is more diverse and interesting then any of its nearest competitors, where all nationalities are represented, and which has become the very 'heart of the world'. In a city that encompasses 'half the world', distant people and places have, it would appear, come closer. While London is itself becoming transformed, migration is also shaping the nature of London's – and the UK's – engagement with the global South and with central and eastern European countries. It is this connection of London – and the UK – with the rest of the world that is the focus of this chapter.

Conceptually, this engagement is mostly understood in relation to questions of development, with growing academic and public policy attention being paid to a migration–development nexus within which mobility emerges as a potential driver of development (Nyberg-Sørensen et al. 2002, Skeldon 2008a). Thus, even though migration does not explicitly feature in contemporary discourses on development as encapsulated by the Millennium Development Goals (MDGs), commentators agree that it remains central to the achievement of many of these ambitions (Piper 2009, Skeldon 2008a). In turn, much of the euphoria surrounding the economic potential of migration and development rests upon the transnational links which migrants maintain with their non-migrant families and communities located in their home countries, which facilitate the flow of resources, values and ideas between a migrant's new home and their country of origin. Of these, it is undoubtedly remittances – and to a lesser extent skills – that have come to dominate discussions, even while commentators are quick to point out that transnational links are much more diverse than these, encompassing the traffic of social, cultural and political flows (Ballard 2003b, Carling 2004, Faist 2008, Levitt and Nyberg-Sørensen 2004).

Like many of its counterparts in the minority world, the UK also subscribes to such positive pronouncements on the migration–development nexus. New Labour has 'expanded its funding on migration, and [is] working towards the goal of increasing the benefits and reducing the risks of international migration' (Representative of the Department for International Development). This said, in practice the UK government's policies on migration and development have tended to conflict with the approach taken to migration itself. Thus, even while rhetoric on the importance of migration for development and poverty-reduction abounds (DFID 2006), as outlined in Chapter 1, the New Labour government has aggressively pursued a 'managed migration' agenda and adopted a points-based immigration regime that is designed to restrict migration and enforce return for many from the poorest parts of the world. This same incoherence is evident in its piecemeal response to the 'brain drain' which, on the one hand, facilitates the flow of skills that are vital for global cities like London, while, on the other, articulating a desire to stem recruitment from particularly beleaguered sectors, such as healthcare, in the global South. Furthermore, a distinct realignment of British geopolitical priorities is also evident in its migration–development agenda, in which migrants coming from an enlarged EU are (guardedly) envisaged as the 'right kinds of migrants', who can contribute more to the development of both their home and host countries than those from elsewhere (Datta 2009a). Thus, even while their movement has been partly facilitated, the opportunities available for unskilled migrants from the global South to migrate legally to the UK are now being dramatically reduced. As we saw in Chapter 4, this has increased tensions between migrants and stimulated the re-racialisation of employment at the 'bottom-end' of the labour market in London.

These debates are fleshed out below, but we begin this chapter by examining the multifaceted and multi-scalar transnational networks that link migrants in

London to their families and home communities. These networks are not only financial, but also social, political and philanthropic in nature. We then consider what these links tell us about London's changing relationship with the rest of the world, focusing first on remittances, and then on skills. Finally, we consider the implications of these connections for developing a more relational sense of care and responsibility in the contemporary world.

Migrants' Transnational Practices: Linking London to the World

Given that 'the financial remittance market is the most visible, exemplary, and easily measurable dimension of migrant transnational development activities' (Robinson 2004: 7), we begin our discussion with a consideration of the remittances that link London to the rest of the world. Recent World Bank figures suggest that worldwide remittances exceeded US$305 billion in 2008 – up from US$2 billion in 1970, US$17.7 billion in 1980, US$31.1 billion in 1990, US$76.8 billion in 2000, US$116 billion in 2003, and US$281 billion in 2007 (World Bank 2006, Ratha et al. 2008). Given that these estimates disregard informal money transfers, the true volume of remittances is likely to be much higher.[1] Globally, the most significant recipient countries were India (US$45 billion), China (US$35 billion), Mexico (US$26.2 billion) and the Philippines (US$18.3 billion) (Ratha and Shaw 2007, Ratha et al. 2008). This partly reflects the fact that some national regimes have promoted the export of labour, with a number of countries – including the Philippines – having developed strong 'cultures of migration' in which official policies facilitate out-migration at all skill levels in the expectation that these *bagong bayani* – 'new heroes' – will send money back home.

Within eastern and central Europe, remittance flows increased from US$7.9 billion in 1995 to an estimated US$38.6 billion in 2007, with the top recipient countries being Romania (US$6.8 billion), Poland (US$5 billion) and Serbia and Montenegro (US$4.9 billion) (Ratha et al. 2008). In turn, the contribution of remittances as a proportion of GDP or foreign exchange earnings is especially significant in smaller countries with large diasporas, such as Haiti (24.8 per cent

1. Carling (2005) reports that estimates of remittances are based on two sources: information collected by central banks and published as part of their balance of payment (BoP), and information from sample surveys of senders and receivers of remittances. While the latter are very useful, they are often small-scale, and are also not conducted on a regular basis. The majority of estimates are therefore based upon BoP data, which relate to three different items: *compensation of employees*, which refers to the wages, salaries and other benefits paid to non-resident workers; *workers' remittances*, which are the transfers made by migrants who are considered residents in the country where they are employed; and *migrant transfers*, which are assets or liabilities that migrants take with them when they move from one country to another (Carling 2005: 6). Problems arise from undercounting (most particularly of informal remittances), over-counting (from a misidentification of imports as remittances), and deductions for temporary workers spending in their countries of origin.

of GDP) and Jamaica (17.4 per cent of GDP) (Brown 2006: 59; see also Bracking 2003, Connell and Conway 2000, Farrant et al. 2006, Ratha et al. 2008).

From Britain alone, remittances were placed at US$4.5 billion in 2006, and were sent to more than 50 countries in the global South (Isaacs 2008, Ratha et al. 2008). The average amount sent was £870 a year, with Nigeria, India, Pakistan, Jamaica and Ghana receiving the greatest amounts (Balakrishnan 2006). The vibrancy of the remittance business is further illustrated by the fact that approximately 2,600 money transfer businesses (MTBs), with some 30,000 outlets, currently operate in the UK – a figure that is significantly higher than the 60 agencies in Spain, 50 in Italy, 30 in Germany, and a mere three in France (*Financial World* 2008).[2] The importance of London in these financial transfers is illustrated by our own data, which reflect the concentration of many migrant communities, especially those originating from the global South, in the city (Chappell et al. 2008). Remittances from the city therefore link London tangibly to a range of countries both in the global South and in east and central Europe (see Fig. 6.1).

A large majority of the households that we interviewed (over 73 per cent) sent remittances – a finding that is partly explained by the fact that 41 per cent reported that they had close dependants living outside the UK. Furthermore, among those who remitted money home, 54 per cent were male migrants and 46 per cent women. Migrants from Africa, and especially sub-Saharan Africa, were the most likely to send money home (81 per cent), followed by migrants from eastern Europe (79 per cent) and Latin America (67 per cent). Some variations were evident in the proportion of income remitted, which ranged from a low of 4 per cent in the case of Ajua, a care worker from Ghana who sent money home to her mother, to 65 per cent for Eduardo, a Brazilian labourer who maintained his two daughters and ex-wife in Brazil (Datta et al. 2007b). The average amount remitted was £100 per month, although this also varied according to the circumstances and reasons for remitting.

But London's migrant communities are not only a source of remittances; they are also, albeit to a lesser extent, potentially the recipients of money transfers which are crucial in tiding migrants over until they are able to find jobs, pay course fees, and support themselves in the city. The receipt of these 'reverse remittances' was particularly evident among migrants who came from relatively well-off families, or who could draw upon the help of relatives and friends in a wider migrant diaspora. Joshua, a care worker from Ghana and part-time student, noted that his uncles in the US had sent him money to pay his university tuition fees; and Carlos, a cleaner from Honduras who was brought up in Colombia, told us that

2. In turn, the proliferation of MTBs in the UK is attributable to the combination of a large migrant population with fairly lax regulations regarding the licensing and monitoring of MTBs. There are initiatives underway to bring MTBs that are currently regulated by Her Majesty's Revenue and Customs (HMRC) under the European Union's Payment Services Directive in 2009, which may result in the closure of some of these MTBs (DFID 2005; *Financial World* 2008).

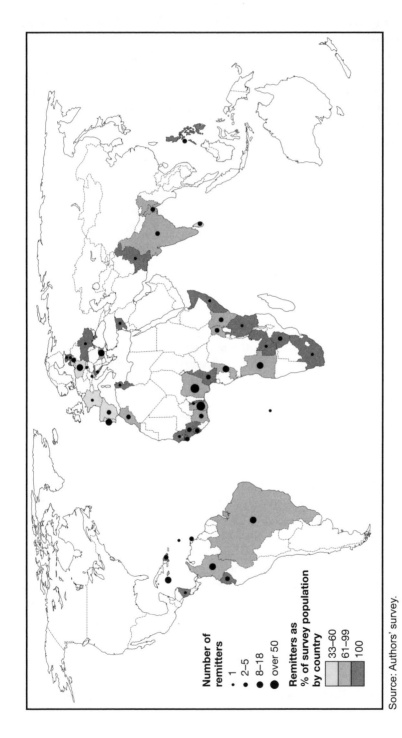

Source: Authors' survey.

Figure 6.1   Remittance flows from London to the rest of the world

Photo 6.1   Advertisement for money-transfer agency, London (photo by Jon May).

his parents sent money to him regularly (up to £300 per month), so that he could cope with living in an expensive city like London. The sending or receiving of remittances thus has a critical impact upon household survival tactics, as we saw in the previous chapter (see Datta et al. 2007a, Datta 2009b).

Of course, it is important to reiterate that transnational links operate at multiple scales, connecting individuals, households, communities and states in both home and host countries (Carling 2005). Thus, for example, financial resources may be transferred from migrants to their own bank accounts in their home countries; to their families; to collectives as charitable donations; and also to home governments, in the form of taxes and/or levies. Individual transfers may also take on a more collective form, through diasporic organisations such as home-town associations, which are often linked to community-development projects, and are increasingly being afforded a prominent role as agents of development (Faist 2008, Farrant et al. 2006, IOM 2007, McIlwaine 2007b, Mohan 2006, 2008, Styan 2007). In our study we came across migrants like Ethel, from Kenya, who observed that a group of Ugandans living in her housing estate in south-east London, had set up an informal system whereby they sent goods and money back to east Africa for family and friends, which was a lot cheaper than using formal channels. Other migrants, predominantly from Ghana, also spoke about their participation in home-town associations that sent money home collectively to fund various development projects (see below).

Financial remittances do not flow in a vacuum. Rather, they are sustained through broader social, cultural and political connections with home countries. Indeed, it is arguably these broader connections that explain why migrants remit for considerable periods of time, and often under financial and emotional duress (Lindley 2007). Migrants' transnational links are part of a wider currency whereby ideas, values and skills circulate in 'diasporic knowledge networks' (Faist 2008: 26, Datta 2009a). Levitt (1998: 926) utilises the concept of 'social remittances' to describe these exchanges, which she defines as 'a local-level, migration-driven form of cultural diffusion'. Such social connections shape non-migrants' knowledge of the places to which their kin have migrated, while also resulting in the cultural diffusion of alternative gender relations, fashion, music and food, which critically shape material demands for Western goods (Levitt 1998). They also facilitate a sense of connection to people and places left behind – a sentiment echoed by Zafia, a Kenyan woman who was working as a carer in London, who said: 'Through the texting and phoning them it feels good, you feel as if you are home because you feel updated.'

In addition to these kinds of connections, much research has illustrated the importance of political links between migrants and their home countries, which are demonstrated by transnational political practices such as expatriate voting, by the fact that political parties canvass in the towns and cities of the global North to raise money and political support, and by migrant support for insurgency movements in their own countries (Portes 2001). While the incidence of these practices was less evident in our research, many migrants did maintain an interest in local politics in their home countries. Thus, José, from Brazil, who worked in the construction sector, told us that it was important to keep in touch not only with his mother, sister and children, who were still in Brazil, but also to 'keep an eye on the politics. It is my country; my money is there. I have my things there and I need to know what is happening over there.'

Such transnational connections operate in transnational social spaces that cut across national borders and involve individuals, households, organisations and firms, linked through a series of social and symbolic ties (Faist 2008). These connections result in the formation of transnational families, which Huang and colleagues define as 'families whose members continue to share strong bonds of collective welfare' (Huang et al. 2008: 3). Coming in various guises – and including 'astronaut' fathers, 'parachute' or 'satellite' kids, and transnational mothers – these new familial formations enable what is described as a 'simultaneity of everyday lives' (ibid.), incorporating both home and host countries, and bringing rewards, but also generating significant emotional, mental and economic costs (Datta et al. 2009). Such simultaneity was evident in the narratives of migrants like Kiryk, a Polish construction sector worker:

> Yeah ... when I am coming back to London I feel like ... it is here that my home is ... but then when I go back to Poland I begin to engage in things there even that I am there just for a while – so it is a sort of rediscovering of myself there.

The kinds of links described above are by no means new; but it is equally clear that the connections that contemporary transnational migrants are able to sustain are unique in their density and flexibility, both of which have been facilitated by the revolution in modern communications (Portes 2001, Vertovec 2004). As Portes (2001: 188) points out, the 'advent of cheap and efficient air transport, telephone and facsimile technology, and above all the internet, endows contemporary immigrants with resources entirely beyond the reach of their predecessors'. We found that the availability of cheap phone cards, as well as special deals with mobile phone companies, effectively meant that many of the migrants we interviewed were able to keep in close and frequent touch with family and events back home. Moreover, while we recognise the importance of not romanticising the extent to which phone calls and the like can sustain 'virtual intimacies', as they are a poor replacement for physically embodied relations (Huang et al. 2008), they were often cited as being extremely important. This was especially the case for transnational mothers and fathers, who reported calling home at least once a week, and sometimes even more frequently. For example, Judith, a care worker from Ghana, phoned her son every day to find out what he was doing. Another care worker, Zelu, who was from Bangladesh, recounted how he had three mobile phones: one of which he used solely to speak to his mother, brother and sister in Bangladesh, who he called every other day to keep in touch with events in their lives. These frequent phone calls were extremely important for him, because 'when I phone to them, [and] I speak with them every time, I feel that they are very close to me'. These calls were also important for the family left behind. As Gladys, a Ghanaian woman working as a cleaner, told us, frequent calls home were necessary:

> Because they want to know how you are faring, what is going on. You know, like mother with a child, the child goes and the mother is concerned about child. Are you going to school? What is happening? Where have you reached? They want to know everything, what is going on like that. So if you can't do every week, two weeks you call them, 'I'm OK, happy with work,' or whatever like that, you tell them Sunday. They really want to know.

Mary, also from Ghana, simply said: 'But I love to hear their voice, so I prefer to phone them to the email.' Indeed, even though phone calls could serve as an avenue through which control was exercised, and we had examples of relatives using the phone to ask for remittances, the technology facilitated transnational connections and ties (Boehm 2004, Lindley 2007).

Furthermore, phone calls were often supplemented by internet contact, as well as by subscriptions to ethnic TV channels, which were often identified as enabling migrants to keep abreast of political events back home. Alvaro, a construction worker from Brazil, told us: 'In the Internet I read *O Globo* [Rio de Janeiro–based] newspaper and my local newspaper, and I keep myself up to date [with] every event that's going on there ... I try to follow all that it's happening.' Other migrants supplemented these transnational links by additional means. Adanya, an Underground cleaner from Nigeria, told us about receiving a video recording from home:

> Like last year, Christmas, my uncle, there was a traditional African chieftaincy, you know, my uncle was chosen as a chief in my country, they videoed everything, they sent me the video coverage and [I] watched it while I was on the phone with them hearing all these happenings, they sent me the video cassettes because it's really nice, African traditions.

In addition to these forms of communication, those migrants whose home countries were geographically close, and whose return to the UK was guaranteed, could also visit their families. Thus, Mirek, who was from Poland, and was working in the construction sector in London, told us: 'Very often I call them, and I am trying to go to Poland for weekend from time to time.'

While these links are interesting in themselves, they are perhaps even more important for what they tell us about London's relations with the rest of the world, which we explore in more detail below.

Winners One and All? Migration and Development

Remittances lie at the heart of the conviction that migration can serve as a catalyst for development, and are viewed as being broadly beneficial for both the global South and North. From the perspective of the former, there is agreement that remittances represent 'new development finance', and can bring important developmental gains at a range of scales from the household and community to the nation-state (Kapur 2003). Indeed, given the sheer volume of money being transferred by migrants (see above), it is hard to dispute the importance of remittances. Second, and perhaps counter-intuitively, the sending of remittances has also been interpreted as being broadly beneficial to the host countries in the global North, although for significantly different reasons. Even though remittances *could* be (and indeed have in the past been) interpreted as a loss of resources and a sign of migrants' lack of integration into host countries, there is a growing conviction that, by facilitating development in home countries, remittances will reduce pressures to migrate, and so relieve the pressure caused by migration on host countries like the UK (but see de Haas 2007, Faist 2008, Hernandez and Coutin 2006).

A strong international narrative therefore prompts nation-states – both North and South – to capitalise on remittances. The British government, as is clear from reports issued by the Department for International Development (2006), clearly supports the potentially positive synergies between remittances and development. This relationship has even grabbed the attention of policy-makers in Westminster – the then chancellor, Gordon Brown, explicitly identifying the importance of remittances to development in his pre-budget speech of 2005, when he declared: 'Remittances have a significant positive economic impact in developing countries ... People from developing countries who are living and working in the UK are an important source of remittances.' Furthermore, remittances have been explicitly tied to development goals, and are viewed as a 'fast and effective way of shifting resources to the developing world, thus giving the means for poverty reduction and sustainable development in accordance with government and DFID roles' (UK Remittances Working Group 2005: 1).

In order to consider whether this confidence in the positive links between remittances and development is well placed, we have explored the impact of remittances at a range of scales, from the household to the state. Remittances evidently play an important role in providing for the basic needs of migrant households in the form of food purchases, health and education. Even while such expenditure has traditionally been rather spuriously cast as being 'unproductive', it is clearly necessary for the survival of households, and can have important long-term effects in terms of poverty alleviation, as we show below. Indeed, remittances appear to function as crucial safety nets that cash-strapped national governments have been incapable of providing (Carling 2004, de Haas 2005, Van Hear and Sørensen 2003). In countries like Zimbabwe, for example, extreme economic deprivation has meant that nearly half of all households are heavily dependent upon migrant remittances for their survival (Styan 2007).

In our research, it was clear that remittance-sending was closely tied to the basic needs of migrant families (Datta et al. 2007b). Perhaps most obviously, this could be seen in the case of transnational mothers and fathers like Patricia and José, who both sent money home regularly for the upkeep of their children. Patricia, a care worker from Jamaica, remitted money home once, and sometimes twice, each month to her father and domestic helper who looked after her 12-year-old daughter. The amount she sent varied between £50 and £100, depending on her daughter's needs – such as the payment of school fees at the start of the school term. José, a construction worker from Brazil, sent money home to his three children who lived with his two ex-wives, commenting that he provided a 'basic basket' for both households, which consisted of clothing, shoes and school expenses. Further reflecting how important remittances are for basic survival, Chris, an architectural technician from Ghana who was working as a cleaner in London, commented that the £150 that he sent home to his wife and children every month for food, school bills, water and electricity bills was 'a lot of [money, but] they can't survive without it'. An important finding was that it was not necessarily only immediate family members who benefited from remittances, but also extended family – a tendency that was especially marked among those from sub-Saharan Africa, most often relating to the payment of education expenses. Alternatively, social ties with wider kin and friendship groups were maintained through the sending of gifts to coincide with important transnational rituals (Cligget 2005, Gardner and Grillo 2002).

Remittances also enabled migrants to deal with their own, and in some cases their families', financial liabilities (Datta 2007, 2009b, Datta et al. 2007b). Debt-financed migration was evident among some of the migrant workers we interviewed, who had borrowed money to purchase air tickets as well as initial spending money for accommodation, food and transport. Indeed, many told us that they had underestimated how costly it would be to survive in London, so that the money that they had brought with them was quickly spent; a fortunate few were able to address this problem by calling on relatives to help them through 'reverse remittances' (see Chapter 5; see also Datta 2009b). Others were indebted because of failed business ventures that had been the catalyst for migrating. For example, Roberto, a Brazilian construction worker, sent money every month to the joint bank account that he held with his mother, and which was mainly used to pay off a loan for a failed venture.

In turn, over a period of time some of the migrants – and/or their families – were able to use remittances to accumulate assets. This finding is echoed in broader research which documents a potential continuum between so-called 'unproductive' and 'productive' investments of remittances in land, housing and small service-based businesses (Carling 2004, Connell and Conway 2000, de Haas 2006, Gardner and Ahmed 2006). This has been recognised by some governments and banks – for example, the Peruvian state recently pioneered a new initiative to tap into the ambitions of migrants and their families. The 'Quinto Suyo' programme enables Peruvian migrants resident in the US, Spain, Italy and Japan to purchase housing for their families in Peru directly, by means of collaborations between Peruvian banks and several foreign intermediaries (Conthe and García 2007). Many respondents in our study told us that while they sent remittances for altruistic reasons in the first instance, once they had met these obligations, they could then concentrate on more self-interested goals. Thus, several migrants reported that they had invested remittances in land and housing, as well as small businesses, the latter being more common among those from middle-income countries – especially Brazil. For example, Pedro, an office cleaner, pointed out that his fellow country people

> are here [with] the idea of earning money and going back to Brazil. I know many here who are like that – they save money here, as much as they can ... and buy a flat over there. They save as much as they can, then they return to Brazil to set up a business. They save to open a hairdresser salon, a bar, or anything else where they can be self-employed. To work in Brazil as an employee, you'll starve to death.

Demonstrating even greater entrepreneurial flair, Alvaro, a construction worker, invested some of his London earnings in a money-lending business in Brazil, which his brother was managing for him and which enabled him to accumulate sufficient savings to purchase land and housing. In order to maximise his profits, he told us:

> I always buy land in parts in the city where there are no utilities, because if I buy a house were there are utilities, in ten years the value will still be the same. So I buy where there is nothing, paying peanuts; then later on, when the area gets the electricity and paved roads, these will increase their value. I always buy following this [rationale].

Other migrants invested their remittances in what can be best described as transnational or diasporic businesses. For example, Chris discussed his plans to set up an architectural practice that would serve the Ghanaian diaspora in London by providing plans for houses that migrants wished to construct in Ghana with the money they sent back home.

Shifting our attention from migrants and their households to the communities from which they originated, our research also identified the collective channelling of remittances through migrant diasporic organisations, reflecting the ability of some migrants to 'scale up' individual inter-household transfers. These remittances are often invested in their communities in the form of schools, infrastructure, church repairs and/or improved health facilities. Increasingly identified as 'agents of development', such diaspora organisations can also be critical in generating human capital growth, which was evident in the accounts of migrants like Kojo, a cleaner from Ghana:

> But there ... are guys from my area, from the same village that I come from [in] Ghana, we meet monthly and then we discuss issues and see how best we can contribute to schools back at home. Some schools lack in science books and nursing books or whatever – those kind of things – and we put money together to buy and then we ship it out to them, so that they can also develop and take care of our community here. 'Cause if you are privileged enough to be here, you can get the money. I can get all the facilities. Why [should they] be sitting there suffering? So we can also help them.

Where diasporic funds are matched by government spending, considerable benefits can accrue to specific communities in terms of infrastructure and other development potential. A prominent example of a fund-matching initiative is the Mexican *tres-por-uno* ('three for one') programme, in which each 'migradollar' sent by migrants from abroad is complemented by three dollars from various governmental levels (Faist 2008).

Yet, perhaps not surprisingly, it is the potentially detrimental consequences of remittances and migration that become more apparent at the community scale. Most obviously, there is evidence that remittances can intensify inequalities between migrant and non-migrant households, with attendant implications for community relations (Boehm 2004, Osella and Osella 2000). For example, while domestic industries such as construction may flourish as a result of migrant investment in housing, they also become highly dependent upon migrant remittances (Portes 2001). Furthermore, so-called 'productive' investments can result in land and housing booms, and consequent inflation in sending areas, which marginalise non-migrant households that may already suffer from multiple economic, social and cultural exclusions because of their lack of access to remittance income (Ballard 2003b, Gardener and Ahmed 2006, Levitt and Nyberg-Sørensen 2004). Indeed, a dependency on remittances may 'infect' entire communities, with particularly detrimental consequences for local economies. For example, Gardner and Ahmed (2006) comment that, in areas of heavy out-migration such as Sylhet in Bangladesh, young people aspire to be migrants rather than farmers, factory workers and so on. Indeed, migrants' investments in their home communities may transform these areas from agricultural to service-based economies, which predominantly serve the needs of migrants and their families rather than those of locals (Portes 2001). The benefits of remittances are thus highly localised and very uneven.

Nevertheless, at the level of the nation-state there has been a tendency to eulogise the potential benefits of money transfers. Within the global South, remittances purportedly hold the potential to enhance the liquidity and the credit-rating of nation-states. They can augment foreign exchange reserves; enlarge tax bases through fees attached to the issue of passports, departure taxes, international telephones, and so on; and contribute to financial development by enabling investments, savings and the development of formal banking systems (Ballard 2003b, Farrant et al. 2006). Remittances are generally regarded as having important 'multiplier effects' – engendering consumption, generating new businesses and employment through investment, and fostering broader development leading to a consensus that 'remittances might play a significant role in national development, or at least national solvency' (Hernandez and Coutin 2006: 188).

State support for remittances is also driven by the fact that this money represents an increasingly important, and purportedly superior, financial flow to the countries of the global South and those of east and central Europe. Remittances overtook overseas development assistance (ODA) in 1995, coming a close second to foreign direct investment (FDI), and outpacing private equity investment by 15 per cent (de Haas 2005, Orozco and Ferro 2007, Ratha et al. 2008). Indeed, in some poorer countries remittances are twice as large as FDI, and outstrip ODA by some 20 per cent – thus representing the most significant financial transfer to cash-strapped governments and states (Black and King 2004). Perhaps most important is the illusion that 'in financial terms, remittances are a free lunch. While other sources of capital carry a cost for the receiving country, be it interest payments for loans or profit repatriation for investments, remittances require no fees or services' (Kapur and McHale 2003: 50). Moreover, in contrast to ODA, FDI and export income, remittances are also apparently resilient and counter-cyclical – in that they still persist at times of political, economic or environmental crisis. Remittances continued to flow during the financial crisis in Mexico in 1995, and those in Indonesia and Thailand in 1998 (Lindley 2007, Ratha 2007). The current recession has already had a dramatic impact on new private capital inflows to emerging economies, which have halved from US$929 billion in 2007 to US$466 billion in 2008, with a predicated further decline to US$165 billion in 2009. But this collapse has to be measured against the fact that, even while there has been a slowdown in the rate of growth of remittance-sending in 2008 – with a particularly marked decline in certain remittance corridors, such as that between the US and Mexico – remittances have continued to grow in most places (*Economist* 2009).[3] Furthermore, in a world in which the 'war on terror' is obscuring the 'war on poverty' (Oxfam 2004), remittances are an attractive

3. It is estimated that remittances may decline in real terms, from 2 per cent of GDP in 2007 to 1.8 per cent of GDP in 2009, with a sharper deceleration expected in 2009. The scale of decline will be geographically varied, with some remittance corridors more affected than others, including those between the US and both Latin America and the Caribbean, between western and eastern Europe, and between central Asia and sub-Saharan Africa (Ratha et al. 2008).

source of development finance over which national governments may have more control (Datta 2009a).

Given this rosy view of remittances, policy-makers in both the global South and North have been exhorted to adjust their policies in order to maximise the flow and developmental potential of remittances. Within the countries of the global South, the emphasis has been on creating policy frameworks that enable the flow of remittances through formal financial channels and their subsequent investment in productive enterprises, and on developing financial products such as diasporic bonds and strengthening diaspora business networks. For example, DFID (2006) reported that the State Bank of India had made five-year bonds available to 'non-resident Indians' that can be redeemed in US dollars or German euros, while also being exempt from Indian income and wealth taxes. The Philippine government has also created incentives, including tax breaks and privileged investment options, for Filipinos living abroad. Governments are also attempting to court their migrant diasporas by offering dual-citizenship, and holding events such as homecoming celebrations (Asiedu 2005, Levitt 2001, Levitt and Nyberg-Sørensen 2004, Mohan 2008, Robinson 2004, Wimaladharma et al. 2004).

These policies have been matched by similar initiatives in host countries like the UK. Working through the UK Remittances Working Group, which it set up in 2004, and then the UK Remittances Taskforce, established in 2006, DFID has had an 'active agenda to remove barriers to the flow of money transfers, lower their costs and make access to money transfer products easier for low-income people' (UK Remittances Working Group 2005: 1). Two significant achievements of the Taskforce have been the establishment of the Send Money Home service, which enables migrants to compare transaction costs across a range of providers, and the creation of a Remittances Charter in 2007 to promote a voluntary code of conduct among money transfer businesses (MTBs). By early 2008, it was estimated that approximately 60 per cent (18,000) of MTBs had signed up to the Charter. In an attempt to deal with 'rogue' MTBs and protect the interests of migrants, there are also initiatives underway to bring MTB activities under the jurisdiction of the forthcoming Payment Services Directive (see footnote 2, also Datta 2009a).

Do Remittances Always Work for Development?

Assessments of whether remittances and migration are indeed beneficial for development at a macro scale are of course dependent upon how development is defined, and upon what remittances are measured against. In terms of their impact on poverty, there is some evidence that the relationship is positive. Presenting evidence from a World Bank study of 71 developing countries, Adams and Page (2005) report that remittances reduce both the level and depth of poverty. Thus, a 10 per cent increase in remittances from each migrant would lead to a 3.5 per cent decline globally in the share of people living in poverty, as well as reducing income inequality. These findings are supported by household surveys reporting reduced poverty head-count ratios in Uganda (by 11 per cent), Bangladesh (6 per cent) and Ghana (5 per cent) (Ratha 2007). Other research indicates that migration from Kerala in India to the Middle Eastern states generated remittances of about US$3 billion in 2000, and was estimated to have resulted in a 12 per cent reduction in poverty across the state (Skeldon 2008a: 8). Migrant workers' remittances can thus play a significant role in the reduction of poverty and the achievement of a key millennium development goal.

However, this apparent success has to be measured against the fact, as de Haas (2006) points out, that remittances do not necessarily go to either the poorest countries or to the poorest people in a country – not least because international migration is dominated by relatively well-off migrants living in middle-income countries. Indeed, half of all remittances to the global South go to lower-middle-income countries, while the other half go equally to upper-middle-income and low-income countries, so that the poorest countries are not receiving the most remittances (Adams and Page 2005, Bracking 2003). As Skeldon (2008a) points out, this reflects trends in migration itself, with only 15 per cent of migrants to OECD countries originating in low-income countries. Rates of out-migration from the global South ranged from a mere 0.5 per cent from low-income countries to 3.3 per cent for lower-middle-income countries, 4.2 per cent for upper-middle-income countries, and 2.8 per cent for high-income countries (Skeldon 2008a: 6).

In turn, evidence suggests that the ability of remittances to generate growth is again dependent upon levels of financial development in home countries as well as the wider socio-economic context (de Haas 2005, Farrant et al. 2006). Indeed, policy-makers have tended to overemphasise the benefits of remittances, much of which continue to be spent on consumption. Therefore, while access to remittances may alleviate credit constraints in countries with poorly developed financial systems, it can also induce reliance upon them (Ratha 2007). The challenge of achieving sustainable growth remains, raising the question of how these potentially positive injections of capital at the household level can be made more sustainable and widespread at a community and national level (de Haas 2005, 2006, Guarnizo 2002).

Not surprisingly, therefore, a creeping scepticism about the alleged beneficial consequences of the migration–development nexus is now evident (Datta 2009a, Datta et al. 2007b, Hernandez and Coutin 2006, Piper 2009, Skeldon 2008a). This was clear in an interview we conducted with a representative of the Institute for Public Policy Research, who told us:

> I don't think we know enough about the relationship [between migration and development]. It's like shining a torch on an elephant in a dark room. We have a few torches, but we have no idea what the relationship is like.

There are also broader questions being voiced about the implications of viewing remittances as a type of development finance, and the impact this will have on development aid and practice. Critics are increasingly sceptical about the ethics of a development discourse in which migration is simultaneously positioned as both a symptom of under-development and a solution to it (Datta et al. 2007b, Hernandez and Coutin 2006, Skeldon 2008a).

Elevating remittances, which are essentially intra-household transfers of money, to the status of other flows of capital, finance and income – such as ODA, FDI and export income – is problematic for a number of reasons (Datta et al. 2007b, Datta 2009a, Hernandez and Coutin 2006). For a start, such comparisons 'elevate these exchanges to the level of state transactions, and permit governments to claim credit for generating remittances' (Hernandez and Coutin 2006: 191). By identifying remittances as national funds, states in both the global South and North open up what are essentially private flows of money between family members to the regulatory framework of global finance, as they attempt to instigate policies to deploy remittances in particular 'development-friendly' ways (Robinson 2004). In addition, as Skeldon (2008a) argues, migrants may be extremely wary of government interference in remittances, which otherwise go in cash or straight to the pockets of migrants' families. Indeed, attempts to channel them into 'worthwhile' investments may lead to an increase in informal transfers, or even in extreme cases, put a stop to remitting altogether.

Comparisons of remittances with ODA also fail to ask how or why remittances have come to substitute for foreign assistance from richer countries to their poorer counterparts (Sriskandarajah 2005). It has to be said that, at least at the level of rhetoric, most policy-makers are aware that the geographies of ODA and remittances do not neatly match, and that one cannot replace the other. In his own address on the subject, quoted above, Gordon Brown went on to say that remittances 'should be seen as an important complement to aid, not a replacement'. Yet if, as Skeldon (2008a) argues, remittances are shaping flows of ODA, the consequences will be very severe for poor non-migrants, since the flow of remittances cannot be explicitly and consistently tied to poverty-reduction.

Until very recently, there has also been a general lack of acknowledgement of the implications of this discourse for the question of the responsibility for development itself (Datta et al. 2007b, Hernandez and Coutin 2006, Skeldon 2008a). With the championing of remittances, migrants are left shouldering the burden of development, while states, both in the global South and North, are able to ignore the structural factors that hinder development on both national and global scales (Ballard 2003b, Datta et al. 2007b, de Haas 2005, Skeldon 2008a). Moreover, the increasingly instrumental role afforded to both migrant men and women – which is reinforced by a strong narrative adopted in many home countries suggesting that migrants have a duty not only to their families, but also to their home nations – ignores the conditions under which remittances are generated and sustained.

Remittance-sending comes at a significant economic cost; it is important to acknowledge the poor working conditions and difficult lives that migrants often encounter in order to support both themselves and their dependants and family left behind. Low wages and the absence of a social wage, as well as a failure to afford migrants the respect and dignity their labour deserves, all contribute towards very stressful working lives. This was quite graphically expressed to us by Pitchens, a cleaner from the Democratic Republic of Congo:

> The image and concept I had of Europe were totally different from the reality on the terrain. We always think life is easy in Europe – you don't see anyone suffering, you don't have to work hard to have more money, and hard jobs don't exist, and so on.

As Pitchens found when he arrived in London, in order to survive while maintaining his transnational financial obligations, he had to devise a range of coping tactics, including working long hours, having two or more jobs, sharing housing, and reducing expenditure on necessities. Other migrants, like Adanya, an Underground cleaner from Nigeria, specifically highlighted the near-impossibility of balancing her low-paid work with her responsibilities as a transnational mother. For yet others, like Mirek, a Polish construction worker, low wages and poor conditions of work in London enforced transnational separation upon him. He told us: 'I would say this. If I had a decent job, that would allow me to have a decent life, so I could bring over my wife and [child].' While remittances may be funded through (scarce) savings, they may also entail entering into debt – or perhaps, even more controversially, they may be funded through state benefit income (Datta 2009b). In addition, such remittances are often generated through the deregulation of human capital, with skilled workers finding themselves in low-skilled, low-paid work in countries like the UK (see below).

Fuelling Uneven Development? Skills, Migration and Development

It is even harder to sustain the notion that migration represents a 'win–win' situation for migrants, and for both home and host countries, when our focus shifts to skills and development. Here it is crucial to recognise that London's position as a global city rests fundamentally on its ability to attract skilled workers from all over the world. The importance of skills to the global economy is demonstrated by the fact that both the volume of skilled migration and its relative share of international migration flows are increasing. Skeldon (2008b) reports that, between 1990 and 2000, the proportion of skilled migrants over the age of 25 living in the countries of the OECD grew from 29.8 per cent to 34.6 per cent. In addition, numerous reports point to the fact that migrants to the UK are on average more highly skilled than the native-born population (Salt and Millar 2006, Sriskandarajah et al. 2007).

This gaining/losing of skills has been interpreted in two ways. On the one hand, there is evidence that the out-migration of particular skilled workers has had negative consequences, especially for smaller and poorer countries that have a small skills base to start with, where the deleterious consequences of the brain-drain are potentially immense (Skeldon 2008b). African states have often taken the lead in voicing their concerns over the brain-drain, especially in relation to the most controversial of skilled labour flows – those involving health workers. While it is important to bear in the mind that the largest suppliers of health personnel are from middle-income countries like India, the loss of doctors and nurses from poorer countries like Zimbabwe, Guinea-Bissau and Uganda is much more harmful (Skeldon 2008b). Indeed, it is estimated that three-quarters of all doctors emigrate from Zimbabwe within a few years of qualifying (Farrant et al. 2006, Ratha et al. 2008). Moreover, although countries like Nigeria and Ghana do not fall within the poor- or small-country category, the scale of out-migration of health personnel they experience is still significant. Black and King (2004) report that some 20,000 Nigerian doctors are working in the US. Furthermore, it is estimated that a third of all African graduates reside outside their country of birth, rising to as many as 42 per cent of skilled Ghanaians and 36 per cent of skilled Nigerians – many of whom, as we have found in London, are only able to secure employment in low-skilled and low-paid work (Grillo and Mazzucato 2008, Styan 2007). Even beyond Africa, it is estimated that three-quarters of all highly-skilled workers in Guyana, Jamaica, Haiti, Trinidad and Tobago, and Fiji have moved to OECD countries (Guerrero and Bolay 2005, Sriskandarajah 2005). While a range of policies have been advanced by international organisations such as UNCTAD (2007) to counter the harmful aspects of skilled migration – including controls on skilled migration flows, compensation policies, support for the growth of human capital in home countries, and the facilitation of diasporic knowledge networks – these measures have, as yet, had very little effect (Faist 2008, Skeldon 2008b, Sriskandarajah 2005).

Our research found that a significant proportion of the migrants working in low-paid employment in London were part and parcel of this flow of skilled migrants. Prior to their migration to London, 43.1 per cent had completed primary and/or secondary education, a further 19 per cent had obtained vocational or professional tertiary education, and 21 per cent academic tertiary education, with some variation by national origin (see Table 6.1). Furthermore, even while the majority of these migrants did not fall into the category of the 'super-skilled', the sample included a significant number of men and women who had pursued professional careers in their own countries as teachers, accountants, civil servants, clerks and health workers.

Table 6.1   Highest level of education by nationality

Country of origin	Total (N)	Primary/secondary education	Tertiary education
Brazil	22	12	10
Bulgaria	9	3	6
Colombia	12	5	7
Congo (DRC)	19	14	5
Ghana	63	31	32
India	8	7	8
Jamaica	11	8	3
Kenya	7	7	0
Lithuania	6	1	5
Mauritius	9	8	1
Nigeria	59	22	9
Portugal	13	10	3
Spain	5	3	2
Uganda	7	1	6

Note: The countries listed are those with at least five individuals in the survey.

Source: Analysis of authors' questionnaire survey (see also Appendix 1).

Such increases in skilled migration are largely attributable to changing immigration regimes in a number of prominent host countries – including the UK, but also France, Germany, Australia and the US – which have adopted immigration regimes that prioritise migrants with skills (Datta 2009a, Guerrero and Bolay 2005, Kapur and McHale 2003, Skeldon 2008a, Sriskandarajah 2005). Recognising the potentially adverse implications of its own cherry-picking of migrants in the interests of the British economy through its points-based regime (see Chapter 1), the British government has, through the Department for International Development, sought to mitigate some of the more harmful aspects of that system. One move in this direction has been support for health systems in sub-Saharan African countries such as Malawi, so as to enable that country to retain its essential health staff. Furthermore, the New Labour government has worked with the National Health Service to develop a 'Code of Practice for the International Recruitment of Healthcare Professionals' (Department of Health 2004), which seeks to restrict the recruitment of health professionals from developing countries unless a specific bilateral arrangement was in place.[4] Responses to such initiatives have in turn been contradictory, with one interviewee from the Institute of Public Policy Research likening them to a 'compassionate racism' curtailing the rights of skilled men and women to migrate, as well as running the risk of engendering irregular migration, which may further compound the problem of wasted assets and skills.

4. While these guidelines were revised in 2004 in an attempt to incorporate private-sector agencies, these agencies continue to work to their own guidelines and to recruit health workers from a proscribed list (see Farrant et al. 2006).

In contrast, a second set of arguments revolves around the premise that the extent of the 'brain-drain' and its impact on the countries of the global South is overplayed (Skeldon 2008b, Sriskandarajah 2005). Optimists argue that instead of focusing on how migration can lead to a loss of skills, we should instead be concentrating on the potential for 'brain-gain' or even, more recently, 'brain circulation'. The latter claim is premised on the diasporic connections that exist between migrants and their home countries, and suggests that opening borders would facilitate temporary movement and increase opportunities to learn across borders (Legrain 2007, RSA Migration Commission 2005). Such gains are understood to be engendered by rising levels of human capital in home countries, as more people pursue higher education, sometimes through international study, with the ambition of migrating themselves, thus potentially creating a larger pool of educated people in the poorer parts of the world (Guerrero and Bolay 2005, Lowell et al. 2004).

The quest to improve educational attainment was certainly evident in our research, with significant numbers of migrant men and women stating that their primary purpose for coming to London was to further their education. To this end, Akelo, a Ghanaian who had come to London in 2000 having completed vocational training as a teacher in Ghana, told us:

> The job in Kumasi was basically teaching, and as it normally happens if you have a degree in teaching, you definitely go for PGCE. So I purposely came over here to upgrade my teaching profession by pursuing my education – that's the main reason why I travelled from Ghana to UK.

Indeed, migrants like Akelo believed that the pursuit of British qualifications was a means of accumulating human and cultural capital, which could be used to further their professional lives both at home (where British qualifications are highly valued) and in London, where they might provide a route out of low-paid work (although, as outlined in Chapter 4, this process can often turn out to be illusory for migrants from the global South).

However, notions of brain-gain rest crucially upon the fact that migrants are able to utilise or build upon their skill levels in host countries. In this context, our research – in tandem with similar enquiries in other parts of the world – points to 'brain wastage', whereby migrants are progressively de-skilled and de-profession-alised through migration (Chappell et al. 2008, Pollard et al. 2008). A number of migrants in our study complained about their experiences of de-skilling. Gabriel, a Brazilian migrant working in construction in London, told us:

> I was disenchanted with many things ... the people's desperation – the Brazilians that I see, poor people trying to make a living. People doing washing up – I see people who worked in banks in Brazil, which is an occupation which affords a good life, but here they

are washing dishes, perhaps the dishes of a guy who used to work in a bank but be below him, but who is earning more than he would in Brazil.

Zelu, a care worker from Bangladesh, had been a practising doctor back home and was especially eloquent about the indignity he sometimes suffered in his current work. Describing an encounter with one of his clients, he told us:

> The very first time I met with him, he asked me, 'You're from Bangladesh?' 'Yes.' 'What did you do? What did you do back to your country?' And I told him, 'To be very honest, I am a doctor in my country.' 'Oh, you bloody doctor, what are you doing here? You are doing my kitchen, my hoovering' ... He underestimate me very much – you can't imagine it – and I did work with him for that day only, and I told the office that I don't feel comfortable with that man.

Furthermore, as we saw in Chapter 4, many migrants also experienced frustration at failing to develop their skills. A primary motive for the migration of men like Gabriel was to learn English, which was seen as having a significant bearing upon his career progression. But the opportunities to do this were limited by long working days, low wages, and the fact that many migrants worked in low-paid sectors dominated by other migrants:

> My father thinks that I am already speaking English! How can I tell him that here it is as if I am in Brazil? I live here in an island of Brazilians. If you want you can spend ten years here and never learn English!

Barbara, a care worker from St Lucia who had worked as a teacher in her home country, and who had migrated to London to acquire an accountancy qualification, told us that the demands of work and home life had left her with little time to pursue this dream: 'Opportunities and things that I wanted to do, I couldn't do it; I think I have wasted a lot of time here and I don't want it to be repeated. I wasted too much time.'

A Changing Ethic of Care and Responsibility?

There has been a growing appreciation – even if largely implicit – that migration works for the UK and can contribute to the economic development of London and the UK. But this realisation has been accompanied by a strong sense that migration needs to be – and perhaps even more critically needs to be seen to be – carefully managed, so as to alleviate public fears of immigrants 'flooding' their shores, especially at a time of recession, and potentially depression. This has led partly to efforts to tie the UK's migration needs to the enlargement of the European Union. As we saw in Chapter 1, this process has meant that a range of new European migrants now enjoy the de facto right to live and work in the

UK (albeit restricted for A2 migrants). While initial numbers from countries like Poland grossly exceeded predicted inflows, raising fears of a 'Polish invasion', the subsequent departure of these migrants as the recession has begun to bite in the UK (it is estimated that almost half of the migrants who arrived from the A8 countries since 2004 have now returned home) makes them 'ideal migrants', who come and go according to the development needs of the host country (Pollard et al. 2008).

Not surprisingly, the government seems to have favoured these kinds of migrants – as is demonstrated by the fact that the points-based immigration regime assumes that it is they who will supply all the low-skilled labour needed in the UK. As we saw in Chapter 4, these migrants are also at an advantage by virtue of being 'white' Europeans with legal status, who are able to move across borders whenever they chose. As the workers themselves are only too aware, being closer to 'us' on a number of registers brings them political, social and economic advantage over those from further afield. This was very forcefully pointed out by Kriyk, a Polish construction worker:

> There are people that would say that Polish wants to work, that [they] do not pose any danger ... like people from the Middle East ... to the society, that are white; to be honest we are the hope for the UK – we are needed here ... I know people respect what I do, that I work hard and I am from Poland – that it is good for the British economy ... We all pay taxes ... Majority of opinions that I came across ... on the British side ... were very pleasant, many people are very well predisposed towards Polish – the fact that one was from Poland, that we are here to work hard ... to work, and not for benefits.

At the same time, the New Labour government has taken a much more draconian approach to migration from the global South. Thus, even while development may have moved up the agenda, and despite the rhetoric that migration is good for development, immigration reform has made it much harder for people from Africa, Asia and Latin America to come to the UK. Indeed, the law now ensures that increasing volumes of this migration will be rendered irregular. This in itself will lead to losses to development, as irregular migrants are more likely to experience de-skilling, and are thus less likely to remit money or return to their home countries. Thus, for example, even while a significant proportion of the migrants from Africa and Latin America who we interviewed declared a desire to return to their home countries, such ambitions were tempered for those who were unable to envisage a route back to London in an era of increasingly restrictive migration regimes (Datta et al. 2009). Tighter border control in the UK is thus, ironically, making it harder for irregular migrants to leave, for fear of not being able to return should they want to do so in future. As Roberto, a construction worker from Brazil, put it:

Since I left Brazil to come over here I went to Brazil only once ... I don't have plans to go back in [the] near future because of my visa. Because I am separating from my wife I am scared of going there, and when I return they do not let me get back in [to Britain]. I don't want to run this risk, so I will incarcerate myself here.

It is precisely the closure of opportunities to migrate and return, and then perhaps migrate again, which could ultimately render migration an obstacle to development, rather than a promoter of it. Such a closure is also indicative, we would argue, of an abdication of care and responsibility for people and places with which London and Britain have long and historic connections.

Furthermore, even while there may be a bias towards certain types of migrants over others (whether on the basis of skills or nationality), this does not always translate into an ethic of care for migrant workers themselves (Datta et al. 2011). Thus, Kiryk thought that, although employers viewed Polish workers positively, this did not always translate into decent wages or working conditions:

[T]here was also the other side of coin – [that] you are OK to work for less, because you are from Poland. [There are] assumptions that Polish worker is strong and unbreakable and does whatever, hence the workload was based on this assumption, but earnings were not proportional to it.

Such experiences were echoed by the majority of the migrants we interviewed: they felt that, while they had contributed to development in London, London had been less generous towards them. José, a Brazilian construction worker, remarked:

They [the government] should put in their head that a person who travels 12,000km to come to a place to work and earn money, we don't come here just to take their money away, because I pay tax. I pay at least £400 per month. That is the minimum I pay ... Where does this money go to? If I buy one glass, I am already paying taxes, because the market pays taxes, so do I ... Not only Brazilians – it is thousands of illegal people. Can you imagine how many trillions they leave to the government? What does the government do with this money?

This chapter has explored how the migration to London of men and women from the global South, and from east and central Europe, is reconfiguring London's relations with the world from which these migrants move. These relations are themselves fundamentally shaped by the transnational links created and maintained by migrants, which intimately bind their families, communities and home countries to London. While it is economic links – remittances – that have received the most public-policy and academic attention, these transnational connections are much more diverse, and lead to the formation of transnational social spaces, with migrants potentially maintaining a foothold in each world.

A key reason for the predominant focus on remittances, and also on skills, is partly the widespread consensus that they collectively hold the potential of releasing the positive synergies between migration and development. But it is also abundantly clear that migrants, their home countries, and their host countries are each dancing to subtly different tunes: migrants are not necessarily interested in the macro-development of their home countries, but rather the improvement of the lives of their children, parents, siblings, and wider extended families; home countries promote migration and remittances, but also bemoan the loss of skilled workers; while host countries like Britain are clearly following migration policies that are more decisively motivated by their own short-term national interests, rather than lofty development ideals.

While migration is clearly linked to development, our discussion in this chapter demonstrates that the UK government's immigration and labour-market policies will impair rather than enhance the synergies between migration and development. Those from the poorest parts of the world have the fewest opportunities to make a new life in a city like London. In turn, the structural position of many of the migrants we encountered from countries in Africa, Asia and Latin America helps to explain their growing involvement in politics in London today, and we explore this development in the following chapter.

7
REMAKING THE CITY: IMMIGRATION AND POST-SECULAR POLITICS IN LONDON TODAY

Galahad watch the colour of his hand, and talk to it, saying, 'Colour, is you causing all this, you know. Why the hell you can't be blue, or red or green, if you can't be white? You know is you that cause a lot of misery in the world. Is not me, you know, is you! I ain't do nothing to infuriate the people and them, is you! Look at you, you so black and innocent, and this time so you causing misery all over the world!'

Sam Selvon (2006 [1956]: 77)

Though the common world is the common meeting ground of all, those who are present have different locations in it, and the location of one can[not] coincide with the location of another ... Being seen and being heard by others derive their significance from the fact that everybody sees and hears from a different position. This is the meaning of public life.

Hannah Arendt (1998 [1958]: 57)

The arrival and settlement of significant numbers of non-white immigrants in the post-war period has changed the demographic profile, culture and civic life of cities across the UK. This chapter explores the ways in which these immigrant communities have entered London's public life, the changing ideological and institutional forms of politics that have allowed them to do so, and the impact of this on the wider society. In brief, we argue that, between the 1950s and the 1980s, immigrants from the Caribbean, India, Bangladesh and Pakistan arrived with strong traditions of collective organisation that were coincident with a growing new Left in Britain. Over time, different organisations were able to forge alliances with each other, securing space for anti-racist politics and practice in the wider body politic. For a period in the 1970s and 1980s, shared political identifications of 'black' and 'anti-racist' united a wide range of individuals, organisations and communities in a struggle for justice. In the wake of this political organisation, the UK largely came to accept itself as a multicultural polity, albeit one in which socio-economic disadvantage continues to shape the lives of most minority ethnic Britons today (Gilroy 2004).

In contrast, as we have seen, London's newer immigrant communities are more diverse, with less sense of a common political identity or a shared political agenda for change. We have shown how London's migrant division of labour is characterised by workers from a plethora of different countries, who are further differentiated by the immigration regime and its relationship to nationality, ethnicity and race. While London's new migrants have established a variety of new community organisations, and though these communities often face common challenges to securing citizenship and adequate access to decent work and welfare, they have as yet remained largely fragmented, with very little political voice. In this context, our research has identified faith as a key site for the formation and mobilisation of social capital. As we saw in Chapter 5, personal relations can be critical to surviving in the city; but here we explore faith organisations as a basis for political organisation as well. Continuing the arguments made in Chapter 5, we suggest that faith can provide an institutional space to develop 'linking social capital', allowing the voices of migrants to reach the wider polity.

This chapter highlights the relatively high levels of active involvement in faith organisations among low-paid migrants in London. We then explore contemporary debates about the role of faith in immigrant communities, and the emergence of a post-secular politics within the UK. In London, faith communities have been playing a key role in the work of a broad-based political coalition called London Citizens, and in the final part of the chapter we introduce this organisation and explore the ways in which it has been able to engage migrant communities in public and political life.

Just as the identifications of 'black' and 'anti-racist' allowed a generation of political activists to create local coalitions to effect political change in the 1970s and 1980s, we argue that a broad-based alliance like London Citizens allows people to work together for change. Moreover, while an earlier generation of immigrant community groups and their allies mobilised against racism in employment, education, housing, immigration policy and the police, in contemporary London the issues on London Citizens' agenda similarly concern matters of state. However, whereas activists in the earlier period mobilised around opposition to racism in a wide range of state institutions, the language of anti-racism is rarely a vehicle for mobilisation today. As we saw in Chapter 4, race is as likely to divide migrants as it is to unite them. Thus, although institutional racism and the impact of immigration status help to explain the fact that it is non-white Londoners who remain concentrated in poor neighbourhoods and low-paying jobs, and often have the least chance of socio-economic progression, there are no powerful organisations that mobilise on the issue of race. Instead, effective political mobilisation has fostered unity and collective purpose in relation to issues that arise from sharing space in the city. In early 2009, London Citizens had campaigns running for a living wage, affordable housing, safer neighbourhoods, and an earned amnesty for irregular migrants. Migrant workers were being mobilised, alongside other Londoners, as part of these ongoing campaigns.

Being Black: Immigrant Politics and the Creation of Multiculturalism

The largest groups of immigrants who first arrived in Britain after the upheavals of the Second World War were fleeing from the imposition of Communism and the legacy of war in eastern Europe. At least 100,000 Poles and 86,000 people from the Baltic, Ukraine and Yugoslavia were settled through the European Voluntary Workers programme without much complaint (McDowell 2005, Ryan 2005). In contrast, the small numbers of black citizens who started to arrive in Britain after the *Empire Windrush* first docked in 1948, with 492 passengers from Jamaica on board, caused much greater public concern. Caribbean, Indian and Pakistani immigrants arrived to settle in hostile territory, and were seen as rivals for women, welfare and work. Such tensions provoked riots in Liverpool and Deptford, London, in 1948, in Birmingham in 1949, and in Notting Hill, London, and Nottingham in 1958. The state responded with tighter controls to limit such immigration through the Commonwealth Immigrants Acts of 1962 and 1968, a further Immigration Act in 1971, and a British Nationality Act in 1981 (Hatton and Wheatley-Price 2005, Paul 1997).

Faced with such naked hostility, black and Asian immigrants tended to settle in areas of declining white populations and growing diasporic communities in inner-city locations (Herbert 2008a, Miles 1988, Peach 1968, Rex and Tomlinson 1979, S. Smith 1989). Over time, these communities developed their own civil society infrastructure, including social clubs, welfare associations, faith institutions and political groups (Carter 1986). For example, a number of branches of the Indian Workers Association were established in London and the West Midlands to support and represent Punjabis in housing, welfare and work (Josephides 1990, de Witt 1969). These organisations were explicitly political, and the Indian Workers Associations (IWA) often played a key part in registering their members to vote, engaging local politicians with community issues, and supporting workers in industrial disputes. In the run-up to the 1966 general election, the IWA could claim to have registered as many as 6,000 voters in the West Midlands alone (de Witt 1969: 3).

The leaders in these local community-based organisations often deployed a shared analysis of colonialism and imperialism in relation to life 'back home', and an understanding of racialised capitalism in relation to their position within the UK (Centre for Contemporary Cultural Studies 1982, Sivanandan 1990). As one of the key leaders of the IWA put it when describing the work of the Campaign Against Racist Laws that was launched in 1979, for example:

> Since we, the first generation, arrived as immigrants in the 1950s our history has been one of constant struggle against a racist society, which invited us for their benefit, which has always used us as their scapegoat, and which all too readily forgets out contributions. It is this circumstance of our repeating history which led to our self-organisation into black/community workers' organizations in defending our communities and securing their rights. The form of this organisation has been a dynamic one, ever changing, dependent on the manner of struggle waged and the footholds established. (Singh Jouhl 1994: 80)

As Avtar Singh Jouhl remarks, the struggle for black Britons to secure their rightful place in British society has been dynamic, involving a challenge to the institutions of the Left – and particularly the trade unions and the Labour Party – as well as the machinery of the state itself.

Over time, activists from the countries of the New Commonwealth were able to forge connections across the different communities of diaspora by creating a shared political identity as black, while also being part of a wider 'anti-racist' movement that embraced their white allies. Black was an identity that reflected a shared experience of colonial oppression at home and racial discrimination abroad. As Goulbourne puts it:

> There is an assumption that Britain's non-white minorities, whether of African or Asian backgrounds, have enough in common to unite in order to overcome the hurdles placed in their way. The word *black* is therefore used generally to denote people who experience discrimination based on their (non-white) skin colour. (Goulbourne 1990: 9; emphasis in original)

This use of a black identity – which was sometimes stretched as far as including the Irish – was extraordinarily successful in fostering connections for political gain. For Paul Gilroy, it enabled a new social movement that in turn contained a wealth of traditions:

> It includes the language of Ethiopianism and Pan-Africanism, and the heritage of anti-colonial resistances as well as the inputs from contemporary urban conflicts. These diverse elements combine syncretically in struggles to reconstruct a collective historical presence from the discontinuous, fractured histories of the African and Asian diasporas. Multiple meanings have grouped around the central symbol of racial alterity – the colour black – and it is difficult to anticipate the outcomes of the political struggle between the different tendencies they represent – ethnic absolutism on the one hand, and a utopian, democratic populism on the other. (Gilroy 1987: 236)

Identification as black thus denoted not only a shared experience, but also a presumption of a shared set of interests that were articulated *within* the institutions of the Left – as the trade unions and the Labour Party were forced to confront their own racism – as well as without. Indeed, living in poor neighbourhoods, New Commonwealth immigrants quickly saw the need to engage with, and become involved in, the Labour Party in order to improve things for them. As Shukra remarks: '[I]f black people wished to participate in the decision-making process which affected their lives, whether on matters of representation, immigration or education, the channel available was the Labour Party' (Shukra 1990: 165–6). Increasing numbers of activists were attracted into the Labour Party as it shifted leftwards in the 1970s, using it as a vehicle to challenge national and local policy on housing, education, employment and the police (Shukra 1990, Solomos 1993). By the 1980s, black community activists were often simultaneously involved in local campaigns – such as the Broadwater Farm support group, or the Viraj Mendis campaign – as well as belonging to the Black Sections movement within the party.

This dynamic accelerated in the aftershock of the urban riots in Bristol, London and Liverpool in the early 1980s. In tandem with the New Left, black activists pushed Labour-controlled councils to start ethnic monitoring in employment and service-delivery, as well as developing more appropriate services – including the translation of information and the provision of interpreting for service encounters, providing culturally appropriate services such as meals on wheels, and implementing racial awareness training for staff (Solomos and Back 2000, Virdee 2006). Pioneered by what were colloquially known as 'loony Left' councils in London, these practices gradually became more widespread. The Greater London Council, Brent, Hackney, Haringey and Lambeth councils were sites of particularly radical local political activity, as ascendant Left activists sought to integrate anti-racism and black self-organisation with the concerns of other social movements focused on gender, sexuality and disability (Boddy and Fudge 1984, Wainwright 1987). The 1980s thus saw the integration of black voices and anti-racist practice into the political mainstream, and what had been protest from the 'outside' turned into engagement with different parts of the state (Goulbourne 1990).

A similar process of contested but gradual engagement took place within the trade union movement. Black workers often faced difficult battles to secure trade union representation at work, and a number of now infamous industrial disputes exposed the racism of British trade unions (Parmar 1982, Phizacklea and Miles 1987, Wrench and Virdee 1996). While black and Asian workers proved more willing to join trade unions than their white British counterparts, it was only during the 1980s, and following efforts at black self-organisation within the unions, that these new members were really accepted.

Of course, it is also important to acknowledge that the emergence of what we now know as multiculturalism has always had its critics. From the Left, there are those who contest the reification of community that multiculturalism seems to imply, as well as the dominance of self-appointed, often male and conservative leaders as spokespeople for what are, in practice, fractured communities (Anthias and Yuval-Davis 1992, Parekh 2000). Others have bemoaned the triumph of reformism over revolution as the black struggle has been tamed by the state (Kundnani 2002, Shukra 1997, Sivanandan 1990). Still others have challenged the neglect of Asian experience, highlighting the need for greater appreciation of the differentiation between diaspora communities within the UK (Modood 1994, Robinson 1990). From the right, and in the wake of the terrorist attacks in London on 7 July 2005, multiculturalism has also been blamed for failing to foster a shared sense of nation and community cohesion (Back et al. 2002). Ethnic diversity is again being constructed as a problem in public and political life (Putnam 2007).

When it was elected in 1997, however, the New Labour government appeared to endorse fully the hegemonic status of multiculturalism within the UK. Government ministers, along with corporate leaders, publicly extolled the virtues of diversity and the dangers of racism. Efforts were made to recruit more minority ethnic politicians and to engage with prominent community groups. In practice, however, New Labour's reforms of local government, and more recent ideological shifts in the wake of the terror attacks in the US and London, have undermined the legacy of political organisation among immigrant communities in cities like London (Back et al. 2002, Kymlicka 2003). On the one hand, the party has adopted the idea of 'partnership', which has involved community organisations in being co-opted on to local committees that tend to endorse existing approaches to policy and services (Marquand 2004, Nanton 1998, Quilley 1999, Taylor 2000). On the other hand, in the wake of anxiety about extremism and security, government ministers have shifted the policy agenda away from multiculturalism towards 'community cohesion', advocating that funding should be given only to groups that work *across* community lines. This is likely to undermine many community organisations – particularly those representing newer immigrant groups – further limiting, or even preventing, their representation and participation in urban political life (Kyambi 2007, Modood 2005, Stubbs 2007).

An earlier generation of black Britons successfully challenged the dominant society and its institutions, to grant greater equality in the public sphere (Joppke 1999, Kymlicka 2003). But this victory remains fragile. Launched by the struggles of earlier immigrants, multiculturalism is still a contested project, and has represented poorly the new migrant communities in cities like London. Indeed, this is partly because the nature of immigration has changed. New arrivals from eastern Europe are often reluctant to engage in debates about integration into British society, often emphasising their European identity and their plans to return. In turn, those from outside the EU often lack the immigration status that would allow them to engage in local and national politics. Even those who have been afforded a pathway into citizenship are now faced with the additional challenges of speaking a required level of English and passing a citizenship test before they are fully welcome to stay (Rutter et al. 2008). As a result, many immigrant communities are now politically weaker and more fragmented than their counterparts were 20 or 30 years ago, and this lack of political capital further reinforces the economic and social exclusions we documented in earlier chapters.

Immigrants and Political Organisation in London Today

As we have seen, the pioneering political activists in immigrant communities during the 1960s, 1970s and 1980s used a 'black' identity to unite a diverse community, and the language of 'anti-racism' to find allies in the white community in the struggle for change. In contrast, today's newer immigrants remain rooted in the languages of their diverse national communities and in their different religious traditions. These newer communities are still setting up civil society organisations, but these are more likely to be tailored to the particular needs of their own national group, and may be more orientated to the home country than to tackling issues within the UK (Al-Ali et al. 2001). Where they are locally focused, such organisations are almost all devoted to supporting individuals and providing information, welfare and social activities, rather than to pursuing political goals relating to developments within the UK.

This situation is partly a result of the fact that newer arrivals – and particularly those concentrated in low-paying, low-status jobs – are much less likely to have full citizenship (McIlwaine 2007b). Estimates suggest that there are as many as half a million irregular migrants in the UK, and that many of these live in London (London School of Economics 2009, Woodbridge 2001). As we saw in earlier chapters, many other migrant workers in London are waiting for their asylum claims to be processed, or are dependent upon student visas or Home Office extensions for leave to remain. But, while this makes it much harder for these immigrants to raise their political voice, it also provides strong motivation to do so (Taran 2000). Recent experience in the US and France highlights the potential to organise the undocumented, who practise citizenship even if they do not possess it, and we explore this further below (Iskander 2007, Jordan and Düvell 2002, Pulido 2007, Varsanyi 2005).

We would contend that, in addition to strong connections to faith, community organisations – however fragile their roots – contain the seeds for further politici-sation. It is now widely argued that, once people associate, they have the chance to develop the social relations, collective trust and skills required for political life (Putnam 2000, Warren 2001). Where immigrants are organised into community and faith organisations, these institutions can provide a space in which to develop the skills and create the social capital needed to foster political participation and action. The likelihood of this happening is also dependent upon the political opportunities afforded to them to become more involved. As Koopmans (2004) has argued, self-organisation can provide a platform for wider engagement, but is not sufficient for it. There are sharp international as well as sub-national variations in migrant access to citizenship, and in the public recognition and respect afforded to immigrant communities, and this wider political opportunity structure can facilitate – or otherwise – the political action of migrants (Jacobs et al. 2004).

Britain is often argued to be more open to public claims-making by immigrant communities than other European polities – not least because of the adoption of the multicultural discourse and practice briefly outlined above. However, the nature of immigrant politics is also a product of the prevailing traditions, expectations, circumstances and leadership of immigrant communities. London's newer communities face a particularly complex set of internal challenges, and they do so in the context of increasing hostility to immigration from outside the EU. As a result, many community organisations have been small-scale, service-orientated, and inward-looking.

In a recent study of the state of community organisation among immigrant communities in the UK, for example, Zetter and his co-authors raised concerns about the limited ambitions of many of these newer organisations. Most are focused on individual support, welfare, and social activities, and are argued to be essentially defensive, reflecting the marginalised position of many new migrants in the UK:

> These organizations perform an essentially defensive role in an environment of hostile immigration policy ... This social capital constitutes the currency of differentiation, fragmentation and exclusion, not a vehicle of social cohesion that Putnam's concept implies. (Zetter et al. 2006: 11)

Such organisations often have limited funding, and have been set up to support what are often beleaguered communities with high numbers of refugees and asylum-seekers and/or significant numbers of irregular migrants. In response to these limitations, activists have recently created a network of local migrant community organisations called the Migrant Rights Network (MRN), which seeks to

> address policy issues which have the potential to affect all immigrants, whether the immigration arose from flight as refugees, economic migration, family reunification, the exercise of EU free movement rights or irregular migration. It will seek to bring migrant groups across ethnic and national categories into dialogue with one another, and to bring the resultant network of collaborating groups into contact with mainstream civil society organizations known to be supportive of the rights of migrants. (Flynn 2006: 24)

This agenda recognises the need for migrant community groups to work together and to find allies in wider civil society. But, whereas an earlier generation of immigrants was able to do this – at least in part – through working in and against the Left, and uniting under the identification of 'black' and/or 'anti-racist', today's community activists have to build such connections from scratch. Moreover, they have to do this at a time when there is wider anxiety about declining levels of membership of civil society organisations, and about the impact this has on political participation within the UK (Putnam 2000). In their recent citizen audit, Charles Pattie and his colleagues (Pattie et al. 2004) found that declining levels of engagement were strongly correlated with class. They argued that the decline of trade unionism and collapsing levels of membership of political parties have had a particularly significant role in eroding the basis on which working-class people can participate in public and political life (see also Power Inquiry 2006, Electoral Commission and Hansard Society 2004). At a time when the secular Left is no longer present in poor communities, there are far fewer opportunities for the powerless to engage with politics, and it will be that much harder for immigrant groups to foster social and political links.

Our research highlighted the relative weakness of trade union organisation among low-paid migrant workers, and the relative strength of religious organisations. While only 20 per cent of those sampled belonged to a union (despite the fact that we used trade union contacts to access various groups), we found that as many as half of the new immigrants we interviewed were strongly embedded in religious organisations. Indeed, in the absence of other political organisations, faith organisations were found to be the most vibrant and active civil-society institutions among newer immigrants in low-paid employment in London.[1]

1. Only 7 per cent of the sample (29 people) reported belonging to any other organisations, and these tended to reinforce national and ethnic networks. The organisations mentioned were overwhelmingly associated with the situation at home, including the Angolan Relief Association, the Croatian Student and Young Professionals Association, and the Zimbabwean Fellowship. Moreover, there were cases where workers belonged to overlapping networks that incorporated faith, ethnicity and political ideas. Mary, from Ghana, reported that her friend from university was now a practising minister in London, so when she had arrived they were quickly introduced to a group that met for a monthly church meeting. This was for people from their home town in the Volta region of Ghana, and it meant they could speak their own dialect and share stories of home. However, this group also overlapped with activities for '[Ghanaians] as a whole', as well as secondary school student reunions. Once a year, this woman met her old colleagues from secondary school for 'a dinner dance and things like that'. Some members of the Ghanaian community were also active in supporting welfare work in Ghana through formal and informal organisations. As we saw in the previous chapter, Kojo, who worked as an Underground cleaner, met friends from his home town to send resources home. Apart from trade union membership, only a handful of respondents reported belonging to more locally focused organisations. One person was a member of the Labour Party, another mentioned a credit union, and another belonged to a gym. In general, migrant workers were concentrated in separate worlds and separate institutions. Moreover, even those who belonged to faith organisations tended to worship with people like themselves.

Faith and integration in Europe and the US

Given that faith institutions remain as increasingly isolated generators of social capital among immigrant groups, we would suggest that it is likely that religion will continue to play a significant role in urban political life in the future. Such arguments mirror those made by researchers in the US, where, similarly, faith organisations are one of the few remaining generators of strong social connections with particular importance for immigrant groups (Putnam 2000). In the US, faith organisations have been found to provide psychological and social support for new immigrants, while also offering a socially acceptable route to integration (Foley and Hoge 2007, Foner and Alba 2008, Hirschman 2004). As a religious society, the US tends to respect and value the practice of faith, and this has allowed immigrants to use the social networks and practices developed in their religious communities, often with co-ethnics, as a basis for connecting with the wider society beyond their church, mosque or temple (Foley and Hoge 2007). For Foner and Alba, religious affiliation 'helps to turn immigrants into Americans and gives them and their children a sense of belonging or membership in the United States'. Faith institutions have been shown to provide a place from which 'immigrants can formulate claims for inclusion in American society' (Foner and Alba 2008: 365).

Such arguments jar with the European experience. Despite the history of Christianity in Europe, and the vestiges of this history that remain in the established church (in Britain), in support for Christian schools (in Britain, France and the Netherlands), in the collection of church taxes (in Germany), and in the state ownership of churches (in France), there is significant popular hostility towards faith and any role it does or might play in public and political life. This is most clearly illustrated in relation to Islam, which has long been seen as a 'barrier or a challenge to integration and a source of conflict with mainstream institutions and practices' (ibid.: 368). Popular commentary often focuses on the 'backward' attitudes of Muslim immigrants and their beliefs, highlighting the supposed repression of women, and the practices of arranged marriage and honour killing. Such hostility has fuelled resentment and isolation, but has also helped to create the strong religious communities that are the subject of fear (Maalouf 2000).

Foner and Alba explain these intercontinental differences between Europe and the US in terms of the religious culture of the host countries, the class background and religious traditions of the immigrant groups themselves, and the approach of the state. Thus, they note that the US has integrated greater numbers of wealthier Christian immigrants than Europe, where poorer Muslim immigrants have been dominant in the post-war period. At the same time, while as many as 44 per cent of Americans worship at least once a week, the figure is nearer 10 per cent in France, Germany, the Netherlands and the UK – although religious observance is much more prevalent among immigrant groups (Foner and Alba 2008: 377). Finally, whereas Christianity has been institutionalised in European countries, the American state has supported religious freedom and equality. As a result, successive waves of immigrants to the US have been able to use religious spaces as a means to enter the public sphere in a way that is much more contested in a country like the UK.

Despite these differences, however, there are signs that the role of religion is changing in Europe (Kastoryano 2004). Immigration has provided new members for existing faith organisations, and religious spaces are increasingly important as places where marginalised immigrant communities can associate, organise and develop a public voice. As a result, politicians in Britain are increasingly recognising the role of religious organisations and including them in the development of national and local policy (Furbey and Macey 2005). For example, some of the privileges afforded to Christian churches are now being extended to minority faiths, with the development of state-funded Jewish, Hindu, Islamic and Sikh schools. Many religious institutions are also now being led and managed by second-generation citizens who have greater confidence to intervene in public debate. Moreover, given the collapse of the secular Left and the resultant vacuum in local political life, as well as the strong social capital embedded in religious communities that include immigrant groups, it is likely that faith organisations will begin to play more of a political role. As Glynn (2002; see also Bhatt 2006) suggests in relation to the political life of Bengali Muslims living in Tower Hamlets, the secular politics of the first generation of immigrants has now given way to a new politics that is intimately connected to religious belief and belonging. Large, successful religious institutions like the East London Mosque provide spiritual, emotional and practical support for thousands of people, playing a critical role simultaneously in the communal, civic and political life of the city.

Of course, there is nothing inevitably progressive about the kind of politics that faith organisations will choose to pursue, and many academic commentators have been extremely hostile to the emergence of a post-secular politics in countries like the UK. Even though they acknowledge the role of religious social capital in filling the gaps left by the failure and retreat of secular alternatives, religion is generally cast in a negative light (Davis 2006, Retort 2005). Yet such readings tend to compress internal differences within faith traditions, ignoring the strength of the universalism, solidarity and anti-materialism that are often embedded in faith (Jamoul and Wills, 2008). Faith organisations can potentially move in any number of political directions, depending on the communities involved, their leadership, the networks of which they are part, and the way in which they are treated. Indeed, as one scholar comments in relation to the local political representation of the vibrant religious organisations he finds in the London borough of Newham: 'The issue [is] about the nature of ... representation and whether the interests pursued are narrow sectarian ones, some shared notion of the common good, or proactive advocacy for the socially excluded sections of the local population' (Smith 2000: 26).

Thus while some faith organisations have mobilised their members on the basis of religious matters that are pertinent only to their particular group – such as in opposition to Salman Rushdie's *The Satanic Verses* – others have started to find common cause with each other and with secular organisations over shared political, social and economic concerns (Furbey and Macey 2005, Jamoul and Wills 2008). There is a long history of community organising among faith organisations in the US, which has been manifested in the Civil Rights movement, the Industrial Areas Foundation, and Barack Obama's recent presidential campaign (Osterman 2003, Warren 2001). This experience suggests that religious organisations can indeed be successfully mobilised around core welfare issues like housing, wages and immigration control.

Drawing below on our research data, we highlight the relatively high rates of religious adherence among low-paid foreign-born workers in London. Turning to London Citizens, we then explore the potential for forging connections between faith organisations and wider civil society around a shared agenda for change.

Faithful Lives: The Role of Religion in Immigrant Lives

Our research interviews revealed very high levels of religious affiliation among low-paid immigrants living in London. As many as 48 per cent of the people we interviewed were actively involved with some kind of religious organisation, with very similar levels of adherence by gender (46 per cent of men and 50 per cent of women). Importantly, the rate of adherence did not drop among those who had secured British citizenship, most of whom had been in the UK for relatively long periods of time – though, as might be expected, the research did reveal the extent of unevenness in religious adherence among migrants, with dramatic differences between different groups.

As Table 7.1 shows, faith was much more significant among immigrants from African countries than it was among those from western Europe, with those from countries in Latin America and eastern Europe lying somewhere in between. Although the small size of the sample and the under-representation of Asian workers makes it difficult to form firm conclusions from the data collected, it is clear that faith was particularly important for immigrants from Brazil, DRC, Ghana, Jamaica, Lithuania and Nigeria.

While it is possible that immigrants become *more* religious following the experience of migration and the attendant need to foster a sense of community – and there is considerable evidence that this is the case in the US (see Foley and

Table 7.1   Religious affiliation by place of birth

Regions of origin	Total in group	% active members of faith organisations
Africa	219	62%
Latin America and Caribbean	74	46%
Eastern Europe	44	25%
Asia	23	22%
Western Europe	53	21%
Further breakdown of national groups with 10 or more people		
Ghana	70	81%
Democratic Republic of Congo	19	63%
Lithuania	10	60%
Nigeria	65	59%
Jamaica	14	50%
Brazil	22	46%
Colombia	17	41%
Bulgaria	11	36%
Portugal	17	24%
Poland	30	3%

Source: Analysis of authors' questionnaire survey (see also Appendix 1)

Hoge 2007, Foner and Alba 2008) – it is clear that most of our respondents brought their faith with them when they moved. Given that the low-paid migrants we spoke to had practised their faith in their home country, it was only logical for them to continue to do so once they arrived and settled in London. Moreover, given the difficult circumstances that confronted them in making a life in the city, faith was often psychologically sustaining. As Paulo, a construction worker from Brazil, explained:

> If I were a less strong man I would have returned to Brazil ... and if I am still standing on my own feet [it] is thanks to my education, to the structure my father has given me ... and of course, going to church. Religious belief has helped me a lot.

As we have seen, the majority of immigrants doing low-paid jobs were grappling with the challenges of being de-skilled in physically demanding jobs, as well as facing life in a strange and sometimes hostile environment. Religious faith helped many of these workers to make sense of this situation and restore value in their work and themselves. For example, faith provided a way to value menial and poorly-paid work as having greater purpose than the pay would suggest. Cleaning a hospital and caring for the elderly were jobs that workers saw as intrinsically valuable, and as jobs that needed to be done well (for more on this in relation to care, see Datta et al. 2011). Coming to terms with the low pay and low status of the work was facilitated by the ability to see it as God's work, as well as a means to survive. Faith thus acted as 'psychological ballast' for many workers, helping them to acclimatise to their new situation and to face the challenges they encountered at work. While the low pay, poor conditions and low visibility they experienced reflected the low status of immigrant jobs and immigrants in British society, faith provided these workers with a mechanism to make their work more valuable to themselves and their clients. In 'working well', they were working for God. And by believing in God, workers found the resources to cope with the difficulties they faced in working for very little return. As Zafia, a carer from Kenya, explained:

> Maybe God has given me this strength so that I can help this person ... In my heart I don't want to work just because of money ... I shall continue praying to God. This is the work that I am doing to assist people who cannot do anything for themselves. I think it's hard and even if I don't feel I have the [desire] to do it, it works for me and it teaches me a lot ... If you are going to take care of them, do as if you are doing for God.

Our research also revealed the extent to which religious affiliation both reflected and reinforced national and ethnic identities. In the vast majority of cases, the low-paid workers we interviewed regularly or always worshipped with people like them. Religious identity was a way of finding and connecting with people from their home country, and the practice of faith was a way of reinforcing these networks in London. This echoes findings from research in the US where 'immigrants worship with co-ethnics in settings with many tangible reminders and expressions of home-country cultures, [and] so a sense of ethnic identity is nurtured and strengthened' (Foner and Alba 2008: 363). In addition, our findings hark back to the historical experience of new immigrant communities in cities like London. Describing the life of Irish immigrants who arrived in east London to escape famine in the nineteenth century, and the experiences of Jews who arrived fleeing violence in Europe after the 1880s, Fishman (1997) documents the significant role of faith institutions and religious belief in the lives of these communities. Writing of the Irish, for example, he observes: 'The unsung hero of Irish East London was the homespun priest. Oftentimes he was both policeman and judge as well as spiritual guide to his flock, the mainstay of moral values' (Fishman 1997: 42). Likewise, for the Jewish community, the synagogue provided 'their salon and their lecture hall. It supplied them not only with their religion, but their art and letters, their politics and their public amusement' (ibid.: 45).

More than 100 years later, our research similarly identifies religion and faith institutions as providing the scaffolding that supports many of London's new immigrant communities (see Davis et al. 2007). While religious belief nurtured the soul and provided a strong alternative value-system for workers, it also had the effect of strengthening ethnic and social networks, creating community and providing a mechanism for information exchange.[2] Thus, we interviewed many workers for whom church provided a social as well as a spiritual point of connection. For example, Christina, a Nigerian care worker, reported that the Pentecostal Church provided a wealth of spiritual, social and ethnic support:

> It's like everybody from my country goes to church – you see people so you don't get lonely. You see people on Sunday from your country, you all chat, you go on your dialect ... You don't get bored or get depressed [about] anything because you just go to church and you see people. You don't even want to come home on Sunday. I go to church very early; I get back at 6 o'clock in the evening but I enjoyed it – everybody around you, seeing people from your own country, you talk in your own language and it's fun. I enjoy it.

Acknowledging that a lot of people find it lonely and difficult to live in London, Christina saw church as filling a gap: 'Once they come to church, it's like everybody is their family. They're happy, and then you can go to people and do all sorts of things. It's good.' Many interviewees from African countries told us that 'church is like family', and for these workers church provided a place where they found comradeship, social solidarity, and a place to feel at home in the city. As Akelo, a Ghanaian man working in the construction sector, reported:

> I go to church every Saturday and that's the most enjoyable part of my life since I have been here ... The church is the biggest community that I've come across because they're lovely people over there – you meet people from Ghana and it's a Ghanaian established church, and everybody is happy to help, happy to welcome, happy to do everything for you.

Likewise Alvaro, from Brazil, explained: 'The church for me is for prayer and for social interaction ... I like the church a lot.'

Hence, while many respondents used the familial and social networks developed in their countries of origin to help them build a new life in London, many others had also engaged in religious networks since arriving in the UK (Ryan et al. 2008). Interviewees talked about using religious networks for help with housing, employment and health. As Zafia, from Kenya, explained, joining a church that involved house fellowships twice a week allowed her to access a spiritual and social community, which helped her make a new life. She reported sharing information about

> life in this country. If you are new, how did you find it? When you came, how did you find it? And also, you can help those who are coming new because they don't know ... like when [I was] in Kenya, I never knew about care work. [This is where] you can start.

2. Religion was also important – in similar ways – to the post-war immigrants who arrived from Bangladesh, the Caribbean, India and Pakistan. However, in contrast to the earlier period, faith organisations now increasingly resemble islands in a sea of unorganised civil society in inner-city locations. Whereas earlier groups of immigrants created a secular political voice, this has not yet been a feature of life for newer arrivals.

Abina, from Ghana, reflected on her own experiences of making friends and finding the support she needed to get a job and find a doctor through the fellowship of faith:

> Where we used to stay in Stratford, we used to go to a church in Leytonstone. There's a Methodist church there, and they have a Ghanaian fellowship, so my husband took me there and I was really impressed. We have meetings ... and we have a Ghanaian group as well.... every second Sunday of the month we meet to socialise. We cook, we take food there to eat, socialise, we eat, we chat ... I made friends from there, and if you have any problem you can phone any of the members – they discuss with you. So it was nice – it was like a family, a small family! ... If you don't know anything, since they be here for a long time, they can explain things to you better.

Others had used church connections to find cheaper or more appropriate housing, and when Antobam decided to come to London from Ghana with her children in 2002, to join her husband, it was fellow church members who helped them find a place to live. Her husband found people to rent with through their fellowship of faith: 'They came together and rented a three-bedroom house. So we were sharing the place with them.'

Religion thus provided very strong social connections for many of the migrants we met who had moved to London from Africa, Latin America and eastern Europe. In Putnam's terms (Putnam 2000, 2007; see also Chapter 5), these research respondents were rich in bonding and bridging social capital – usually within national and ethnic groups, and less commonly with a mixture of other migrants and citizens in more established faith institutions; but this did not necessarily foster linking social capital to the wider society. In contrast to experience in the US, faith did not necessarily act as a stepping stone to integration and active citizenship. However, partly linked with the fact that social capital in all its forms intersects with and underpins the creation of civil society organisations (see McIlwaine 2007b), our research did highlight the potential for using religious communities as a basis for political mobilisation among migrant communities in London, through their role in fostering bonding and bridging social capital. As we discuss below, a relatively new, broad-based organisation called London Citizens has helped immigrant workers to raise their voices in the public sphere by mobilising religiously-generated social capital alongside secular partners. Here we explore the Living Wage and regularisation campaigns that have had particular salience for newer migrants living and working in London.

Post-Secular Politics in London Today

As we have seen, British society – like that of Europe more generally – is largely hostile to religious engagement in political life. Yet in diverse, poor, inner-city neighbourhoods it is increasingly the case that faith groups are the strongest and most vibrant institutions of civil society. For example, Smith (2000) has identified as many as 300 different religious organisations in the London borough of Newham, many of them the product of new immigration. He found the Baptist and Methodist churches had attracted considerable numbers of Jamaicans, Ghanaians and Nigerians; the Anglicans had attracted Pakistanis, Ugandans and Barbadians; while the Catholics had members from the Caribbean, as well as from Francophone Africa, Goa (India) and Vietnam. Pentecostal Christianity was also strong, with particular growth in the West African Aladura Church, the Holy Order of the Cherubim and Seraphim, the Christ Apostolic Church, and the Celestial Church of Christ. The borough was also home to five major Hindu temples, four gurdwaras, two Buddhist centres, and a large number of mosques. Given that these institutions are supported by people who often have little, if any, political voice in the wider society, such religious organisations are effectively in the front line of any effort to represent, organise and mobilise immigrant communities. The social capital embedded in faith organisations may be critical to the articulation of immigrant voices in the wider polity of Britain today.

Since 1989, the Citizens Organising Foundation has developed a model of broad-based community organising that began in the US. The approach has it origins in the work of the Industrial Areas Foundation, developed by Saul Alinsky in 1930s Chicago, which has since grown into a nation-wide network of at least 130 local broad-based alliances across the US (Warren 2001). Local broad-based alliances are created to empower local communities – or teach the art of politics – by working together over shared concerns. This model of politics depends on different groups bringing their own traditions to the table of public life in order to find common ground. Shared interests are identified on the basis of common geography, and in poor communities the key issues tend to be education, employment, crime, housing, immigration and welfare. Likewise, the aim of an alliance like London Citizens is to foster solidarity through active campaigning around these issues, demonstrating that politics can make a difference to community life.

In Britain, the East London Communities Organisation (TELCO) is now the longest-running broad-based community alliance, with more than a decade of successful campaigning under its belt. When it joins forces with newer alliances created in south and west London, TELCO forms the largest contingent of London Citizens, which at the time of writing involves more than 100 different community groups. The bedrock of the alliance is composed of faith organisations, including Anglicans, Roman Catholics, Methodists, Pentecostals, a Buddhist centre, a Sikh gurdwara, and a number of mosques, together with trade union branches, schools, student unions, a university department (Queen Mary's Geography Department) and community centres. London Citizens is thus more institutionally diverse than its counterparts in the US, where community organising has tended to be more dependent on affiliation from religious organisations. London Citizens is also extraordinarily culturally diverse, embracing a range of institutions that have very different historical geographies and membership types.

As would be expected from our findings about the salience of religion among low-paid migrant workers, London Citizens includes very significant numbers of foreign-born residents, as well as more established Londoners. In addition, recent campaigns around low pay and an amnesty for irregular migrants have helped to increase the representation and participation of migrant communities. The demand for a living wage was developed to tackle subcontracted employment relations, and the Strangers into Citizens campaign grew out of this campaign as the lack of workers' political rights eroded their power to act.

The Living Wage campaign

This book has chronicled London's migrant division of labour and demonstrated the extent to which our low-paid services now rely on foreign-born workers, most of whom work under subcontracted employment arrangements. Even if trade unions had the resources and commitment to organise such workers, they would face the harsh realities of high rates of labour turnover, complex shift patterns, extraordinary ethnic and national diversity, language difficulties, and relatively high rates of illegal employment (Wills 2005). More than this, however, trade unions have traditionally sought to organise workers in relation to their employer, negotiating to improve the terms of the contract they have. In a subcontracted economy, many workers have no industrial relations contact with their 'real' employer. While the hospital trust, the bank or the retailer sets the terms of the cleaning contract and determines the profit the contractor is able to make (even down to specifying materials, headcount and wage levels in many cases), the workers themselves have no channel through which to bargain over these terms. Even if the subcontracted workers were to organise themselves to try and improve their pay and conditions of work, they would probably price their immediate employer out of the market: at the subsequent round of re-tendering, their contractor would lose out to a cheaper non-unionised firm (Hale and Wills 2005, Wills 2005, 2009).

The idea of a Living Wage campaign was developed to overcome this 'representational gap' between subcontracted workers and their 'real' employers by linking subcontracted workers with a broad alliance of community organisations. First developed in the mid-1990s by a sister organisation to London Citizens – Baltimoreans United in Leadership Development – this model spread across more than 100 cities and counties in the US, before being launched in London in 2001 (Luce 2004, Walsh 2000, Wills 2004, 2009). The campaign uses the notion of a 'living wage' to set a new moral standard for low-wage jobs that better reflects the real cost of living in London. At its best, the model involves working with trade unions to organise subcontracted cleaners collectively, and then mobilising a broad alliance of community groups to put pressure on the 'real' employers to ensure that a living wage is passed on to the staff. Senior managers in London's hospitals, banks, universities, charities, hotels and art galleries have been held to account – often through media pressure – for the terms and conditions of the subcontracted workers who empty their bins, clean their toilets, and polish their floors.

It is estimated that half a million workers – many of them new migrants – fall into the gap between the national minimum wage and what is needed to live in London (Veruete-McKay 2007). So far, only a fraction of these (estimated at about 5,000 – see Table 7.2) have secured the living wage as a result of the campaign. However, the campaign has helped trade unions to deliver improvements for workers, to recruit new members, and produce a new generation of workplace leaders. As we have seen, London's migrant workers already have strong connections to faith organisations, and by building an alliance that incorporates both faith and labour, London Citizens has secured much greater power to act (see Wills 2004, 2009).

Since 2005, and following pressure from the campaign, the mayor of London has taken over responsibility for the publication of an annually updated living wage figure for London (GLA 2005a, 2006, 2007, 2008). As it has progressed, however, the Living Wage campaign has also revealed the extent of London's dependence on irregular workers. As a result, the Strangers into Citizens campaign was born.

Photo 7.1   London Citizens' Living Wage campaign at the Department for Families, Children and Schools, October 2008 (photo by Chris Jepson).

Table 7.2 Estimates of the numbers covered and the wages gained in the London Living Wage campaign (February 2009)

Sector: workplaces	Date	Numbers (estimated)	Total gained
Hospitals: Homerton, Mile End, Royal London,* Whipps Cross	Phased in by 2006	1,000	2006: £3.088 million 2007: £3.145 million 2008: £3.220 million
Canary Wharf/City Barclays, HSBC, Deutsche Bank, Morgan Stanley, Lehman Bros, PWC, KPMG, Macquarie and others	2005 onwards – rolling	1,700 (approx. 3,000 cleaners in total but estimate 800 covered at C. Wharf and 900 in City)	2005: not calculated, but all workers included for 2006–08 2006: £2.705 million 2007: £2.673 million 2008: £2.737 million
Finance Barclays (London-wide)	mid 2007	1,000	2007: six months only £1.572 million 2008: £3.220 million
Higher education QMUL and LSE SOAS from September 2008	2007 (phase in to 2009 at LSE)	250 (QM and LSE) 50 (SOAS)	2007: six months only to reflect QM and LSE phase-in, £163,800 2008: four months SOAS £22,360
Third sector IPPR, CPAG, Big Issue, UnLtd, ACEVO	2005 onwards	50	2006: £66,300 2007: £65,520 2008: £67,080
Olympics	2007 onwards	**	3,000 workers on site (2008) 134 not living wage (in review)
GLA family (City Hall, LDA, LFPEA, Police, TfL)	2006 onwards	100	2006: £132,600 2007: £262,080
	2008	800	2008: £1.207 million
Retail Westfield shopping centre	2008	**	Information pending
Department for Children, Families and Schools	April 2009	**	Information pending
Total		4,950**	£24,346,740

Notes: *The Royal London is included here even though the staff were taken back in-house as part of a PFI deal. This happened after negotiations for a living wage to be paid to cleaners on-site. **The living wage will only reach significant numbers on the Olympics site, Westfield and the DCFS during 2009. The GLA family has introduced living wages as re-contracting has allowed. The largest is the Facilities Management Services contract with the Metropolitan Police Service, covering 800 cleaners by 2008 (GLA 2008). Ealing Council has agreed to implement a living wage for their dinner staff, but this is being introduced gradually and will be recorded once they reach a living wage. Talks with the Hilton Group (17 hotels) are ongoing, small increases have been made in pay, and cuts have been made in the number of agencies used.

Source: Authors' calculations (see Appendix 4)

Photo 7.2   Colombian migrants calling for regularisation at May Day march, 2007 (photo by Cathy McIlwaine).

The Strangers into Citizens campaign

In the wake of an increasingly hostile immigration regime, and without citizenship or the legal right to work, many of Britain's migrants are understandably reluctant to take part in political organisation. Even those with extensive political experience from their home countries are reluctant to jeopardise their security by antagonising

Photo 7.3 Mobilising through faith, Justice for Cleaners, Westminster's Roman Catholic cathedral, 2007 (photo by Chris Jepson).

their employers and/or exposing themselves to the state by joining political campaigns. Vijay, a carer who had extensive experience of political organisation in Mauritius, told us that he was too dependent upon the good will of his employer to get more involved in union activities. While his student visa allowed him to work 20 hours per week during term-time, he was regularly exceeding these hours. He was frightened that if he became involved in trade union organising or political activity – as he had done at home – his employer could reduce his hours, make him redundant, or even report him to the authorities for breaking the law. Moreover, he was acutely aware that the British trade unions were not strong enough to support him should he end up losing his job:

The problem is that I'm a student and I would have a lot of difficulties ... if you give [the employer and authorities] too much fodder. It's better to keep targeted on your things and fix on why you come here instead of being too active. It's not about fear, it's more about whether, when you get into trouble, [someone will] help you.

Many of the workers we interviewed were in a similar position: working as tourists, students, or without any papers at all. While living wages might be important to these workers, they were secondary to their ongoing anxiety about the threat of detention and removal from the UK.

The Brazilian community that we introduced in Chapter 3 (see Box 3.1) was particularly supportive of this campaign – not least because very few of its members had the legal status required to work. For communities like this, the immigration regime had implications for their very presence in London. As many as 90 per cent of the 423 people surveyed in the Brazilian community had been in the UK for less than five years, and half were aged under 34. Despite their size, such communities are currently under threat, and without significant changes in the immigration regime this insecurity will only increase.

Recognising the extent of illegal working, the threat that deportation poses to the cohesion of immigrant communities, and the prohibitive cost of managing the detention and removal regime, London Citizens decided to launch a campaign for regularisation in 2007. What became known as Strangers into Citizens began with a mass, march and rally to celebrate the contribution of migrant workers to London's economy. In May 2007, London's Catholic cathedral was packed to capacity, with more than 2,000 people who went on to join an even larger crowd that raised its voices and demands in the street. Indeed, an estimated 15,000 people, many of them irregular migrants, attended the final rally in Trafalgar Square, coming with their churches, trade union branches, community groups, sports clubs, families and friends. The campaign is now aiming to secure a new pathway to citizenship for many of the workers we encountered in our research. After living and working in the UK for more than four years, it is proposed that migrant workers produce references attesting to their economic contribution in order to secure a two-year work permit. Once granted leave to live and work in the country, these migrants would then be able to build up a right to full citizenship, and so gain secure access to public and political life.

At the time of writing, the Strangers into Citizens campaign was ongoing. Its proposals had been endorsed by the leader of the Liberal Democrats, various back-bench members of parliament, and the new Conservative mayor of London, Boris Johnson. The campaign had also won support from various campaigning organisations and a number of think tanks (IPPR 2006, JCWI 2006). Regardless of the eventual outcome, however, the campaign had already been successful in mobilising newer immigrants in pursuit of their political rights. Moreover, it had done so by linking migrants to the wider polity. Faith and labour leaders have been campaigning together, seeking to strengthen the economic and political rights of those whose labour keeps the city afloat. As the archbishop of Westminster, Cardinal Cormac Murphy-O'Connor, said at a mass for migrant workers held in May 2006:

> While our nation benefits economically from the presence of undocumented workers, too often we turn a blind eye when they are exploited by employers ... Is it not time to consider, as other countries have done, ways of regularising their situation – those who are working in the country and do not have a criminal record – to the benefit of our economy and to enable them to play a fuller part in society?

The Living Wage and Strangers into Citizens campaigns have provided a vehicle for immigrants to act as citizens, with many members of these campaigns motivated by their lack of citizenship (Varsanyi 2005). Many low-paid immigrants are asking to be given a place in British society, and our research shows just how much London's economy would suffer without them.

This chapter has explored the changing forms and impact of immigrant politics in London. Whereas colonial and ex-colonial subjects arrived in Britain with full citizenship prior to the increasingly draconian immigration regime that was implemented after 1962, significant numbers of the migrants who have arrived since the 1990s come from non-Commonwealth countries without the right of citizenship. These differences are central to understanding the political traditions, expectations and rights that people bring with them. Migrants from the Caribbean, India, Pakistan and Bangladesh arrived in the Motherland speaking English, importing both the proud traditions of anti-colonial struggle and the political entitlement of British citizenship. In contrast, today's immigrants have tended to arrive in smaller groups from a wider range of locations. While some have been able to join strong and established communities crafted by earlier settlers, many have remained relatively isolated, with little means of support. Our research findings have highlighted the particular importance of faith organisations for these later migrants, identifying high levels of active membership, social support and solidarity in religious organisations. London Citizens has effectively used such religiously generated bonding and bridging social capital as a mechanism to generate linking social capital, which can be used for collective political organisation.

Thus, while the New Left provided a language and institutional infrastructure in which to conduct political organisation during the 1960s and into the 1980s, today's new arrivals face a relative vacuum of political organisation at the grassroots. The political potential of new immigrant communities remains largely hidden in the sacred spaces of churches, gurdwaras, mosques and temples, small community organisations, and mixed social networks. The activities of London

Citizens demonstrate the potential to mobilise these diverse and often relatively isolated communities in a shared struggle for change. But, unlike in the past, this is less likely to be focused on the issue of race. Rather, ethnically differentiated groups are now finding a shared interest in tackling the challenges that arise from living in inner-city communities (recent campaign issues have included affordable housing and the need for street safety and youth training opportunities, as well as the scourge of low wages).

Moreover, while an earlier generation of activists used a black identity as a means to forge a collective large enough to secure political change, today's immigrants have engaged in collective organisation as members of a plethora of different organisations and groups. While the language of the Left was used by the earlier generation to work 'in and against the state', today's activists in London Citizens come to the table with a variety of traditions, including those of the secular Left (through trade union branches), Buddhism, Christianity, Hinduism and Islam, as well as community-focused service providers (third-sector welfare organisations, schools, and university departments). On the surface, London Citizens practises a less ideological form of politics, but each participating group brings its own ideological analysis and traditions with it to the public arena. This is a politics that comes from sharing space in the city and recognising the need for solidarity across difference in the interest of common concerns. It is also a post-secular politics that grants a place at the table for institutions of faith. London Citizens remains controversial, but it has been politically effective. It reaches and engages London's immigrants where they are already organised – in their faith, trade union, and community organisations – allowing them to be heard in public and political life.

8

JUST GEOGRAPHIES OF (IM)MIGRATION

We opened this book with a quotation from Robert Winder in which he advocated that we think of the nation as a lake – one that is constantly re-colonised by the organisms brought to it by the incoming stream. The use of this fluvial metaphor implies that, over time, the new melds with the old and the ecology of the lake undergoes often imperceptible change; the people who were immigrants gradually become an accepted part of the whole. Yet Winder's book considers immigration over the centuries. In contrast, this book has focused on the rather short term. We have looked at the role that unprecedented levels of in-migration have played in helping to reshape London's labour market since the 1980s. As we will show here, this more restricted time-frame renders such analogies more problematic. Our research has shown that immigration is currently characterised by divergent streams of arrival which are stratified in a hierarchy that privileges the skilled over those classified as unskilled, and the European over the non-European. Moreover, given the particular situation in London, migrants in the lower echelons of the hierarchy often find themselves in employment and residence with other migrants, having few opportunities to meld with the longer-established society. The twin processes of deregulation and international migration have generated rapid change in the labour market, raising tensions and divisions between migrant groups, as well as between migrants and the wider society.

In this final chapter we summarise our findings, before exploring their wider implications. So far we have provided evidence to show that London – and, by extension, other parts of the UK and the rest of the world – are now characterised by having a migrant division of labour. Immigrants are arriving in Britain from a wider array of countries than ever before, codified by an immigration regime that differentiates new arrivals in a hierarchy related to skills, nationality and welfare entitlement. As a result, foreign-born workers from the EU are privileged over those from further afield; and, among the latter, those classified as highly skilled are privileged over the others. This situation means that immigration status is itself now a key determinant of labour-market position and prospects. Furthermore, while immigration status intersects with enduring ethnic and gender divisions of labour, it often 'trumps' these older distinctions. As we showed in Chapter 4, the structural position of new immigrants can be such that ethnicity and gender no longer map on to the labour market as they did in the past. Black African men from middle-class backgrounds are to be found doing traditionally feminised jobs, just as eastern European immigrants are altering the ethnic balance of what used to be coded as black people's jobs.

These trends reflect the power of the contemporary state to shape the labour supply, and we argue that it is no longer possible to understand the labour market without attention to national immigration regimes. We have found that, in London at least, employers have proved very adept at responding to changes in the labour supply. New arrivals have been brought into the labour market through a complex web of recruitment agencies and personal networks that channel workers into employers' ever-changing hiring queues. The energy of new migrants has been put to work in the service of the city, and foreign-born workers are now performing essential tasks to an unprecedented degree. As we showed in Chapters 2 and 3, many workplaces are now almost entirely dependent upon foreign-born staff.

Yet our research has also exposed the disjuncture between the official immigration regime and the world that exists on the ground. We have highlighted the extent to which a global city like London now depends upon an army of foreign-born workers who are largely absent from government thinking. We have documented London's dependence upon a large population of workers from countries in the global South – and in the case of care work, cleaning, and construction, sub-Saharan Africa and Latin America in particular. Though the numbers of new arrivals from the officially sanctioned countries of central and eastern Europe are certainly rising – often prompting considerable tension with more established communities, as we suggested in Chapter 4 – current immigration policy flies in the face of this reality. While there have been only limited opportunities for people from sub-Saharan Africa and Latin America to come to the UK legally in recent years, the number of workers from these regions now employed at the 'bottom end' of London's labour market suggests that immigration policy has had little success. Instead, as we have documented, people from these regions are to be found across the low-paid labour market – often working with tourist or student visas, and sometimes without any official permission at all. While some have secured their legal status through the asylum system, it is striking that the largest numbers are from countries that do not feature in the asylum regime – such as Brazil, Ghana and Nigeria. Although these communities have been keeping the city working for the past 20 years, many of their members are now threatened by tighter immigration control.

In the previous chapter we explored the ways in which the workers embodying London's migrant division of labour are now organising to respond to the conditions of their employment. The demand for regularisation – the demand of the Strangers into Citizens campaign – reflects the political position of these marginalised communities that are increasingly vulnerable to legal restraint. As many as 20,000 such workers and their allies assembled in Trafalgar Square in May 2009 to make their voices heard in what remains an ongoing campaign. In this chapter, we continue this focus on politics, and bring the book to a conclusion by exploring other possible responses to the migrant division of labour. Most obviously, we locate this narrative within the changing landscape of global political economy. Since we began the project behind this book, the world economy has gone 'from boom to bust', and the political pendulum has swung away from the market and back to the state. Just a few months ago, London and the rest of the UK attracted large numbers of migrants who were eagerly accommodated in the growing subcontracted low-wage economy. At the time of writing, however, unemployment is rising, confidence in the main political parties is at an all-time low, and there are growing fears about migrants stealing 'our jobs'. In what follows, we explore the role of the state and the British trade union movement before making the case for improved labour standards here, as well as further afield. We suggest that the economic crisis poses opportunities for rethinking the dominant model of political economy, for improving labour standards at home and abroad, and thereby reconfiguring the landscape in which labour migration takes place.

Immigration, the State and the British Trade Union Movement

As we saw in Chapter 1, the British government has recently sought to manage migration in the national interest. Taking a largely instrumental approach to the supply of foreign labour – viewing labour power as a commodity to be imported and exported like any other – this has been a strategy designed to succour business, as well as to appease the wider electorate. But managing a commodity as complex as labour power is less than straightforward. As Marx argued more than 100 years ago, labour can only ever be a pseudo-commodity. The commodity, labour power, has to be extracted from the worker, and this in turn depends upon management, industrial relations, and the balance of power at work. In the case of foreign-born workers, such processes are strongly dependent upon the role of the state. Government policy and the actions of government officers determine the nature of the immigrant labour supply, the terms of entry, and access to employment itself. As we have seen – at least in Britain – government has legislated to develop a new armoury of policy and practice, implemented by a host of public and private officials, to manage and stratify immigrant workers. The points-based system, biometric ID cards, and a new phalanx of enforcement officers have proved essential to assessing, ranking and controlling the foreign-born labour supply. Indeed, the policy has required the recruitment of a wide battery of hitherto uninvolved officials in the form of employers, university administrators, educators, health officials, transport inspectors and welfare providers. These individuals are now legally required to scrutinise potential workers, international students, those with illnesses, passengers, and would-be claimants to identify those who are entitled, and to exclude those who are not. The British government has apparently been very proactive in managing (and trying to control) migration and its consequences for the British economy and local communities within the UK. The state has thereby played a critical role in mediating labour supplies and workplace employment relations.

Yet, taking a broader geographical perspective, the UK can also be seen as one of the most liberal – some would say neo-liberal – in its approach to immigration reform. Among the 15 members of the old EU, only Britain, Ireland and Sweden opened their borders to potential workers from new accession states in May 2004. In contrast to countries like Austria, France and Germany, where there were deep-seated fears about the impact of an increased supply of labour in the context of local unemployment, the UK opened its borders to all (Krings 2009). Reflecting strong employer demand as well as the large numbers of those from the accession countries seeking to better themselves, unprecedented numbers of workers arrived. Most took up employment in low-wage services and manufacturing jobs that would previously have been done by younger workers, women, the low-skilled, and more settled immigrant groups (Drinkwater et al. 2009, MacKenzie and Forde 2009, Stenning and Dawley 2009).

Moreover, like the state, the British trade union movement has been remarkably positive about these new supplies of labour. The Trades Union Congress (TUC) has reiterated the official view that such immigration has had few, if any, negative effects on local workers and their communities (TUC 2007). Together with government and a range of think-tanks, the TUC has drawn on a series of econometric studies to suggest that the increase in economic activity associated with new supplies of labour, and the process of labour-market segmentation whereby these workers are 'contained' in particular jobs that complement rather than displace local the labour supply, have prevented any negative effects on employment and jobs (Blanchflower et al. 2007, Dustmann et al. 2005, Gilpin et al. 2006). This approach partly reflects the hard-won battle, summarised in Chapter 7, to ensure that unions challenge xenophobia and racism throughout their organisations.

In contrast to the situation in many European countries, however, the British unions have proved to be very weak in their defence of wages and conditions at the 'bottom end' of the labour market. As we saw in Chapter 2, wages have fallen in real and relative terms for those in routine, low-paid jobs in London over the past 20 years. Despite the welcome introduction of the national minimum wage following the election of a New Labour government in 1997, many workers earn wages at the statutory minimum rate. As we saw in Chapter 3, very few of the workers we met doing important jobs in cleaning, care and hospitality received anything like a living wage, and they were generally without access to sick pay or a company pension – or, indeed, a trade union. The deregulated labour market has devalued these jobs, and as a result, many unskilled natives are no longer doing this work. While the British trade unions have sought to lobby government for increases in the NMW (Grimshaw 2008), an end to privatisation and increased regulation of agency work, this has had very little effect.

A number of British unions have recognised that their ability to influence the terms and conditions of work now depends upon grassroots organisation. In what has become known as the 'organising agenda', a number of trade unions have trained and employed organisers to try and increase membership levels and win union recognition campaigns (Heery 1998, Gall 2003). Such organising efforts have inevitably involved attempts to organise previously under-represented constituencies, including migrant workers in London (Holgate 2005, Wills 2005). Yet, in practice, the challenges of this work are immense. As we have shown, for London at least, the migrant division of labour is constituted by workers from a super-diversity of different locations, with implications for workplace cohesion, communication and divisions between ethnic groups. In addition, labour mobility has provided the best route to advancement, meaning that labour turnover in low-paid employment is usually remarkably high (see Chapter 3). In addition, work is often mediated by labour agencies, and those with regular jobs are inevitably employed though subcontracted labour arrangements, reducing their power to act. People tend to work for long hours and share childcare as a means of survival, squeezing their time to do anything else. Most seriously of all, there are also many who do not have the immigration status required to stay, and are necessarily fearful of getting involved in union organising.

This obviously represents a very difficult population in which to establish traditional trade union organisation. While some unions have sought to learn the lessons from successful organising activities in other parts of the world – and particularly in North America – new campaigns have had only a marginal impact on migrant workers in London. The Transport and General Workers' Union (TGWU – now part of the merged union Unite) and UNISON have been part of the coalition led by London Citizens to secure a living wage and regularisation, but these unions have failed to engage fully with the campaign, and the rest have largely abstained (Holgate 2009, Wills et al. 2009b). The TGWU has also been unusual in pioneering a relationship with the North American Service Employees' International Union (SEIU) to share best practice in relation to organising techniques, trying to connect campaigns across space – but even this has been slow to produce any major results (see Anderson et al. 2009, Wills 2008). So far, at least, it has proved remarkably difficult to cement traditional trade union organisation within the low-paid, subcontracted economy that frames the lives of many of London's foreign-born workers today.

In many ways, the challenges of organising in deregulated and subcontracted labour markets make it all the more remarkable that British trade union leaders have remained so positive about the supply of immigrant labour. National union officials have tended to echo official government policy in relation to immigration, even going further, arguing for full labour market access to Bulgarians and Romanians from 2008. Yet much of the wider population – and, presumably, trade union members – have been anxious about increasing numbers of migrants. Whatever the outcome of econometric research, anecdotes about local workers being replaced by foreigners – reinforced by the headlines in much of the tabloid press – have tended to reinforce a popular fear of outsiders. As we saw in Chapter 1, immigration and race relations have become a major concern for voters during the past decade – and, in the wake of recession, anxiety is only likely to grow. At the time of writing, the British National Party had 53 councillors in elected positions in England, winning as many as 12 seats on Barking and Dagenham Council in May 2006 (Muir 2008). Though geographically uneven, such electoral preferences reflect increasing disquiet about the impact of immigration on local labour markets at a time of rising unemployment across the UK.

As a manifestation of this sense of unease, workers at the Lindsey Oil Refinery in North Lincolnshire walked out in an unofficial strike in protest over the employment of approximately 200 foreign workers in February 2009. These workers caught the nation by surprise by being able to mount successful industrial action that spread across the country – involving 20 other sites, including Scotland, Northern Ireland and Wales – and lasting well over a week. Lincolnshire – an area not known for strong trade union organisation or militancy – became a strike headquarters for a nation of aggrieved skilled construction workers. Strikers protested that a local employer (albeit a French-owned multinational firm) was able to subcontract work to a foreign-owned company that then shipped in their 'own' workers – in this case, from Italy. Given the free movement of workers within the EU, and despite the operation of the EU Posted Workers Directive that provides limited guarantees that local wage rates will be respected, local workers were alarmed that it was cost-effective for the contractor to import and accommodate up to 200 workers rather than recruiting local workers.

The powerful combination of subcontracting and increased labour mobility with which we opened this book was exposed on the picket lines outside Lindsey Oil Refinery in this dispute. Workers were demonstrating for their right to a job – and, as we have seen in relation to London, local workers were facing or drawing the dole while foreigners were being employed. In this case, the dispute was so intense because the jobs were relatively skilled, and because the contractor directly recruited the labour abroad. More commonly, as we have seen in London, wages and conditions have been driven down to a level at which locally available workers are unwilling to work, and the foreign-born are recruited through a gradual process of change. The net effect, however, is largely the same. Foreigners become a preferred source of labour, while locals sit on the dole. When this happens gradually, as we have documented in this book in relation to London, there is little direct conflict. But when it happened on a large scale, in the early days of economic recession and redundancies, it provoked a dramatic response.

In Lincolnshire, the strikers repeated the ill-judged rhetoric of Prime Minister Gordon Brown, demanding 'British jobs for British workers', and some major concessions were made. Yet, as we have seen, the British government cannot stop immigration from the EU – and in this case the dispute was sparked by the nature of the European Procurement Directive, which allows firms to compete for contracts within the EU and to include the relocation of workers as part of the job. While the European Posted Workers Directive requires such contractors to recognise and respect the local terms and conditions of employment, this has proved rather hard to interpret, and very hard to police. Indeed, recent judgements made by the European Court of Justice have upheld the rights of contractors over their trade union opponents in relation to the Viking, Laval and Ruffert cases, in which companies imported foreign-born labour and undercut local terms and conditions of work (Cavalier 2008, Woolfson 2007, Woolfson and Sommers 2006).

Such developments, which undermine rates of pay and working conditions, are clearly exercising the trade union movement. If and when migrant labour becomes a tool to reduce the cost of labour and displace more expensive local workers from their employment, tension with non-immigrant workers is inevitable. This book has documented that, in London at least, the market has achieved more subtle reform. As labour standards have fallen, natives have voted with their feet, and migrants have become the preferred labour supply. The hidden hand of the market has worked behind the backs of the trade unions, and they are left bereft of the power to act. Our research suggests that trade unions need to refocus and rethink their efforts to improve labour standards for those doing low-paid employment. This would not only improve the lives of the migrants doing the jobs – as demonstrated by the impact of the Living Wage campaign – but also create the grounds for unity with the non-immigrant workers displaced from these jobs. Moreover, improved labour standards would probably have more impact on the supply of foreign-born labour than the laws determining border control. Improved labour standards would stimulate more local labour supplies (in Marx's terminology, introduced in Chapter 1, these could be characterised as the 'stagnant, latent and floating' labour reserves). This increased supply of local labour would undermine demand for those born abroad, with a resulting effect upon rates of immigration itself. Indeed, it is significant that the open-borders policy adopted by

Sweden did not result in a similar influx of migrant labour to that seen within the UK. In Sweden, the tight regulation of wages and conditions – with a major role for the trade union movement – has largely prevented strong employer demand for immigrant workers, as non-immigrant workers are doing the jobs.

Thus, as we have seen, the UK's subcontracted, low-wage economy has created the conditions in which migrant workers have become a perfect labour supply. In addition, the immigration regime has itself helped to create a situation in which migrant workers are necessarily differentiated from the native labour supply. Migrants have provided a means to fill posts without increasing wages or improving conditions, thereby boosting the rent that flows to both immediate employers and the 'real' employers at the top of contracting chains. Tackling the subcontracted economy and improving labour standards would thus operate to protect workers' interests, while also eroding employer demand for a migrant labour supply.

So far, however, there are few prominent voices demanding increased labour regulation within the UK. While there is now greater enthusiasm for rethinking neo-liberalism, political leaders have largely sought to prop up rather than transform the ailing economy. Moreover, as we have seen, there are dangers that political activists can make ground by fostering hostility to outsiders. As yet, there is little sign that the recession will act as a stimulus for the development of a new political agenda that could unite migrants with the settled population. Our research suggests that a focus on labour standards could be critical here, contributing to a wider debate about the redistribution of wealth.

The Politics of Place Beyond Place

The imperative to improve labour standards is just as important – if not more so – in the rest of the world. As we saw in Chapter 1, international migration has been at least partly stimulated by the nature of economic development in poorer parts of the world. Inequality, poverty, the paucity of opportunity, and political crisis are key drivers for migration from the South to the North. Hundreds of people are dying every year – often in terrible circumstances, without their families being informed – trying to reach Europe and North America to make a new life. Improved labour standards – particularly along the global commodity chains that feed the markets in the wealthy parts of the world – could be critical in saving at least some of these lives. In the spirit of Doreen Massey's (2004, 2007) arguments about the 'politics of place beyond place', our research highlights the responsibilities that London and the UK have to the distant communities on which we depend for our labour, as well as for the goods we consume.

As we saw in Chapter 6, it is heartening that the New Labour government has championed its commitment to international development, augmenting the role of the Department for International Development. The government has doubled its development assistance, with the aim of meeting the UN target of 0.7 per cent of Gross National Product being spent on aid by 2013. Yet, despite these laudable ambitions, there is ample evidence that development is already slipping down the agenda as the richer countries make frantic efforts to kick-start their economies to meet national-level demands. When the powerful leaders of the G20 gathered in London during the week we finished this book, voices from the global South bemoaned their integration into a global neo-liberal economy that was in dramatic decline. For them, the global recession constituted nothing short of an 'emergency for development' (World Bank 2009) – and, perhaps more critically, the global stimulus packages pursued by countries like the US raised the combined threats of protectionism and reductions in development aid.

This resurgence of nationalism in the face of economic decline will have profound implications for our sense of care and responsibility for the rest of the world. Indeed, as we argued in Chapter 6, contemporary evidence suggests that, while the UK has made some attempt to unlock the developmental potential of migration – most notably through the facilitation of financial remittances – the priority has been on British interests both at home and abroad. This national interest clearly determines both the extent of development activity itself and the newly reinforced limits to contemporary in-migration from the developing world. Thus, even while global cities like London have benefited immensely from migrant labour – particularly from the so-called unskilled migrants we have described in this book – the possible gains of such migration for development remain strictly curtailed.

However, it is equally clear that there are other national interests in play. The moment of economic crisis is an opportunity to proselytise greater commitment to human development both within and beyond the UK. A renewed agenda to promote equality and redistribution would benefit workers and their communities in both the global North and the South. A more egalitarian agenda could replace the neo-liberal vision of global growth built on a subcontracted and grossly unequal economy. Echoing the arguments made by Keynesian thinkers in the wake of economic collapse before the Second World War, economic activity would itself be stimulated through improved labour standards, the greater distribution of wealth, and greater global equality. A commitment to paying living wages and respecting core labour standards in every location would be an important first step on this road.

It is rarely acknowledged that London has been sustained by centuries of uneven development. In this book we have highlighted the extent of London's dependence on the rest of the world for its low-paid labour supply. Recognising this dependence, as well as its consequences and its associated responsibilities, could be a core part of efforts to rethink and remake contemporary political economy in London, the UK and the rest of the world.

APPENDICES

Appendix 1: Data Sources Used in this Book

The bulk of the research material presented in this volume was generated as part of the Global Cities at Work project based at Queen Mary, University of London, between 2005 and 2007. This involved a number of different research techniques conducted using varied sets of data. At the largest scale, we worked with Yiannis Kaplanis from the London School of Economics to interrogate the Labour Force Survey, exploring changes in employee numbers and the proportions of migrants for a number of occupational categories for the periods 1993–04, 1999–2000 and 2005–06. In each case, we looked at the data for London and the rest of the UK, allowing us to contrast trends in the city with the nation as a whole. We also used the Annual Survey of Hours and Earnings to focus on wages, and although this data set is not weighted and does not record the numbers of foreign-born staff, it is thought to be more consistent in relation to the figures on pay. While there are difficulties in ensuring consistency across this period of time, due to changes in the occupational codes that are used, we matched these as carefully as possible (full details are provided in Appendix 2, below).

We also had to create new data sets to get to grips with the nature of low-paid jobs and the characteristics of the people employed in them. We thus conducted a large-scale questionnaire survey in two separate parts. In the first phase (summer 2005) we contacted workers employed in four different sectors of the economy that were known to rely on significant numbers of low-paid workers: cleaning (offices and London Underground), hospitality (hotels and catering), domiciliary care, and food processing. This part of the research was conducted in partnership with London Citizens, and we designed the questionnaire for use by eleven student interns during July 2005. The questionnaire was completed through face-to-face encounters with workers who were approached randomly outside their workplaces, or through snowballing following an initial contact. The questionnaire included information about the terms and conditions of employment, work and migration histories, household circumstances, and plans for the future. This stage of the research included all workers (341 cases) regardless of nationality, and the data allowed us to make some assessment of the degree of dependence on migrant workers in particular jobs. In this phase of the research we put all 341 cases onto the database, and then later removed the UK-born respondents, storing that data in a separate file.

In the second stage of the research we used the same questionnaire with a further cohort of workers. These were selected as part of a separate interview survey, and the final data set included 429 responses from foreign-born workers in London. This second group included only foreign-born workers, and we asked them to complete the questionnaire prior to an in-depth interview that explored their migration and labour-market histories, current employment, household structures, coping strategies, relations with 'home', and immigration status. These in-depth interviews were conducted with 103 workers in 2007. Some of the participants were identified from the first phase of the questionnaire survey, but we also sought to extend the research into particular communities, as well as into the construction sector. We found respondents by advertising in the Brazilian media, and we collaborated with Boguslaw Potoczny (a Polish student), Monika Percic (a Slovakian student) and Eva Matamba (a British–Congolese researcher), who each used snowballing to contact workers in their own communities. These interviews were generally conducted in first languages (Brazilian Portuguese, various Congolese languages, Polish, and Slovak) and were conducted in people's homes, at Queen Mary, or in local cafés. These encounters were digitally recorded and later translated into English. The full set of 103 transcripts were coded using computer software.

Given that the research project was designed to examine the nature of a migrant division of labour as seen from the perspective of low-paid cleaning, caring, construction, food processing and hospitality workers and employers in London, it was also imperative to include the views and experiences of employers. It proved easier to make initial contact with employers' associations, and we conducted a number of semi-structured interviews with representatives of the cleaning, care, construction and hospitality sectors. These interviews followed a similar schedule in every case, and we were able to make initial contacts with a number of employers through these and other channels. In total, we conducted eleven interviews with employers and their representatives, covering topics such as changes in employment patterns, the importance and problems of employing migrants, the role of British-born workers, and challenges for the future (see Appendix 3, below). These interviews were recorded and transcribed, and analysed manually.

In-depth interviews with representatives of seven community organisations also helped to unpack the wider implications of our research. We were able to consider the issues that were particular to local communities (such as the Brazilians, Congolese and Polish), while also identifying issues common to all those concentrated in low-paid employment. This phase of the work also involved interviewing 13 representatives from a number of government departments that have a role in managing migration and low-wage employment, including the Department for Work and Pensions, the Treasury, the Department for International Development, and the Home Office. We also spoke to senior officials from a number of London-wide organisations, such as the Greater London Authority and the Local Government Association, and from think-tanks and relevant service providers, including the Child Poverty Action Group, the Citizens Advice Bureau, and the Institute for Public Policy Research. We also included organisations that campaign around the issues of migrants and employment, including the Migrant Rights Network and London Citizens (see Appendix 3, below).

In the final stages of the project we were able to work with London Citizens to analyse a data set collected by members of a Brazilian Catholic community in London. As part of the Strangers into Citizens campaign, some of the church leaders worked with London Citizens to develop a very simple questionnaire exploring people's migration and work histories, family circumstances, and immigration status. A total of 423 questionnaires were completed, and we constructed a new database to analyse this material, which is summarised in Box 3.1 in Chapter 3.

Some of the research presented in this book – particularly that in Chapter 7 – was collected as part of a related ESRC-funded research project called 'Work, Identity and New Forms of Political Mobilisation: An Assessment of Broad-Based Organising and London's Living Wage Campaign'. This project involved interviews with workers and workplace activists involved in the London Living Wage campaign, as well as participation in the campaign and interviews with leaders and organisers of the London Citizens alliance. Much of this material is presented elsewhere (see Wills 2008, 2009, Jamoul and Wills 2008), but the data presented in Table 7.2 and access to information on the Living Wage and the Strangers into Citizens campaigns was secured through participant observation in the coalition itself.

Appendix 2: Technical Information about the Use of Large Data Sets

As outlined above, this book draws upon original analysis of two large data sets: the Labour Force Survey and the Annual Survey of Hours and Earnings. Each is outlined below, before an explanation of the occupational categories and indicators used in the analysis we presented in Chapter 2.

Labour Force Survey (LFS)

The LFS is a quarterly sample survey of 60,000 households living at private addresses in Britain, which provides a wide range of data on labour-market statistics, including employees and the self-employed. The survey seeks information on respondents' personal circumstances and their labour-market status during a specific reference period – normally one week or four weeks (depending on the topic) – immediately prior to the interview. The self-employed account for some 13 per cent of the sample.

The LFS is based on a systematic random sample design that targets all persons aged 16 and over, to make it representative of the whole of Britain. Each quarter's LFS sample of 60,000 private households is made up of five 'waves', each of approximately 12,000 households. Each wave was interviewed in five successive quarters. Households were interviewed face-to-face when first included in the survey, and by telephone thereafter. The sample data are weighted to reflect population estimates produced by the Office for National Statistics. In regard to pay, the data refer to employees only (i.e. there is no pay information about the self-employed).

The New Earnings Survey (NES) and the Annual Survey of Hours and Earnings (ASHE)

The NES was used until 2004 to provide information about the earnings of the workforce in Great Britain (i.e. excluding Northern Ireland). In 2004 it was replaced by the Annual Survey of Hours and Earnings, to provide better coverage of the labour force, as well as including imputations for non-response and the weighting of earnings estimates. The ASHE provides information about the levels, distribution and make-up of earnings and hours worked for employees in all industries and occupations in Britain. It is based on a sample size of approximately 150,000 employees per year, and the results are presented as absolute numbers (i.e. they are not weighted).

Standard Occupational Classification and Occupational Categories

The type of job done by a worker can be classified into a particular occupational group. Occupations are coded according to the current Standard Occupational Classification (SOC), which is maintained by the Occupational Information Unit (OIU) of the Office for National Statistics. SOC90 was employed throughout the 1990s, and consisted of the following main categories:

1. Managers and administrators
2. Professional occupations
3. Associate professional and technical occupations
4. Clerical and secretarial occupations
5. Craft and related occupations
6. Personal and protective service occupations
7. Sales occupations

8. Plant and machine operatives
9. Other occupations

The SOC90 was replaced in 2001 by a new classification, SOC 2000, which was created by classifying jobs in terms of their skill level and content, where skill is defined by the nature and duration of the qualifications, training, and work experience required to perform a particular job:

1. Managers and senior officials
2. Professional occupations
3. Associate professional and technical
4. Administrative and secretarial occupations
5. Skilled trades occupations
6. Personal service occupations
7. Sales and customer service occupations
8. Process, plant and machine operatives
9. Elementary occupations

The data presented in this volume involved selecting the occupational categories that are known to include large numbers of low-paid employees, for which comparable data were available from the 1990s. The aim was to provide a picture of the trends in employment and wages over the period, to allow us to contextualise the findings from our own questionnaire survey of migrant workers. Notable omissions are occupations that either lack data for the period covered, such as hotel housekeepers, or occupations where the available data are inconsistent, such as 'waiters and waitresses'. As indicated in the tables presented in Chapter 2, the best data were available for the occupational categories of chefs and cooks, catering assistants, care assistants, and cleaners and domestics.

Key indices in these data sets that were critical to our analysis include foreign-born and wages:

Foreign-born: The LFS has allowed us to calculate the percentages of these occupational categories occupied by foreign-born workers, and we have used this to understand London's migrant division of labour, accepting that this includes settled immigrants and British citizens who were born abroad.

Wages: Median values (i.e. the central values of a distribution) have been used for the variable 'real hourly pay rate' (RHP), instead of mean values, in order to avoid distortion by extreme values. This variable was deflated with the Retail Price Index in the first year of the historical periods examined (1993 and 2001) to provide the value of the wage rate, in any one year, equivalent to the value of the base year.

Appendix 3: Interviews with Employers, Policy-Makers and Community Groups

The following is a full list of the organisations where interviews were conducted, at the dates shown. For reasons of confidentiality, some of these organisations are not fully identified.

Organisation (by category and chronology)	Date
Employers	
Cleaning and Support Services Association	3 May 2006
Managers from one cleaning company contract	28 September 2006
at Canary Wharf	4 December 2006
British Hospitality Association	17 November 2006
Construction Confederation	24 November 2006
Home Care Association	5 December 2006
Personnel manager, food manufacturer, East London	18 December 2006
Director, Home Care Services company, London	20 March 2007
HR director, large construction company HQ	11 July 2007
Policy-makers and think-tanks	
HM Treasury	8 December 2006
Department for Work and Pensions	11 December 2006
Child Poverty Action Group	13 December 2006
Policy officer, Greater London Authority	12 January 2007
Citizens Advice Bureau HQ	26 January 2007
Policy Studies Institute	26 January 2007
Institute for Public Policy Research	26 January 2007
Department for International Development	22 March 2007
Local Government Association	5 April 2007
Home Office	5 April 2007
Doughty Chambers (specialists in immigration law)	14 May 2007
Local Authorities Coordinators of Regulatory Services (LACORS)	15 May 2007
Community organisations	
Federation of Poles	13 December 2006
Carila	3 April 2007
Associação Brasileira no Reino Unido	8 May 2007
Community for Congolese Refugees	9 May 2007
Central Association of Nigerians in the United Kingdom (CANUK)	15 May 2007
Ghana Black Stars Network	18 June 2007
A priest from a Brazilian Roman Catholic church, London	22 June 2007

Appendix 4: A Note about the Living Wage Calculations in Table 7.2

The figures in Table 7.2 are calculated using the difference between the NMW and LLW, except for those working in Canary Wharf and the City, as research suggests that these workers were already paid about £1 more than the LLW – half the difference has been used for this group.

There is a mismatch between the award date for the NMW and the LLW (the former is in October and the latter is in May), and this will affect the detail of the calculations. The differences between the annual rates of the NMW and the LLW are shown below:

	NMW*	LLW**	Difference	Half difference
2003	£4.50	£6.50	£1.90	£0.95
2004	£4.85	£6.50	£1.65	£0.83
2005	£5.05	£6.70	£1.65	£0.83
2006	£5.35	£7.05	£1.70	£0.85
2007	£5.52	£7.20	£1.68	£0.84
2008	£5.73	£7.45	£1.72	£0.86

* Set by the government-funded Low Pay Commission – <www.lowpay.gov.uk>.
** Calculated by the GLA from 2005 – <www.london.gov.uk/mayor/economic_unit/workstreams/living-wage.jsp>.

Workers are assumed to work 36 hours per week for 52 weeks per year: a total of 1,872 hours each year (though many also work long hours of overtime, which are not included here). The workers at Queen Mary, SOAS and the LSE, those in the Third Sector, and those in the GLA family are assumed to work 15 hours per week, as the vast majority were part-time: a total of 780 hours per year. The difference between the NMW and the LLW is applied to each hour worked for each worker for the years when the improvement in pay was agreed.

The information has been collated through participation in the campaign, regular contact with London Citizens' organisers, and background research (see also Wills 2004, 2008, 2009).

REFERENCES

Adams, R., and J. Page (2005) 'Do international migration and remittances reduce poverty in developing countries?' *World Development* 33: 1645–69.

Al-Ali, N., R. Black, and K. Koser (2001) 'The limits to "transnationalism": Bosnian and Eritrean refugees as emerging transnational communities', *Ethnic and Racial Studies* 24 (1): 578–600.

Allen, J., and N. Henry (1997) 'Ulrich Beck's *Risk Society* at work: labour and employment in the contract services industries', *Transactions of the Institute of British Geographers* 22: 180–96.

Anderson, A., P. Hamilton, and J. Wills (2009) 'The multi-scalarity of trade union practice', in S. McGrath-Champ, A. Herod, and A. Rainnie (eds) *Handbook of Employment and Society: Working Space* (Cheltenham: Edward Elgar).

Anderson, B. (2000) *Doing the Dirty Work? The Global Politics of Domestic Labour* (London: Zed Books).

—— (2007) 'A very private business: exploring the demand for migrant domestic workers', *European Journal of Women's Studies* 14 (3): 247–64.

Anderson, B., M. Ruhs, B. Rogaly, and S. Spencer (2006) *Fair Enough? Central and East European Migrants in Low-Wage Employment in the UK* (Oxford: COMPAS).

Andreotti, A. (2006) 'Coping strategies in a wealthy city of Northern Italy', *International Journal of Urban and Regional Research* 30 (2): 328–45.

Anthias, F., and N. Yuval-Davis (1992) *Racialized Boundaries: Race, Nation, Gender, Colour and Class and the Anti-Racist Struggle* (London: Routledge).

Arendt, H. (1998) [1958] *The Human Condition* (New York: Anchor Books).

Ashforth, B., and G. Kreiner (1999) '"How can you do it?" Dirty work and the challenge of constructing a positive identity', *Academy of Management Review* 24 (3): 413–34.

Asiedu, A. (2005) 'Some benefits of migrants' return visits to Ghana', *Population Space and Place* 11: 1–11.

Back, L., M. Keith, A. Khan, K. Shukra, and J. Solomos (2002) 'New Labour's white heart: politics, multiculturalism and the return of assimilation', *The Political Quarterly* 4: 445–54.

Baker, P., and Y. Mohieldeen (2000) 'The language of London's school children', in P. Baker and J. Eversley (eds) *Multilingual Capital* (London: Battlebridge).

Balakrishnan, A. (2006) 'Workers abroad send poor more money than world aid donors', *Guardian*, 27 July 2006.

Ballard, R. (2003a) 'The South Asian presence in Britain and its transnational connections', in B. Parekh, G. Singh, and S. Vertovec (eds) *Culture and Economy in the Indian Diaspora* (London: Routledge).

—— (2003b) *Remittances and Economic Development* (London: House of Commons Select Committee for Migration and Development).

Banks, R., and R. Scanlon (2000) 'Major economic trends in the 1980s and 1990s: London', in *The London–New York Study* (London: City of London Corporation).

Batnitzky, A., L. McDowell, and S. Dyer (2008) 'A middle-class global mobility? The working lives of Indian men in a west London hotel', *Global Networks* 8: 51–70.

Bayart, J. (1993) *The State in Africa: The Politics of the Belly* (Longman: Harlow).

Beaverstock, J. (2004) '"Managing across borders": knowledge management and expatriation in professional service legal firms', *Journal of Economic Geography* 4 (2): 157–79.

Beaverstock, J., and J. Smith (1996) 'Lending jobs to global cities, skilled international labour migration, investments banking and the City of London', *Urban Studies* 33 (8): 1377–94.

Beckman, B. (1992) 'Empowerment or repression? The World Bank and the politics of African adjustment', in P. Gibbon (ed.) *Authoritarianism, Democracy and Adjustment: The Politics of Economic Reform in Africa* (Uppsala: Nordiska Afrikainstitutet).

Bell, B. (1997) 'The performance of immigrants in the United Kingdom: evidence from the General Household Survey', *Economic Journal* 107: 333–45.

Benería, L., and M. Roldán (1987) *The Crossroads of Class and Gender: Industrial Homework, Subcontracting and Household Dynamics in Mexico City* (Chicago: University of Chicago Press).

Benton-Short, L., M. Price, and S. Friedman (2005) 'Globalisation from below: ranking world cities', *International Journal of Urban and Regional Research* 29 (4): 945–95.

Berkeley, R., O. Khan, and M. Ambikaipaker (2006) *What's New About New Immigrants in Twenty-First Century Britain?* (London: Joseph Rowntree Foundation).

Bhatt, C. (2006) 'The fetish of the margin: religious absolutism, anti-racism and postcolonial silence', *New Formations* 59 (autumn): 98–115.

Bivand, P., B. Gordon, and D. Simmonds (2003) *Making Work Pay in London* (London: Centre for Social Inclusion).

Black, R., and R. King (2004) 'Editorial introduction: migration, return and development in West Africa', *Population, Space and Place* 10: 75–83.

Black, R., M. Collyer, R. Skelton, and C. Waddington (2005) *A Survey of the Illegally Resident Population in Detention in the UK* (Home Office Online Report, 20 May).

—— (2006) 'Routes to illegal residence: a case study of immigration detainees in the United Kingdom', *Geoforum* 37 (4): 552–64.

Blanchflower, D., J. Saleheen, and C. Shadforth (2007) *The Impact of the Recent Migration from Eastern Europe on the UK Economy* (Bank of England research paper) available at <www.bankofengland.co.uk/publications/speeches/2007/speech297.pdf>.

Bloch, A., and L. Schuster (2005) 'At the extremes of exclusion: deportation, detention and dispersal', *Ethnic and Racial Studies* 28 (3): 491–512.

Boddy, M., and C. Fudge (eds) (1984) *Local Socialism* (London: Macmillan).

Boehm, D. (2004) *Gender(ed) Migrations: Shifting Gender Subjectivities in a Transnational Mexican Community*, Working Paper 100, Center for Comparative Immigration Studies (San Diego: University of California).

Bonnett, A. (2000) *White Identities: Historical and International Perspectives* (Harlow: Addison-Wesley Longman).

Bracking, S. (2003) 'Sending money home: Are remittances always beneficial to those who stay behind?' *Journal of International Development* 15: 633–44.

Braverman, H. (1974) *Labor and Monopoly Capitalism* (New York: Monthly Review Press).

Brown, C. (1984) *Black and White Britain: The third PSI survey* (London: Heinemann Educational Books).

Brown, S. (2006) 'Can remittances spur development? A critical survey', *International Studies Review* 8: 55–75.

Brubaker, R. (2003) 'The return of assimilation? Changing perspectives on immigration and its sequels in France, Germany, and the United States', in C. Joppke and E. Morawska (eds) (1999) *Toward Assimilation and Citizenship: Immigrants in Liberal Nation-States* (Basingstoke: Palgrave Macmillan).

Buck, N. (1994) *Social Divisions and Labour Market Change in London: National, Urban and Global Factors* (Paper for the ESRC London Seminar, 28 October 1994).

Buck, N., I. Gordon, P. Hall, and M. Kleinman (2002) *Working Capital: Life and Labour in Contemporary London* (Routledge: London).

Cantle, T. (2008) *Community Cohesion: A New Framework for Race and Diversity* (Basingstoke: Macmillan, second edition).

Carling, J. (2004) *Policy Options for Increasing the Benefits of Remittances*, Working Paper 8 (Oxford: COMPAS).

—— (2005) *Migrant Remittances and Development Cooperation*, PRIO Report 1 (Oslo: International Peace Research Institute).

Carter, T. (1986) *Shattering Illusions: West Indians in British Politics* (London: Lawrence & Wishart).

Castles, S. (2004) 'Why migration policies fail', *Ethnic and Racial Studies* 27 (2): 205–27.

Castles, S., and G. Kosack (1973) *Immigrant Workers and Class Structure in Western Europe* (Oxford: Oxford University Press).

Cavalier, S. (2008) 'Procurement: Public Services and Fair Employment', presentation to Working with Government conference (Cardiff: Cardiff University, 7 April).

Centre for Contemporary Cultural Studies (1982) *The Empire Strikes Back: Race and Racism in 1970s Britain* (London: Hutchinson Education).

de Certeau, M. (1984) *The Practice of Everyday Life* (Berkeley: University of California Press).

Chalcraft, J. (2007) 'Labour in the Levant', *New Left Review* 45: 27–47.

Chambers, I. (1994) *Migrancy, Culture, Identity* (London: Routledge).

Chant, S., and C. McIlwaine (1995) 'Gender and export-manufacturing in the Philippines: continuity or change in female employment? The case of Mactan Export Processing Zone', *Gender, Place and Culture* 2 (2): 147–76.

Chappell, L., D. Sriskandarajah, and T. Swinburn (2008) *Building a New Home: Migration in the UK Construction Sector*, Working Paper 2, Economics of Migration project (London: IPPR).

Cheong, P. (2006) 'Communication context, social cohesion, and social capital building among Hispanic immigrant families', *Community, Work and Family* 9 (3): 367–87.

Cheong, P., R. Edwards, H. Goulbourne, and J. Solomos (2007) 'Immigration, social cohesion and social capital: a critical review', *Critical Social Policy* 27 (1): 24–49.

Clarke L., and M. Gribling (2008) 'Obstacles to diversity in construction: the example of Heathrow Terminal 5', *Construction Management and Economics* 26 (10): 1055–65.

Clarke, S., S. Garner, and R. Gilmore (2008) *Mobility and Unsettlement: New Identity Construction in Contemporary Britain*, ESRC Identities and Social Action programme – key findings available at <www.identities.org.uk>, last accessed 16 January 2009.

Cliggett, L. (2005) 'Remitting the gift: Zambian mobility and anthropological insights for migration studies', *Population, Space and Place* 11: 35–48.

Collyer, M. (2005) 'When do social networks fail to explain migration? Accounting for the movement of Algerian asylum-seekers to the UK', *Journal of Ethnic and Migration Studies* 31 (4): 699–718.

Commission on Integration and Cohesion (COIC) (2007) *Our Shared Future* (London: Department for Communities and Local Government).

Connell, J., and D. Conway (2000) 'Migration and remittances in island microstates: a comparative perspective on the South Pacific and the Caribbean', *International Journal of Urban and Regional Research* 24 (1): 52–78.

Conthe, P., and A. García (2007) 'New mechanisms for developing primary and secondary housing finance markets: the case of Peru', *Housing Finance International* (June): 46–56.

Cornelius, W. (2005) 'Controlling "unwanted" immigration: lessons from the United States, 1993–2004', *Journal of Ethnic and Migration Studies* 31 (3): 775–94.

Cox, R., and R. Narula (2003) 'Playing happy families: rules and relationships in au pair employing households in London', *Gender, Place and Culture* 10 (4): 333–44.

Cox, R., and P. Watt (2002) 'Globalization, polarization and the informal sector: the case of domestic workers in London', *Area* 34 (1): 39–47.

Cranford, C. (2005) 'Networks of exploitation: immigrant labor and the restructuring of the Los Angeles janitorial industry', *Social Problems* 52 (3): 379–97.

Dale, A., N. Shaheen, V. Kalra, and E. Fieldhouse (2002) 'The labour market prospects for Pakistani and Bangladeshi women', *Work, Employment and Society* 16 (1): 5–25.

Daniel, W. (1968) *Racial Discrimination in England* (Harmondsworth: Penguin Books).

Datta, K. (2007) *Money Matters: Financial Exclusion among Low-Income Migrants in London* (London: Department of Geography, Queen Mary, University of London).

—— (2009a) 'Transforming South–North relations? International migration and development', *Geography Compass* 3 (1): 108–34.

—— (2009b) 'Risky migrants? Low-paid migrants coping with financial exclusion in London', *European Urban and Regional Research* (forthcoming).

—— (2009c) *The Remittance Industry and Financial Inclusion among Low-Paid Migrants in London*, Working Paper (London: Department of Geography, Queen Mary, University of London).

Datta, K., C. McIlwaine, Y. Evans, J. Herbert, J. May, and J. Wills (2007a) 'From coping strategies to tactics: London's low-pay economy and migrant labour', *British Journal of Industrial Relations* 45 (2): 409–38.

—— (2007b) 'The new development finance or exploiting migrant labour? Remittance-sending among low-paid migrant workers in London', *International Development Planning Review* 29 (1): 43–67.

—— (2009) 'Men on the move: narratives of migration and work among low-paid migrant workers in London', *Social and Cultural Geography* (forthcoming).

—— (2011) 'A migrant ethic of care? Negotiating care and caring among migrant workers in London's low-pay economy', *Feminist Review* (forthcoming).

Davis, F., J. Stankeviciute, D. Ebbutt, and R. Kaggwa (2007) *The Ground of Justice: The Report of a Pastoral Research Enquiry into the Needs of Migrants in London's Catholic Community* (Cambridge: Von Hugel Foundation).

Davis, M. (2006) *Planet of Slums* (London: Verso).

Dench, G., K. Gavron, and M. Young (2006) *The New East End: Kinship, Race and Conflict* (London: Profile Books).

Dench, S., J. Hurstfield, D. Hill, and K. Akroyd (2006) *Employers' Use of Migrant Labour* (London: Home Office).

Department for Communities and Local Government (DCLG) (2008) *Review of Migrant Integration Policy in the UK* (London: HMSO).

Department of Health (2004) 'Code of Practice for the International Recruitment of Healthcare Professionals', available at <www.dh.gov.uk/en/Publicationsandstatistics/Publications/PublicationsPolicyAndGuidance/DH_4097730>, last accessed August 2009.

Department for International Development (DFID) (2005) *UK Remittance Market Profile*, Business Intelligence (London: DFID).

—— (2006) *Moving Out of Poverty: Making Migration Work Better for Poor People* – Draft Policy Paper, available at <www.dfid.gov.uk/pubs/files/migration-policy-paper-draft.pdf>, last accessed December 2006.

De Witt, J. (1969) *Indian Workers Association in Britain* (Oxford: Oxford University Press).

Dickinson, S., G. Thompson, M. Prabhakar, J. Hurstfield, and C. Doel (2008) 'Migrant Workers: Economic issues and opportunities', *Viewpoint Series* 2 (August) (Cambridge: SQW Consulting).

Doeringer, P., and M. Piore (1971) *Internal Labor Markets and Manpower Analysis* (Heath: Lexington).

Doyal, L., G. Hunt, and J. Mellow (1980) *Your Life in their Hands: Migrant Workers in the NHS* (London: Department of Sociology, Polytechnic of North London).

Drinkwater, J., J. Eade, and M. Garapich (2009) 'Poles Apart? EU enlargement and the labour market outcomes of immigrants in the UK', *International Migration* 47 (1): 161–90.

Duffy, M. (2005) 'Reproducing labour inequalities: challenges for feminists conceptualizing care at the intersections of gender, race and class', *Gender and Society* 19 (1): 66–82.

Dustmann, C., F. Fabbri, I. Preston, and J. Wadsworth (2003) *Labour Market Performance of Immigrants in the UK Labour Market* (London: Home Office).

Dustmann, C., and F. Fabbri (2005) 'Immigrants in the British labour market', *Fiscal Studies* 26 (4): 423–70.

Dustmann, C., T. Hatton, and J. Preston (2005) 'The impact of immigration on the British labour market', *Economic Journal* 115: 324–41.

Dutton, E., C. Warhurst, C. Lloyd, S. James, J. Commander, and D. Nickson (2008) 'Just like the elves in Harry Potter: room attendants in UK hotels', in C. Lloyd, G. Mason, K. Mayhew (eds) *Low-Paid Work in the United Kingdom* (New York: Russell Sage Foundation).

Düvell, F., and B. Jordan (2003) 'Immigration control and the management of economic migration in the United Kingdom: organisational culture, implementation, enforcement and identity in processes in public services', *Journal of Ethnic and Migration Studies* 29 (2): 299–336.

Dyer, S., L. McDowell, and A. Batnitzky (2008) 'Emotional labour/body work: the caring labours of migrants in the UK's National Health Service', *Geoforum* 39 (6): 2030–8.

Eade, J. (2000) *Placing London: From Imperial Capital to Global City* (New York: Berghan Books).

Eade, J., S. Drinkwater, and M. Garapich (2007) *Class and Ethnicity: Polish Migrant Workers in London* (Swindon: ESRC).

Economic Development (2006) 'City Economy Digest', *Economic Development* 1: 1–8.

Economist (2009) 'Remittances: trickle-down economics', *Economist*, 19 February 2009.

Edwards, R., M. Reich, and D. Gordon (eds) (1975) *Labor Market Segmentation* (Lexington: D.C. Heath).

Ehrenreich, B., and A. Hochschild (eds) (2002) *Global Woman: Nannies, Maids and Sex Workers in the New Economy* (London: Granta Books).

Electoral Commission & Hansard Society (2004) *An Audit of Political Engagement* (London: Hansard Society).

Evans, L., and S. Bowlby (2000) 'Crossing boundaries: racialised gendering and the labour market experiences of Pakistani women in Great Britain', *Women's Studies International Forum* 23 (4): 461–74.

Evans, Y., J. Wills, K. Datta, J. Herbert, C. McIlwaine, and J. May (2007a) '"Subcontracting by stealth" in London's hotels: impact and implications for labour organising', *Just Labour: A Canadian Journal of Work and Society* 10 (spring): 85–97.

Evans, Y., J. Wills, K. Datta, J. Herbert, C. McIlwaine, J. May, O. Araújo, A. Franca, and A. France (2007b) *Brazilians in London: A Report for the Strangers into Citizens Campaign* (London: Department of Geography, Queen Mary, University of London).

Faist, T. (2008) 'Migrants as transnational development agents: an inquiry into the newest round of the migration–development nexus', *Population Space and Place* 14: 21–42.

Farrant, M., A. MacDonald, and D. Sriskandarajah (2006) 'Migration and development: opportunities and challenges for policymakers', IOM Migration Research series no. 22 (Geneva: International Organisation for Migration).

Favell, A., and R. Hansen (2002) 'Markets against politics: migration, EU enlargement and the idea of Europe', *Journal of Ethnic and Migration Studies* 28: 581–601.

Fielding, A. (1992) 'Migration and social mobility: south-east England as an escalator region', *Regional Studies* 26: 1–15.

Financial World (2008) *Money on the Move*, available at <www.financialworld.co.uk/archive/2008/2008_11nov>, accessed 13 November 2008.

Fishman, W. (1997) 'Allies in the promised land: reflections on the Irish and the Jews in the East End', in A. Kershen (ed.) *London: The Promised Land? The Migrant Experience in a Capital City* (Aldershot: Avebury).

Florida, R. (2002) *The Rise of the Creative Class and How It's Transforming Work, Leisure and Everyday Life* (New York: Basic Books).

Flynn, D. (2005) 'New borders, new management: the dilemmas of modern immigration policies', *Ethnic and Racial Studies* 28 (3): 463–90.

—— (2006) *Migrant Voices, Migrant Rights: Can Migrant Community Organizations Change the Immigration Debate in Britain Today?* (London: Barrow Cadbury Trust).

Foggo, D., and E. Habershon (2006) 'Invasion by Poles hits "lazy" Britain', *The Times*, 14 May 2006.

Foley, M., and D. Hoge (2007) *Religion and the New Immigrant* (New York: Oxford University Press).

Foner, N., and R. Alba (2008) 'Immigrant religion in the US and Western Europe: bridge or barrier to inclusion?' *International Migration Review* 42 (2): 360–92.

Frankenberg, R. (1993) *White Women, Race Matters: The Social Construction of Whiteness* (London: Routledge).

—— (ed.) (1997) *Displacing Whiteness: Essays in Social and Cultural Criticism* (London: Duke University Press).

Freeman, G. (1995) 'Modes of immigration politics in liberal democratic states', *International Migration Review* 29 (4): 881–902.

Friedmann, J., and G. Wolff (1982) 'World city formation', *International Journal of Urban and Regional Research* 6: 306–44.

Furbey, R., and M. Macey (2005) 'Religion and urban regeneration: a place for faith?' *Policy and Politics* 33: 95–116.

Gall, G. (ed.) (2003) *Union Organising* (London: Routledge).

Gamburd, M. (2000) *The Kitchen Spoon's Handle: Transnationalism and Sri Lanka's migrant housemaid* (Ithaca: Cornell University Press).

Garapich, M. (2008) 'Odyssean refugees, migrants and power: construction of the "other" and civic participation within the Polish community in the United Kingdom', in D. Reed-Danahay and C. Brettell (eds) *Citizenship, Political Engagement and Belonging: Immigrants in Europe and the United States* (New Brunswick, N.J. and London: Rutgers University Press).

Gardner, K., and Z. Ahmed (2006) 'Place, social protection and migration in Bangladesh: a London village in Biswanath', Working Paper T18 (Development Research Centre on Migration, Globalisation and Poverty: University of Sussex).

Gardner, K., and R. Grillo (2002) 'Transnational households and ritual: an overview', *Global Networks* 2 (3): 179–90.

Gerreffi, G., and M. Korzeniewicz (eds) (1994) *Commodity Chains and Global Capitalism* (Connecticut: Praeger).

Gilpin, N., N. Henty, S. Lemos, J. Portes, and C. Bullen (2006) *The Impact of Free Movement of Workers from Central and Eastern Europe on the UK Labour Market*, Working Paper 29 (London: Department for Work and Pensions).

Gilroy, P. (1987) *'There Ain't No Black in the Union Jack': The Cultural Politics of Race and Nation* (London: Hutchinson).

—— (2004) *After Empire* (London: Routledge).

Glenn, E. (1992) 'From servitude to service work: historical continuities in the racial division of paid reproductive labor', *Signs: Journal of Women in Culture and Society* 18 (1): 1–43.

Glynn, S. (2002) 'Bengali Muslims: the new East End radicals?' *Ethnic and Racial Studies* 25 (6): 969–88.

Goos, M., and A. Manning (2003) 'McJobs and MacJobs: the growing polarisation of jobs in the UK', in R. Dickens, P. Gregg, and J. Wadsworth (eds), *The Labour Market under New Labour* (Basingstoke/New York: Palgrave Macmillan).

Gordon, I. (2004) 'Capital needs, capital growth and global city rhetoric in Mayor Livingstone's London Plan', *GaWC Research Bulletin* 145 – available at <www.lboro. ac.uk/gawc/rb/rb145.html>, accessed 21 September 2005.

Gordon, I., and C. Whitehead (2007) *The Impact of Recent Immigration on the London Economy* (London: City of London Corporation).

Goulbourne, H. (ed.) (1990) *Black Politics in Britain* (Aldershot: Avebury).

Greater London Authority (GLA) (2002) *London Divided* (London: GLA).

—— (2005a) *A Fairer London: The 2005 Living Wage in London* (London: GLA).

—— (2005b) *Women in London's Economy* (London: GLA).

—— (2005c) *London: The World in a City: An Analysis of the 2001 Census Results* (London: GLA Data Management and Analysis Group Briefing, 6 May).

—— (2006) *A Fairer London: The 2006 Living Wage in London* (London: GLA).

—— (2007) *A Fairer London: The 2007 Living Wage in London* (London: GLA).

—— (2008) *A Fairer London: The 2008 Living Wage in London* (London: GLA).

Grillo, R., and V. Mazzucato (2008) 'Africa < > Europe: a double engagement', *Journal of Ethnic and Migration Studies* 34 (2): 175–98.

Grimshaw, D. (2008) *The UK: A Progressive Statutory Minimum Wage in a Liberal Market Economy Context*, Report to the International Labour Organisation.

Guarnizo, L. (2002) 'The economics of transnational living', *International Migration Review* 36 (2): 355–88.

Guerrero, G., and J. Bolay (2005) *Enhancing Development through Knowledge Circulation: A Different View of the Migration of Highly Skilled Mexicans*, Global Migration Perspectives 51 (Global Commission for International Migration).

Gugerty, M. (2007) 'You can't save alone: commitment in rotating savings and credit associations in Kenya', *Economic Development and Cultural Change* 55 (2): 251–82.

de Haan, A., and S. Maxwell (1998) 'Poverty and social exclusion in the North and South', *IDS Bulletin* 29 (1): 1–9.

de Haas, H. (2005) 'International migration, remittances and development: myths and facts', *Third World Quarterly* 26: 1269–84.

—— (2006) 'Migration, remittances and regional development in Southern Morocco', *Geoforum* 37: 565–80.

—— (2007) 'Turning the tide? Why development will not stop migration', *Development and Change* 38 (5): 819–41.

Hage, G. (1998) *White Nation: Fantasies of White Supremacy in a Multicultural Society* (Kent: Pluto).

Hale, A., and J. Wills (eds) (2005) *Threads of Labour: Garment Industry Supply Chains from the Workers' Perspective* (Oxford: Blackwell).

Hamnett, C. (1994a) 'Socio-economic change in London: professionalisation not polarisation', *Built Environment* 20: 193–203.

—— (1994b) 'Social polarisation in global cities: theory and evidence', *Urban Studies* 31: 401–24.

—— (1996) 'Social polarisation, economic restructuring and welfare state regimes', *Urban Studies* 33 (8): 1407–30.

—— (2003) *Unequal City: London in the Global Arena* (London: Routledge).

Hamnett, C., and M. Cross (1998) 'Social change, social polarisation and income inequality in London, 1979–1993', *Geo-Journal* 46: 39–50.

Hardt, M., and A. Negri (2005) *Multitude: War and Democracy in the Age of Empire* (London: Penguin).

Hartigan, J. (1999) 'Establishing the fact of whiteness', in R. Torres, L. Mirón, and J. Inda (eds) *Race, Identity, and Citizenship: A Reader* (Oxford: Blackwell).

Harvey, D. (2005) *A Brief History of Neoliberalism* (Oxford: Oxford University Press).

Hatton, T., and S. Wheatley-Price (2005) 'Migration, migrants and policy in the UK', in K. Zimmermann (ed.) *European Migration: What Do We Know?* (Oxford: Oxford University Press).

Heery, E. (1998) 'The relaunch of the TUC', *British Journal of Industrial Relations* 36: 339–60.

Henderson, J., P. Dicken, M. Hess, N. Coe, and H. Yeung (2002) 'Global production networks and the analysis of economic development', *Review of International Political Economy* 9 (3): 436–64.

Henry, N., C. McEwan, and J. Pollard (2002) 'Globalization from below: Birmingham – postcolonial workshop of the world?' *Area* 34 (2): 117–27.

Herbert, J. (2008a) *Negotiating Boundaries in the City: Migration, Ethnicity and Gender in Britain* (Aldershot: Ashgate).

—— (2008b) 'Masculinity and migration: life stories of East African Asian men', in L. Ryan and W. Webster (eds) *Gendering Migration: Masculinity, Femininity, and Ethnicity in Post-War Britain* (Aldershot: Ashgate).

Herbert, J., J. May, J. Wills, K. Datta, Y. Evans, and C. McIlwaine, (2008) 'Multicultural living? Experiences of everyday racism among Ghanaian migrants in London', *European Urban and Regional Studies* 15 (2): 103–17.

Hernandez, E., and S. Coutin (2006) 'Remitting subjects: migrants, money and states', *Economy and Society* 35 (2): 185–208.

Herod, A., and L. Aguiar (2006) 'Introduction: cleaners and the dirty work of neo-liberalism', *Antipode* 38 (3): 425–34.

Hickman, M., H. Crowley, and N. Mai (2008) *Immigration and Social Cohesion in the UK: The Rhythms and Realities of Everyday Life* (York: Joseph Rowntree Foundation).

Hicks, J., and G. Allen (1999) *A Century of Change: Trends in UK statistics since 1900*, Research Paper 99/111 (London: House of Commons Library).

Hill, H. (2003) *The London Deficit – A Business Perspective: An Investigation into London's Contribution and Support* (London: London Chamber of Commerce and Industry).

Hirsch, J. (1999) 'En el norte la mujer manda: gender, generation, and geography in a Mexican transnational community', *American Behavioral Scientist* 42 (9): 1332–49.

Hirschman, C. (2004) 'The role of religion in the origins and adaptation of immigrant groups in the United States', *International Migration Review* 38 (3): 1206–33.

Hjarnø, J. (2003) *Illegal Immigrants and Developments in Employment in the Labour Markets of the European Union* (Aldershot: Ashgate).

HM Treasury (2006) *Employment Opportunity for All: Analysing Labour Market Trends in London* (London: HMSO).

—— (2007) *Employment Opportunity for All: Tackling Worklessness in London* (London: HMSO).

Holgate, J. (2005) 'Organising migrant workers: a case study of working conditions and unionisation at a sandwich factory in London', *Work, Employment and Society* 19 (3): 463–80.

—— (2009) 'Contested terrain: London's Living Wage campaign and the tension between community and union organising', in J. McBride and I. Greenwood (eds) *The Complexity of Community Unionism: A Comparative Analysis of Concepts and Contexts* (Basingstoke: Palgrave Macmillan).

Hollifield, J. (1992) *Immigrants, Markets and States: The Political Economy of Postwar Europe* (Cambridge: Harvard University Press).

—— (2004) 'The emerging migration state', *International Migration Review* 38 (3): 885–912.

Holmes, C. (1997) 'Cosmopolitan London', in A. Kershen (ed.) *London: The Promised Land? The Migrant Experience in a Capital City* (Aldershot: Avebury).

Home Office (2006) *A Points-Based System: Making Migration Work for Britain*, Paper 6741 (London: Home Office).

—— (2008) *Asylum Statistics UK 2007*, Home Office Statistical Bulletin 11/08 (London: Home Office).

—— (no date) '"No recourse to public funds" What does it mean?', available at <www.ukba.homeoffice.gov.uk/sitecontent/documents/residency/publicfunds.pdf>, accessed 6 August 2009.

Home Office and Commonwealth Office (2007) *Managing Global Migration: A Strategy to Build Stronger International Alliances to Manage Migration* (London: Home Office).

Hondagneu-Sotelo, P., and E. Avila (1997) '"I'm here, but I'm there": the meanings of Latina transnational Motherhood', *Gender & Society* 11 (5): 548–71.

House of Lords (Select Committee of Economic Affairs) (2008) *The Economic Impact of Immigration, Volume 1* (London: HMSO).

Huang, S., B. Yeoh, and T. Lam (2008) 'Asian transnational families in transition: the liminality of simultaneity', *International Migration* 46 (4): 3–13.

Hudson, K. (2006) 'The new labor market segmentation: labor market dualism in the new economy', *Social Science Research* 36: 286–312.

Hudson, M., J. Phillips, K. Ray, and H. Barnes (2007) *Social Cohesion in Diverse Communities* (London: Joseph Rowntree Foundation).

Iganski, P., and G. Payne (1996) 'Declining racial disadvantage in the British labour market', *Ethnic and Racial Studies* 19 (1): 113–34.

Iglicka, K. (2005) *EU Membership Highlights Poland's Migration Challenges*, Country Profiles, Migration Information Source (Warsaw: Centre for International Relations), available at <www.ippr.org.uk/publicationsandreports/publication.asp?id=446>.

International Organisation for Migration (IOM) (2005) *World Migration 2005: Costs and Benefits of International Migration* (Geneva: IOM).

—— (2007) *Migration, Development and Poverty Reduction* (Geneva: IOM).

—— (2008) *World Migration 2008: Managing Labour Mobility in the Evolving Global Economy* (Geneva: IOM).

Institute for Public Policy Research (IPPR) (2006) *Irregular Migration in the UK: An IPPR Factfile* (London: IPPR).

IPPR–CRE (2007) *The Reception and Integration of New Migrant Communities* (London: IPPR).

Ipsos MORI (2008) *Political Monitor, Recent Trends: The Most Important Issues Facing Britain Today*, available at <www.ipsos-mori.com/polls/trends/issues12.shtml>, accessed 18 March 2008.

Isaacs, L. (2008) *Research on Migrant Remittances and Linkage to Broader Access to Financial Services*, report for the UK Remittances Task Force (Developing Markets Associates Limited).

Iskander, N. (2007) 'Informal work and protest: undocumented immigrant activism in France 1996–2000', *British Journal of Industrial Relations* 45: 309–34.

Jackson, C. (1999) 'Men's work, masculinities and gender divisions of labour', *Journal of Development Studies* 36 (1): 89–108.

Jackson, P. (1992) 'The racialisation of labour in post-war Bradford', *Journal of Historical Geography* 18: 190–209.

Jacobs, D., K. Phalet, and M. Swyngedouw (2004) 'Associational membership and political involvement among ethnic minority groups in Brussels', *Journal of Ethnic and Migration Studies* 30 (3): 543–59.

Jamoul, L., and J. Wills (2008) 'Faith in politics', *Urban Studies* 45 (10): 2035–56.

Jarvis, H. (2005) 'Moving to London time: household co-ordination and the infrastructure of everyday life', *Time and Society* 14 (1): 133–54.

Jayaweera, H. (1993) 'Racial disadvantage and ethnic identity: the experience of Afro-Caribbean women in a British city', *New Community* 19 (3): 383–406.

Joint Council for the Welfare of Immigrants (JCWI) (2006) *Recognising Rights, Recognising Political Realities: The Case for Regularising Irregular Migrants* (London: JCWI).

Johnston, R., and A. McIvor (2007) 'Narratives from the urban workplace: oral testimonies and the reconstruction of men's work in the heavy industries in Glasgow', in R. Rodger and J. Herbert (eds) *Testimonies of the City: Identity, Community and Change in a Contemporary Urban World* (Aldershot: Ashgate).

Jones, T. (1993) *Britain's Ethnic Minorities* (London: Policy Studies Institute).

Joppke, C. (1999) 'How immigration is changing citizenship: a comparative view', *Ethnic and Racial Studies* 22 (4): 629–52.

—— (2004) 'The retreat of multiculturalism in the liberal state: theory and policy', *British Journal of Sociology* 55 (2): 237–57.

Jordan, B., and F. Düvell (2002) *Irregular Migration: The Dilemmas of Transnational Mobility* (Cheltenham: Edward Elgar).

Josephides, S. (1990) 'Principles, strategies and anti-racist campaigns: the case of the Indian Workers Association', in H. Goulbourne (ed.) *Black Politics in Britain* (Aldershot: Avebury).

Kaplanis, I. (2007) *The Geography of Employment Polarisation in Britain* (London: IPPR).

Kapur, D. (2003) *Remittances: The New Development Mantra?* (paper delivered to the G24 Technical Group Meeting).

Kapur, D., and J. McHale (2003) 'Migration's new pay-off', *Foreign Policy* 139: 48–57.

Kastoryano, R. (2004) 'Religion and incorporation: Islam in France and Germany', *International Migration Review* 38 (3): 1234–55.

Katungi, D., E. Neale, and A. Barbour (2006) *People in Low-Paid Informal Work: 'Need Not Greed'* (Bristol: The Policy Press).

Kelly, P. (2000) *Landscapes of Globalisation: Human Geographies of Economic Change in the Philippines* (London and New York: Routledge).

Kelly, P., and T. Lusis (2006) 'Migration and the transnational habitus: evidence from Canada and the Philippines', *Environment and Planning A* 38: 831–47.

King, A. (1990) *Global Cities: Post-Imperialism and the Internationalization of London* (London: Routledge).

Klein, N. (2002) *No Logo: No Space, No Jobs* (London: Picador).

Kofman, E., A. Phizacklea, P. Raghuram and R. Sales (2000) *Gender and International Migration in Europe: Employment, Welfare and Politics* (London: Routledge).

Koopmans, R. (2004) 'Migrant mobilisation and political opportunities: variation among German cities and a comparison with the UK and the Netherlands', *Journal of Ethnic and Migration Studies* 30 (3): 449–70.

Kosic, A., and A. Triandafyllidou (2003) 'Albanian immigrants in Italy: migration plans, coping strategies and identity issues', *Journal of Ethnic and Migration Studies* 29 (6): 997–1014.

Krings, T. (2009) 'A race to the bottom? Trade unions, EU enlargement and the free movement of labour', *European Journal of Industrial Relations* 15 (1): 49–69.

Kundnani, A. (2002) *The Death of Multiculturalism*, available at <www.irr.org.uk/2002/april/ak000001.html>, accessed 5 March 2006.

Kushner, T. (2004) *We Europeans? Mass-Observation, 'Race' and British Identity in the Twentieth Century* (Aldershot: Ashgate).

Kyambi, S. (2007) 'Migrants and social inclusion: what would a progressive approach look like?', in D. Flynn and Z. Williams (eds) *Towards a Progressive Immigration Policy* (London: COMPAS).

Kymlicka, W. (2003) 'Immigration, citizenship, multiculturalism: exploring the links', *Political Quarterly* 74: 195–208.

Lagnado, J. (2004) 'The London service sector and migrant labour in the 1990s: Colombians in contract cleaning', unpublished MSc dissertation, Open University.

Lambert, B. (2000) '40 percent in New York born abroad', *New York Times*, 24 July 2000.

Laurie, N., C. Dwyer, S. Holloway, and F. Smith (1999) *Geographies of New Femininities* (Harlow: Pearson).

Lautenthal, B. (2007) 'The emergence of pro-regularization movements in Western Europe', *International Migration* 45 (3): 101–33.

Learning and Skills Council (2005) *2004 National Employment Survey* (London: Learning and Skills Council).

Lee, G., and J. Wrench (1987) 'Race and gender dimensions of the youth labour market: from apprenticeship to YTS', in G. Lee and R. Loveridge (eds) *The Manufacture of Disadvantage: Stigma and Social Closure* (Milton Keynes: Open University Press).

Legrain, P. (2007) *Immigrants: Your Country Needs Them* (London: Little, Brown).

Leontaridi, M. (1998) 'Segmented labour markets', *Journal of Economic Surveys* 12 (1): 103–9.

Levinson, A. (2005) *The Regularisation of Unauthorised Migrants: Literature Survey and Case Studies* (Oxford: COMPAS).

Levitt, P. (1998) 'Social remittances: migration driven local-level forms of cultural diffusion', *International Migration Review* 32 (94): 926–48.

—— (2001) 'Transnational migration: taking stock and future directions', *Global Networks* 1: 195–216.

Levitt, P., and N. Nyberg-Sørensen (2004) 'Global migration perspectives: the transnational turn in migration studies', Global Migration Perspectives No 6 (Global Commission on International Migration).

Lewis, G., and S. Neal (2005) 'Introduction: contemporary political contexts, changing terrains and revisited discourses', *Ethnic and Racial Studies* 28: 423–44.

Lindley, A. (2007) *The Early Morning Phonecall: Remittances from a Refugee Diaspora Perspective*, Working Paper 47 (Oxford: COMPAS).

Lindsay, C., and R. McQuaid (2004) 'Avoiding the "Mcjobs": unemployed job seekers and attitudes to service work', *Work, Employment, Society* 18 (2): 297–319.

London School of Economics (LSE) (2007) *The Impact of Recent Immigration on the London Economy* (London: City of London Corporation).

—— (2009) *Economic Impact on London and the UK of an Earned Regularisation of Irregular Migrants in the UK* (London: LSE).

Lopez, D., E. Popkin, and E. Telles (1996) 'Central Americans: at the bottom, struggling to get ahead', in R. Waldinger and M. Bozorgmehr (eds) *Ethnic Los Angeles* (New York: Russell Sage).

Lowell, L., A. Findlay, and E. Stewart (2004) *Brain Strain: Optimizing Highly Skilled Migration from Developing Countries* (London: IPPR).

Lucas, R. (1996) 'Industrial relations in hotels and catering: neglect and paradox?' *British Journal of Industrial Relations* 34 (2): 267–86.

Luce, S. (2004) *Fighting for a Living Wage* (Ithaca: Cornell University Press).

Lupton, B. (2000), 'Maintaining masculinity: men who do "women's work"', *British Journal of Management* 11: S33–S48.

Lyon, F. (2005) 'Managing co-operation: trust and power in Ghanaian associations', *Organization Studies* 2 (1): 31–52.

Maalouf, A. (2000) *In the Name of Identity: Violence and the Need to Belong* (London: Penguin).

Mahler, S., and P. Pessar (2001) 'Gendered geographies of power: analyzing gender across transnational spaces', *Identities* 7 (4): 441–59.

Marks, M. (2006) 'A protected, cosy old club', *Guardian*, 27 October 2006.

Marquand, D. (2004) *Decline of the Public* (Cambridge: Polity).

Martin, S., and D. Parker (1997) *The Impact of Privatisation: Ownership and Corporate Performance in the UK* (London: Routledge).

Marx, K. (1954) [1887] *Capital: Volume One* (Moscow: Progress Publishers).

Massey, D. (1995) *Spatial Divisions of Labour: Social Structures and the Geography of Production* (Basingstoke: Palgrave Macmillan).

—— (2004) 'Geographies of responsibility', *Geografiska Annaler* 86 (1): 5–18.

—— (2007) *World City* (Cambridge: Polity).

Massey, D., J. Arango, G. Hugo, A. Kouaouci, A. Pellegrino, and J. Taylor (1998) *Worlds in Motion: Understanding International Migration at the End of the Millennium* (Oxford: Clarendon Press).

Mathews, G., and M. Ruhs (2007) 'Are you being served? Employer demand for migrant labour in the UK's hospitality sector', Working Paper (Oxford: COMPAS).

May, J., K. Datta, Y. Evans, J. Herbert, C. McIlwaine, and J. Wills (2008) 'Travelling neoliberalism: Polish and Ghanaian migrant workers in London', in A. Smith, A. Stenning, and K. Willis (eds) *Social Justice and Neoliberalism: Global Perspectives* (London: Zed).

May, J., J. Wills, K. Datta, Y. Evans, J. Herbert, and C. McIlwaine (2007) 'Keeping London working: global cities, the British state, and London's new migrant division of labour', *Transactions of the Institute of British Geographers* 32: 151–67.

MacInnes, T., and P. Kenway (2009) *London's Poverty Profile*, London: City Parochial Foundation.

MacKenzie, R., and C. Forde (2009) 'The rhetoric of the "good worker" versus the realities of employers' use and the experience of migrant workers', *Work Employment Society* 23 (1): 142–59.

McDowell, L. (1991) 'Life without Father and Ford: the new gender order of post-Fordism', *Transactions of the Institute of British Geography* 16: 400–19.

—— (2001) 'Father and Ford revisited: gender, class and employment change in the new millennium', *Transaction of the Institute of British Geography* 26: 448–64.

—— (2004a) 'Masculinity, identity and labour market change: some reflections on the implications of thinking relationally about difference and the politics of inclusion', *Geografiska Annaler* 86: 45–56.

—— (2004b) 'Work, workfare, work/life balance and an ethic of care', *Progress in Human Geography* 28 (2): 145–63.

—— (2005) *Hard Labour: The Forgotten Voices of Latvian Migrant 'Volunteer' Workers* (London: UCL Press).

—— (2008) 'Thinking through work: complex inequalities, construction of difference and trans-national migrants', *Progress in Human Geography* 32 (4): 491–507.

McDowell, L., and D. Massey (1984) 'A Women's Place?', in D. Massey and J. Allen (eds) *Geography Matters! A Reader* (Cambridge: Cambridge University Press, 197–217).

McGregor, J. (2007) 'Joining the BBC (British Bottom Cleaners): Zimbabwean migrants and the UK care industry', *Journal of Ethnic and Migration Studies* 33 (5): 801–24.

McIlwaine, C. (2005) *Coping Practices among Colombian Migrants in London*, Working Paper (London: Department of Geography, Queen Mary, University of London).

—— (2007a) *Living in Latin London: How Latin American Migrants Survive in the City*, Working Paper (London: Department of Geography, Queen Mary, University of London).

—— (2007b) 'From local to global to transnational civil society: re-framing development perspectives on the non-state sector', *Geography Compass* 1 (6): 1252–81.

—— (2008) *Subversion or Subjugation: Transforming Gender Ideologies among Latin American Migrants in London*, Working Paper (London: Department of Geography, Queen Mary, University of London).

—— (forthcoming) 'Migrant machismos: exploring gender ideologies and practices among Latin American migrants in London in multi-scalar perspective', *Gender, Place and Culture*.

McIlwaine, C., K. Datta, Y. Evans, J. Herbert, J. May, and J. Wills (2006) *Gender and Ethnic Identities among Low-Paid Migrant Workers in London*, Working Paper (London: Department of Geography, Queen Mary, University of London).

McKay, S. (2007) 'Filipino sea men: constructing masculinities in an ethnic labour niche', *Journal of Ethnic and Migration Studies* 33 (4): 617–33.

McKay, S., and A. Winkleman-Gleed (2005) *Migrant Workers in the East of England* (London: Working Lives Research Centre, London Metropolitan University).

McKie, L., S. Bowlby, and S. Gregory (2001) 'Gender, caring and employment in Britain', *Journal of Social Policy* 30 (2): 233–58.

Menjívar, C. (2000) *Fragmented Ties: Salvadoran Immigrant Networks in America* (Berkeley: University of California Press).

Metcalf, D. (2007) *Why Has the British National Minimum Wage Had Little or No Impact on Employment?* CEP Discussion Paper 781 (London: LSE).

Migrants' Rights Network (2007) *Migrant Rights News 1: September*, available at <www.migrantsrights.org.uk/enews/September.htm>, accessed 23 April 2007.

—— (2008) *Papers Please: The Impact of a Government Campaign on the Employment Rights of Vulnerable Migrants* (London: MRN).

Miles, R. (1982) *Racism and Migrant Labour* (London: Routledge & Kegan Paul).

—— (1988) 'Racism, Marxism and British politics', *Economy and Society* 17 (3): 428–60.

Miles, R., and M. Brown (1989) *Racism* (London: Routledge).

Milkman, R. (2000) *Organising Immigrants: The Challenge for Unions in Contemporary California* (Ithaca: Cornell University Press).

Model, S. (2002) 'Immigrants' social class in three global cities', in M. Cross and R. Moore (eds) *Globalization and the New City: Migrants, Minorities and Urban Transformations in Comparative Perspective* (Basingstoke: Palgrave Macmillan).

Modood, T. (1994) 'The end of a hegemony: the concept of "black" and British Asians', in J. Rex and B. Drury (eds) *Ethnic Mobilisation in a Multi-Cultural Europe* (Aldershot: Avebury).

—— (2005) 'Remaking multiculturalism after 7/7', *Open Democracy*, 29 September 2005, available at <www.opendemocracy.net>, accessed 5 May 2006.

Modood, T., R. Berthoud, J. Lakey, J. Nazroo, P. Smith, S. Virdee, and S. Beishon (1997) *Ethnic Minorities in Britain: Diversity and Disadvantage* (London: Policy Studies Institute).

Mohan, G. (2006) 'Embedded cosmopolitanism and the politics of obligation: the Ghanaian diaspora and development', *Environment and Planning A* 38: 867–83.

—— (2008) 'Cosmopolitan states of development: homelands, citizenships, and diasporic Ghanaian politics', *Environment and Planning D* 26: 464–79.

Mohan, G., E. Brown, B. Milward, and A. Zack-Williams (2000) *Structural Adjustment: Theory, Practice and Impacts* (London: Routledge).

Mohan, J. (1999) *A United Kingdom? Economic, Political and Social Geographies* (London: Arnold).

Morris, L. (2002) *Managing Migration: Civic Stratification and Migrants Rights* (London: Routledge).

Mount, F. (2004) *Mind the Gap: Class in Britain Now* (London: Short Books).

Muir, R. (2008) *One London: Change and Cohesion in Three London Boroughs: An IPPR Report for the Government Office for London* (London: IPPR).

Murji, K., and J. Solomos (2005) *Racialization: Studies in Theory and Practice* (Oxford: Oxford University Press).

Nanton, P. (1998) 'Community politics and the problem of partnership: ethnic minority participation in urban regeneration networks', in S. Saggar (ed.) *Race and British Electoral Politics* (London: UCL Press).

Nee, V., and J. Sanders (2001) 'Understanding the diversity of immigrant incorporation: a forms-of-capital model', *Ethnic and Racial Studies* 24 (3): 386–411.

Norgaard, H. (2003) 'The global city thesis: social polarisation and changes in the distribution of wages', *Geografiska Annaler* 85: 103–19.

Nyberg-Sørensen, N., N. Van Hear, and P. Engberg-Pedersen (2002) 'The migration–development nexus: evidence and policy options – state-of-the-art overview', *International Migration* 40: 3–43.

Office for National Statistics (ONS) (2005) *Annual Survey of Hours and Earnings* (Newport: ONS), available at <www.statistics.gov.uk>.

—— (2008) 'Net migration to the UK was 237,000 in 2007', News Release, 19 November 2008, available at <www.statistics.gov.uk/pdfdir/ppmg1108.pdf>, last accessed September 2009.

Ogden, P. (ed.) (1992) *London Docklands: The Challenge of Development* (Cambridge: Cambridge University Press).

Oldroyd, M. (1894) *A Living Wage* (Leeds: McCorquodale and Co. Ltd).

Orozco, M., and A. Ferro (2007) 'Worldwide trends in international remittances', *Migrant Remittances* 4 (5): 1–5.

Osella, F., and C. Osella, C. (2000) 'Migration, money and masculinity in Kerala', *Journal of the Royal Anthropological Institute* 6: 117–33.

Osterman, P. (2003) *Gathering Power: The Future of Progressive Politics in America* (Boston: Beacon Press).

Oxfam (2004) *Paying the Price: Why Rich Countries Must Invest Now in a War on Poverty* (Oxford: Oxfam).

Parekh, B. (2000) *Rethinking Multiculturalism: Cultural Diversity and Political Theory* (London: Macmillan).

Parmar, P. (1982) 'Gender, race and class: Asian women in resistance', in Centre for Contemporary Cultural Studies (eds) *The Empire Strikes Back: Race and Racism in '70s Britain* (London: Hutchinson).

Parrenas, R. (2001) *Servants of Globalization: Women, Migration and Domestic Work* (Stanford: Stanford University Press).

Pattie, C., P. Seyd, and P. Whiteley (2004) *Citizenship in Britain: Values, Participation and Democracy* (Cambridge: Cambridge University Press).

Paul, K. (1997) *Whitewashing Britain: Race and Citizenship in the Post-War Era* (London: Cornell University Press).

Peach, C. (1968) *West Indian Migration to Britain: A Social Geography* (Oxford: Oxford University Press).

Peck, J. (1989) 'Reconceptualising the local labour market: space, segmentation and the state', *Progress in Human Geography* 13: 42–61.

—— (1996) *Work-place* (London: Guilford).

—— (2001) *Workfare States* (New York: Guilford).

Peil, M. (1995) 'Ghanaians abroad', *African Affairs* 94 (376): 345–67.

Perkin, H. (1996) *The Third Revolution: Professional Elites in the Modern World* (London: Routledge).

Phillimore, J., and L. Goodson (2006) 'Problem or opportunity? Asylum-seekers, refugees, employment and social exclusion in deprived urban areas', *Urban Studies* 43 (10): 1715–36.

Phizacklea, A. (ed.) (1983) *One Way Ticket: Migration and Female Labour* (London: Routledge).

Phizacklea, A., and R. Miles (1987) 'The British trade union movement and racism', in G. Lee and R. Loveridge (eds) *The Manufacture of Disadvantage: Stigma and Social Closure* (Milton Keynes: Open University Press).

Piggott, G. (ed.) (2008) *Focus on London* (London: GLA).

Piore, M. (1979) *Birds of Passage: Migrant Labour and Industrial Societies* (Cambridge: Cambridge University Press).

Piper, N. (2009) 'The complex interconnections of the migration–development nexus: a social perspective', *Population, Space and Place* 15: 93–101.

Pollard, N., M. Latorre, and D. Sriskandarajah (2008) *Floodgates or Turnstiles? Post-EU Enlargement Migration Flows to and from the UK* (London: IPPR).

Portes, A. (1998) 'Social capital: its origins and applications in modern sociology', *American Review of Sociology* 24 (1): 1–24.

—— (2001) 'Introduction: the debates and significance of immigrant transnationalism', *Global Networks* 1 (3): 181–93.

Portes, A., and R. Rumbaut (2001) *Legacies: The Story of the Immigrant Second Generation* (Berkeley: University of California Press and Russell Sage Foundation).

—— (2006) *Immigrant America: A Portrait* (Berkeley, CA: University of California Press).

Power Inquiry (2006) *The Decline in Political Participation and Involvement in Britain: An Introduction* (London: Power Enquiry).

Pribilsky, J. (2004) '"Aprendemos a convivir": conjugal relations, co-parenting and family life among Ecuadorian transnational migrants in New York City and the Ecuadorian Andes', *Global Networks* 4 (3): 313–34.

Price, M., and L. Benton-Short (2007) 'Immigrants and world cities: from the hyper-diverse to the bypassed', *GeoJournal* 68 (2/3): 103–17.

Prothero R. (2007) *An Expenditure-Based Approach to Employment Sectors in London*, GLA Economics Working Paper 25 (London: GLA).

Pulido, L. (2007) 'A day without immigrants: the racial and class politics of immigrant exclusion', *Antipode* 39 (1): 1–7.

Putnam, R. (1993) 'The prosperous community: social capital and public life', *American Prospect* 4 (13): 18–21.

—— (2000) *Bowling Alone: The Collapse and Revival of American Community* (New York: Simon & Schuster).

—— (2007) '*E Pluribus Unum*: diversity and community in the twenty-first century', *Scandinavian Political Studies* 30 (2): 137–74.

Quilley, S. (1999) 'Entrepreneurial Manchester: the genesis of elite consensus', *Antipode* 31 (2): 185–211.

Raghuram, P. (2004) 'Migration, gender and the IT sector: intersecting debates', *Women's Studies International Forum* 27: 163–76.

Raghuram, P., and E. Kofman (2004) 'Out of Asia: skilling, re-skilling and de-skilling of female migrants', *Women's Studies International Forum* 27: 95–100.

Rakodi, C. (1999) 'A capital assets framework for analysing household livelihoods strategies: implications for policy', *Development Policy Review* 17: 315–42.

Ratcliffe, P. (1981) *Racism and Reaction: A Profile of Handsworth* (London: Routledge).

Ratha, D. (2007) *Leveraging Remittances for Development*, Policy Brief (Washington, D.C.: Migration Policy Institute).

Ratha, D., and W. Shaw (2007) *South–South Migration and Remittances*, World Bank Working Paper 102 (Washington, D.C.: World Bank).

Ratha, D., S. Mohapatra, and S. Plaza (2008) 'Beyond aid: new sources and innovative mechanisms for financing development', in Sub-Saharan Africa, Policy Research Working Paper 4609, Migration and Remittances Team, Development Prospects Group (World Bank).

Reimer, S. (1998) 'Working in a risk society', *Transactions of the Institute of British Geographers* 23: 116–27.

Retort (2005) *Afflicted Powers: Capital and Spectacle in a New Age of War* (London: Verso).

Rex, J., and R. Moore (1967) *Race, Community and Conflict: A Study of Sparkbrook* (London: Oxford University Press).

Rex, J., and S. Tomlinson (1979) *Colonial Immigrants in a British City: A Class Analysis* (London: Routledge & Kegan Paul).

Robinson, J. (2002) 'Global and world cities: a view from off the map', *International Journal of Urban and Regional Research* 26 (3): 531–54.

Robinson, R. (2004) *Globalization, Immigrants' Transnational Agency and Economic Development in their Homelands* (Canadian Foundation for the Americas).

Robinson, V. (1990) 'Boom and gloom: the success and failure of South Asians in Britain', in C. Clarke, C. Peach and S. Vertovec (eds) *South Asians Overseas: Migration and Ethnicity* (Cambridge: Cambridge University Press).

Roediger, D. (1991) *The Wages of Whiteness: Race and the Making of the American Working Class* (New York: Verso).

Rogaly, B. (2006) *Intensification of Workplace Regimes in British Agriculture: The Role of Migrant Workers*, Sussex Migration Working Paper 36, available at <www.sussex.ac.uk/migration/documents/mwp36.pdf>.

Rouse, R. (1992) 'Making sense of settlement: class transformation, cultural struggle, and transnationalism among Mexican migrants in the United States', *Annals of the New York Academy of Sciences* 645 (1): 25–52.

Rowbotham, S. (2006) 'Cleaners' organising in Britain from the 1970s: a personal account', *Antipode* 38 (3): 608–25.

RSA Migration Commission (2005) *Migration: A Welcome Opportunity* (London: RSA).

Ruhs, M. (2006) *Greasing the Wheels of the Flexible Labour Market: East European Labour Immigration in the UK*, Working Paper 38 (Oxford: COMPAS).

Ruhs, M., and B. Anderson (2006) *Semi-Compliance in the Migrant Labour Market* (Oxford: COMPAS).

Rutter, G., M. Latorre, and D. Sriskandarajah (2008) *Beyond Naturalisation: Citizenship Policy in an Age of Supermobility: A Research Report for the Lord Goldsmith Citizenship Review* (London: IPPR).

Ryan, B. (ed.) (2005) *Labour Migration and Employment Rights* (London: Institute for Employment Rights).

Ryan, L., R. Sales, M. Tilki, and B. Siara (2008) 'Social networks, social support and social capital: the experiences of recent Polish migrants in London', *Sociology* 42 (4): 672–90.

Saggar, S. (2003) 'Immigration and the politics of public opinion', *Political Quarterly* 74: 178–94.

Salt, J., and J. Millar (2006) 'Foreign Labour in the United Kingdom', *Labour Market Trends* (October): 335–55.

Samers, M. (1998) 'Immigration, "ethnic minorities" and "social exclusion" in the European Union: a critical perspective', *Geoforum* 29 (2): 123–44.

—— (2002) 'Immigration and the Global City Hypothesis: towards an alternative research agenda', *International Journal of Urban and Regional Research* 26 (2): 389–402.

Sassen, S. (1991) *The Global City: New York, London, Tokyo* (Princeton: Princeton University Press).

—— (1996) 'New employment regimes in cities: the impact on immigrant workers', *New Community* 22 (4): 579–94.

—— (2001) *The Global City: New York, London, Tokyo* (Princeton: Princeton University Press, second edition).

Sayer, A. (2005) *The Moral Significance of Class* (Cambridge: Cambridge University Press).

Schmitt, J., and J. Wadsworth (2007) 'Changes in the relative economic performance of immigrants to Great Britain and the United States, 1980–2000', *British Journal of Industrial Relations* 45 (2): 1–28.

Schrover, M., J. Van der Leun, and C. Quispel (2007) 'Niches, labour market segregation, ethnicity and gender', *Journal of Ethnic and Migration Studies* 33 (4): 529–40.

Scott, J. (1985) *Weapons of the Weak: Everyday Forms of Peasant Resistance* (New Haven and London: Yale University Press).

Seebohm Rowntree, B. (1918) *The Human Needs of Labour* (London: Thomas Nelson & Sons Ltd.).

Selvon, S. (1975) *Moses Ascending* (London: Penguin Books).

—— (2006) [1956] *The Lonely Londoners* (London: Penguin Books).

Shukra, K. (1990) 'Black sections in the Labour Party', in H. Goulbourne (ed.) *Black Politics in Britain* (Aldershot: Ashgate).

—— (1997) 'The death of a black political movement', *Community Development Journal* 32 (3): 233–43.

Simon, D. (2001) 'Neo-liberalism, structural adjustment and poverty reduction strategies', in V. Desai and R. Potter (eds) *The Companion to Development Studies* (Arnold: London).

—— (2008) 'Neo-liberalism, structural adjustment and poverty reduction strategies', in V. Desai and R. Potter (eds) *The Companion to Development Studies* (London: Arnold, second edition).

Simpson, R. (2004) 'Masculinity at work: the experiences of men in female dominated occupations', *Work, Employment and Society* 18 (2): 349–68.

Singh Jouhl, A. (1994) '1992 and the mobilisation of black people', in J. Rex and B. Drury (eds) *Ethnic Mobilisation in a Multi-Cultural Europe* (Aldershot: Avebury).

Sivanandan, A. (1990) *A Different Hunger: Writings on Black Resistance* (London: Pluto Press).

Skeggs, B. (2003) *Class, Self, Culture* (London: Routledge).

Skeldon, R. (2008a) 'International migration as a tool in development policy: a passing phase?' *Population and Development Review* 34 (1): 1–18.

—— (2008b) 'Of skilled migration, brain drains and policy responses', *International Migration* 47 (4): 3–29.

Smith, A. (1989) 'Gentrification and the spatial contribution of the state: the restructuring of Dockland', *Antipode* 21: 232–60.

Smith, A., and A. Stenning (2006) 'Beyond household economies: articulations and spaces of economic practice in postsocialism', *Progress in Human Geography* 30 (2): 190–213.

Smith, D. (1976) *The Facts of Racial Disadvantage: A National Survey* (London: Political and Economic Planning).

—— (1977) *Racial Disadvantage in Britain* (Harmondsworth: Penguin Books).

Smith, G. (2000) 'Global systems and religious diversity in the inner city: migrants in the East End of London', *International Journal on Multicultural Societies* 2 (1): 16–39.

Smith, S. (1989) *The Politics of 'Race' and Residence: Citizenship, Segregation, and White Supremacy in Britain* (Cambridge: Polity).

Snel, E., and R. Staring (2001) 'Poverty, migration, and coping strategies: an introduction', *Focaal: European Journal of Anthropology* 38: 7–22.

Soldatenko, M. (1999) 'Made in the USA: Latinas/os? Garment work and ethnic conflict in Los Angeles' sweat shops', *Cultural Studies* 13 (2): 319–34.

Solomos, J. (1993) 'The local politics of race equality: policy innovation and the limits of reform', in M. Cross and M. Keith (eds) *Racism, the City and the State* (London: Routledge).

Solomos, J., and L. Back (2000) 'Rethinking the politics of race: participation, representation and identity in Birmingham', in S. Body-Gendrot and M. Martiniello (eds) *Minorities in European Cities: The Dynamics of Social Integration and Social Exclusion at the Neighbourhood Level* (Basingstoke: Macmillan).

Somerville, W. (2007) *Immigration under New Labour* (Bristol: Policy Press).

Sparke, M. (2006) 'A neo-liberal nexus: economy, security and the biopolitics of citizenship on the border', *Political Geography* 25: 151–80.

Spence, L. (2005) *Country of Birth and Labour Market Outcomes in London: An Analysis of Labour Force Survey and Census Data* (London: GLA).

Spencer, S., and B. Cooper (2006) *Social Integration of Migrants in Europe: A Review of the European Literature, 2000–2006* (Oxford: COMPAS).

Spencer, S., M. Ruhs, B. Andersen, and B. Rogaly (2007) *Migrants' Lives Beyond the Workplace* (York: Joseph Rowntree).

Spicer, N. (2008) 'Places of exclusion and inclusion: asylum-seeker and refugee experiences of neighbourhoods in the UK', *Journal of Ethnic and Migration Studies* 34 (3): 491–510.

Sriskandarajah, D. (2005) 'Migration and development: a new research and policy agenda', *World Economics* 6 (2): 1–6.

Sriskandarajah, D., H. Crawley, A. Dhudwar, M. Gill, M. Grell, F. Hopwood, and E. Robinson (2004) *Labour Migration to the UK: An IPPR Factfile* (London: IPPR).

Sriskandarajah, D., L. Cooley, and T. Kornblatt (2007) *Britain's Immigrants: An Economic Profile* (London: IPPR).

Stack, C. (1974) *All Our Kin: Strategies for Survival in a Black Community* (New York: Harper & Row).

Stark, O., and D. Bloom (1985) 'The new economics of labor migration', *American Economic Review* 75 (2): 173–8.

Stedman-Jones, G. (1971) *Outcast London: A Study in the Relationship between Classes in Victorian Society* (London: Penguin).

Stenning, A., and S. Dawley (2009) 'Poles to Newcastle: grounding new migrant flows in peripheral regions', *European Urban and Regional Studies* (forthcoming).

Stenning, A., T. Champion, C. Conway, M. Coombes, S. Dawley, L. Dixon, S. Raybould, and R. Richardson (2006) *Assessing the Local and Regional Impacts of International Migration* (Centre for Urban and Regional Development Studies, University of Newcastle), available at <www.ncl.ac.uk/curds/publications/pdf/A8Final.pdf>, accessed 7 April 2008.

Stiell, B., and K. England (1999) 'Jamaican domestics, Filipina housekeepers and English nannies: representations of Toronto's foreign domestic workers', in J. Momsen (ed.) *Gender, Migration and Domestic Service* (London and New York: Routledge).

Stubbs, S. (2007) 'Britishness and the habits of solidarity', in D. Flynn and Z. Williams (eds) *Towards a Progressive Immigration Policy* (London: COMPAS).

Styan, D. (2007) 'The security of Africans beyond borders: migration, remittances and London's transnational entrepreneurs', *International Affairs* 83 (6): 1171–91.

Taran, P. (2000) 'Human rights of migrants: challenge of the new decade', *International Migration* 38 (6): 7–46.

Taylor, M. (2000) 'Communities in the lead: power, organizational capacity and social capital', *Urban Studies* 37 (5/6): 1019–35.

Tebbit, N. (1984) 'Tebbit predicts last battle to break union shackles', *The Times*, 10 October 1984, available at <www.timesonline.co.uk>.

Theodore, N., A. Valenzuela, and E. Melendez (2006) 'La Esquina: day laborers on the margins of New York's formal economy', *Working USA* 9: 407–23.

Treanor, J. (2006) 'Revolution hailed but City warned of a looming fight for supremacy', *Guardian*, 27 October 2006.

TUC (2007) *The Economics of Migration: Managing the Impact* (London: TUC).

—— (2008) *Hard Work, Hidden Lives: The Full Report of the Commission on Vulnerable Employment* (London: TUC).

Tufts, S. (2004) 'Building the "Competitive City": Labour and Toronto's bid to host the Olympic games', *Geoforum* 35: 47–58.

—— (2006) '"We make it work": the cultural transformation of hotel workers in the city', *Antipode* 38 (2): 350–73.

UK Remittances Working Group (2005) *UK Remittance Market* (London: Profile Business Intelligence).

United Nations Conference on Trade and Development (UNCTAD) (2007) *New Initiatives to Mitigate Brain Drain in the Least Developed Countries*, LDC Report Highlights No. 4 (Geneva: UNCTAD).

United Nations Fund for Population Activities (UNFPA) (2007) *State of the World's Population 2007: Unleashing the Potential of Urban Growth* (New York: UNFPA).

Valentine, G. (2008) 'Living with difference: reflections on geographies of encounter', *Progress in Human Geography* 32 (3): 323–37.

Van Hear, N. (1998) *New Diasporas: The Mass Exodus, Dispersal and Regrouping of Migrant Communities* (London: University College London Press).

Van Hear, N., and N. Sørensen (eds) (2003) *The Migration–Development Nexus* (Geneva: the United Nations and International Organisation for Migration).

Varsanyi, M. (2005) 'The paradox of contemporary immigrant political mobilization: organized labor, undocumented migrants and electoral participation in Los Angeles', *Antipode* 37 (4): 775–95.

Vasta, E. (2007) *Accommodating Diversity: Why Current Critiques of Multiculturalism Miss the Point* (Oxford: COMPAS).

Vasta, E., and Kandilige, L. (2007) *London the Leveller: Ghanaian Work Strategies and Community Solidarity* (Oxford: COMPAS).

Vertovec, S. (1994) 'Multicultural, multi-Asian, multi-Muslim Leicester: dimensions of social complexity, ethnic organisation and local government interface', *Innovation* 7 (3): 259–76.

—— (2004) 'Cheap calls: the social glue of migrant transnationalism', *Global Networks* 4: 219–24.

—— (2007a) *New Complexities of Cohesion in Britain: Super-Diversity, Transnationalism and Civil Integration* (Oxford: COMPAS).

—— (2007b) 'Super-diversity and its implications', *Ethnic and Racial Studies* 30 (6): 1024–54.

Veruete-McKay, L. (2007) *Patterns of Low Pay in London* (London: GLA Economics, Living Wage Unit).

Virdee, S. (2006) '"Race", employment and social change: a critique of current orthodoxies', *Ethnic and Racial Studies* 29 (4): 605–28.

Wainwright, H. (1987) *Labour: A Tale of Two Parties* (London: Hogarth Press).

Waldinger, M., and M. Lichter (2003) *How the Other Half Works: Immigration and the Social Organization of Labor* (Berkeley: University of California Press).

Wall, K., and J. José (2004) 'Managing work and care: a difficult challenge for immigrant families', *Social Policy and Administration* 38 (6): 591–621.

Wallace, C. (2002) 'Household strategies: their conceptual relevance and analytical scope in social research', *Sociology* 36 (2): 275–92.

Walsh, J. (2000) 'Organizing the scale of labour regulation in the United States: service-sector activism in the city, *Environment and Planning A* 32: 1593–610.

Warren, M. (2001) *Democracy and Association* (Princeton: Princeton University Press).

—— (2003) *Dry Bones Rattling: Community Building to Revitalize American Democracy* (Princeton: Princeton University Press).

Watson, M., and P. Danzelman (1998) *Asylum Statistics UK, 1997* (London: Home Office Statistics Bulletin, 14/98).

Webb, S., and B. Webb (1911) [1897] *Industrial Democracy* (London: Longmans, Green & Company).

Webster, W. (1998) *Imagining Home: Gender, 'Race' And National Identity, 1945–64* (London: UCL Press).

Wetherell, M. (ed.) (2009) *Identities and Social Action* (Basingstoke: Palgrave Macmillan).

Wheatley-Price, S. (2001) 'The employment adjustment of male immigrants in England', *Journal of Population Economics* 14: 193–220.

White, J. (1998) 'Old wine, cracked bottle? Tokyo, Paris and the Global City Hypothesis', *Urban Affairs Quarterly* 33 (4): 451–77.

White, M., S. Hill, C. Mills, and D. Smeaton (2004) *Managing to Change? British Workplaces and the Future of Work* (Basingstoke: Palgrave Macmillan).

Whitehead, A. (2001) 'Continuities and discontinuities: the political construction of the working man in rural sub-Saharan Africa: the "lazy man" in African politics', in C. Jackson (ed.) *Men at Work: Labour, Masculinities, Development* (London: Frank Cass).

Whitewell, C. (2002) *'New Migration' in the 1990s: A Retrospective* (Sussex Centre for Migration Research).

Williams, C., and J. Windebank (1999) *A Helping Hand: Harnessing Self-Help to Combat Social Exclusion* (York: York Publishing Services).

Williams, L. (2006) 'Social networks of refugees in the United Kingdom: tradition, tactics and new community spaces', *Journal of Ethnic and Migration Studies* 32 (5): 865–79.

Wills, J. (2003) *On the Frontline of Care: A Research Report to Explore Home-Care Employment and Service Provision in Tower Hamlets* (London: UNISON).

—— (2004) 'Campaigning for low-paid workers: the East London Communities Organisation (TELCO) Living Wage campaign', in W. Brown, G. Healy, E. Heery, and P. Taylor (eds) *The Future of Worker Representation* (Oxford: Oxford University Press).

—— (2005) 'The geography of union organising in low-paid service industries in the UK: lessons from the T&G's campaign to unionise the Dorchester Hotel, London', *Antipode* 37: 139–59.

—— (2008) 'Making class politics possible: organizing contract cleaners in London', *International Journal of Urban and Regional Research* 32 (2): 305–24.

—— (2009) 'Subcontracted employment and its challenge to labor', *Labor Studies Journal* (forthcoming).

Wills, J., with N. Kakpo, and R. Begum (2009) *The Business Case for the Living Wage: The Story of the Cleaning Service at Queen Mary* (London: Queen Mary, University of London), available at <www.geog.qmul.ac.uk/staff/willsj.html>.

Wills, J., J. May, K. Datta, Y. Evans, J. Herbert, and C. McIlwaine (2009a) 'London's migrant division of labour', *European Journal of Urban and Regional Studies* 16 (3): 257–71.

—— (2009b) 'Religion at work: the role of faith-based organisations in the London Living Wage campaign', *Cambridge Journal of Regions, Economy and Society* 2 (3).

Wimaladharma, J., D. Pearce, and D. Stanton (2004) 'Remittances: the new development finance?' *Small Enterprise Development* 15 (1): 12–19.

Winder, R. (2004) *Bloody Foreigners: The Story of Immigration to Britain* (London: Little Brown).

Winkleman-Gleed, A. (2006) *Migrant Nurses: Motivation, Integration and Contribution* (Oxford: Radcliffe Publishing).

Woodbridge, J. (2001) *Sizing the Unauthorized (Illegal) Migrant Population in the United Kingdom, 2001*, Home Office Online Report 29/05 (London: Home Office).

Woolcock, M. (1998) 'Social capital and economic development: toward a theoretical synthesis and policy framework', *Theory and Society* 27 (2): 151–208.

Woolfson, C. (2007) 'Labour standards and labour migration in the new Europe: post-communist legacies and perspectives', *European Journal of Industrial Relations* 13 (2): 199–218.

Woolfson, C., and J. Sommers (2006) 'Labour mobility in construction: European implications of the Latvian Laval Un Partneri dispute with Swedish labour', *European Journal of Industrial Relations* 12 (1): 49–68.

World Bank (2006) *Global Economic Prospects: Economic Implications of Remittances and Migration* (Washington, D.C.: World Bank).

—— (2009) *Global Economic Prospects: Forecast Update* (Washington, D.C.: World Bank).

Wrench, J., and S. Virdee (1996) 'Organizing the unorganized: race, poor work and trade unions', in P. Ackers, C. Smith, and P. Smith (eds) *The New Workplace and Trade Unionism: Critical Perspectives on Work and Organization* (London: Routledge).

Wright, T., and A. Pollert (2006) *The Experience of Ethnic Minority Workers in the Hotel and Catering Industry: Routes to Support and Advice on Workplace Problems* (London: ACAS).

Zetter, R., D. Griffiths, N. Sigona, D. Flynn, T. Pasha, and R. Beyon (2006) *Immigration, Social Cohesion and Social Capital: What are the Links?* (York: Joseph Rowntree Foundation).

Zolberg, A. (1999) 'Matters of state: theorizing immigration policy', in C. Hirschman, P. Kasinitz, and J. de Wind (eds) *The Handbook of International Migration: The American Experience* (New York: Russell Sage Foundation).

Zontini, E. (2004) 'Immigrant women in Barcelona: coping with the consequences of transnational lives', *Journal of Ethnic and Migration Studies* 30 (6): 1113–44.

INDEX

Compiled by Sue Carlton

Page numbers followed by 'n' refer to footnotes

Joint Council for the Welfare of
   Immigrants (JCWI) 16
Justice for Cleaners 184

Kaplanis, Yiannis 35
King, R. 155
Koopmans, R. 170
Kushner, Tony 9n

labour agencies 72–4, 81–2, 83, 89, 157n,
   189, 192
Labour Force Survey 26, 30, 42
labour market
   casualisation of 51
   demand for foreign-born workers 6,
      18–19, 20, 53–7, 101, 194–5
   deregulation 2–6, 17, 37, 93, 95, 192,
      193
   and flexibility 52, 57–8, 75
   influence on immigration policies 48–50
   segmentation 44, 60, 77, 95, 96–100,
      101, 119, 191
   see also London, new migrant division
      of labour; migrant division of labour
Labour Party
   Black Sections movement 167
   and immigrants rights 166
   and racism 167
   see also New Labour
labour power
   as commodity 190
   exploitation 47
   intensification of 127–9
   surplus 6–7
   see also reserve army of labour
labour standards, improving 190, 194–5,
   196
Latin Americans 102, 134, 189
Lebanon, Syrian migrants 47
Levitt, P. 144
Liberal Democrats 185
Lichter, M. 20n, 53
Lindsey Oil Refinery 193
Liverpool
   race riot (1948) 10, 165
   urban riot (1980s) 167
London
   decline in manufacturing industries 32,
      51

as global city 28–9
as global financial centre 28, 50–1
impact of global neo-liberalism 23–4
income inequality 33–4, 35–7
low-paid labour *see* low-paid
   foreign-born workers (London)
new migrant division of labour 1–2, 24,
   27, 28–58, 67, 77, 91–3, 188
   ethnic and gender divisions 27, 29,
      46, 60, 77, 79, 95–120, 189
   and race 104–12
   role of immigration policy 52–7, 100,
      107–8
   see also migrant division of labour
Notting Hill race riot (1958) 10, 165
polarisation of labour market 30, 33–5,
   37, 52, 57
political organisation of migrant
   communities 27, 163–74, 178–87,
   189–90
   post-secular politics 178–86
and poverty 24–6, 131
   child poverty 22, 67
professionalisation of labour force 33,
   34–5, 50
super-diversity 29, 30, 34, 38–44, 60,
   75–7, 95, 138, 192
Trafalgar Square riot (1886) 25
urban riots (1980s) 167
London Citizens 25, 164–5, 174, 178,
   179–81, 186–7
and campaign for living wage 26, 165,
   180–1, 192
   see also London Living Wage (LLW),
   campaign for
campaign for regularisation (Strangers
   into Citizens) 16, 25, 64, 65, 165,
   185, 192
London Living Wage (LLW) 60, 65, 77,
   87, 192
campaign for 26, 27, 60n, 165, 178,
   180–3, 186, 192, 194
London Stock Exchange, deregulation of
   51
London Transport 45
low-paid foreign-born workers (London)
   1, 21–6, 27, 29, 42–4, 59–93, 189
   areas of residence 70–1